The Day Care Book

THE WHY, WHAT, AND HOW OF COMMUNITY DAY CARE

The Day Care Book

THE WHY, WHAT, AND HOW OF COMMUNITY DAY CARE

by Vicki Breitbart

with articles by:

Lucille Abbott, Judy Kleinberg,
Alice Lake, Ann Cook and Herbert Mack,
Margaret Randall, Louise Gross, Virginia Rankin, Georgene Gardner,
Marcia Sprinkle and Norma Lesser, Marnette O'Brien,
Phyllis Taube Greenleaf, and Anna Salter

Designed and illustrated by
Marcia Salo Rizzi

New York: Alfred A. Knopf, 1974

THIS IS A BORZOI BOOK PUBLISHED BY ALFRED A. KNOPF, INC.

The persons whose photographs appear in this book are not necessarily those described in the text; nor were the photographs necessarily taken in the day care centers described in the text.

Thanks to the following for permission to reprint from their works:

The Association for Childhood Education International, Washington, D.C., for "Some Thoughts on Communal Childrearing," by Louise Gross. Copyright © 1972 The Association of Childhood Education International.

The Boston Association for the Education of Young Children, for "Politics in the Preschool," by Anna Salter. Copyright © 1971 Anna Howard.

The Connecticut Commission on the Arts, for photographs by Joe Linsalata in their publication *Artists in the Classroom.*

McCall's, for "The Day Care Business," by Alice Lake. Copyright © 1970 McCall's.

Off Our Backs, for "The Children's House," by Marcia Sprinkle and Norma Lesser. Copyright © 1970 Off Our Backs.

Second Wave, for "On the Road to Child Care for All," by Marnette O'Brien, and "Public Child Care: Our Hidden History," by Judy Kleinberg. Copyright © 1971 Female Liberation, Inc.

Social Policy, published by Social Policy Corporation, New York, N.Y., for "Business in Education: The Discovery Center Hustle," by Ann Cook and Herbert Mack. Copyright © 1970 Social Policy Corporation.

Up from Under, for "Starting a Play Group," by Georgene Gardner, and "Well, I passed the park today . . . ," by Lucille Abbott. Copyright © 1971 Up from Under.

And to the following for permission to use their works:

Phyllis Taube Greenleaf, for "Liberating Young Children from Sex Roles." Copyright © 1973 Phyllis T. MacEwan.

Margaret Randall, for "Child Care: Not from One Generation to the Next but from One Social System to Another." Copyright © 1973 Margaret Randall.

Virginia Rankin, for "Children in Communes." Copyright © 1973 Virginia Rankin.

Library of Congress Cataloging in Publication Data

Breitbart, Vicki, comp. The day care book.
Bibliography: p. 1. Day nurseries—United States—Addresses, essays, lectures.
2. Children—Care and hygiene—Addresses, essays, lectures. I. Title.
HV854.B7 362.7'1'0973 73-7294 ISBN 0-394-48070-8

Manufactured in the United States of America.

FIRST EDITION

Acknowledgments

There are many people in this country who are working to create positive child care alternatives; I have met some in child care centers, others in meetings, demonstrations, and sit-ins. I don't know all their names, but their ideas, their feelings for children, and their strength of purpose have influenced the writing of this book. Certainly all the members of the Women's Child Care Collective, the Committee for Community Controlled Day Care, the Boston Area Child Care Action Group, the Bank Street College Center for Day Care Training, and the Day Care Consultation Service have changed both the image and the reality of day care for me and countless others. Specifically, I have listened to and learned a lot from Kathy Gruber, Ann Siekman, Janet Page, Bob Gangi, Shirley Johnson, Dorothy Pitman Hughes, Phyllis Greenleaf, Sheli Wortis, Susan Ginsberg, Amabel McKay, Mary Klein, and Lorraine Smithberg. I am also thankful to Norm Fruchter and Dan Okrent for helping to make this book possible. I am grateful to Pam Booth, Leslie Cagan, Gay Falk, Rachel Fruchter, Waltraud Ireland, Liz Long, Honor Moore, and Brenda Way for helping me understand what it means to be a woman, and to everyone in the Red Paint Child Care Center for helping to make it possible for me to try. For their encouragement, cooperation, and humanity, I am always grateful to Eric Breitbart, Susan Cowley, Ruth Gallo, Polly Howells, Allan Jacobs, Susan Kanor, Bev Leman, and Jini Tanenhaus. I also thank my parents, but most of all I want to thank Lela Breitbart, who helped make the alternatives clear and who in time will create her own.

Some of the proceeds from this book will go to child care action groups.

Contents

PART 2 Other Ways of Getting There

PART 3 How to Start Your Own Child Care Center

The Day Care Book

THE WHY, WHAT, AND HOW OF COMMUNITY DAY CARE

Introduction

In this country, child care is supposed to be the family's job. This may have been possible in the past. Well into the 1900's, extended family groups that included grandparents, aunts, and cousins lived under the same roof or near enough for frequent visits and family dinners. Several adults shared the responsibilities and joys of child rearing and children were exposed to different people with different styles of relating. But this situation has changed.

Today, the extended family is a rarity. Relatives are either geographically separated or, with the change in values from one generation to the next, are psychologically distant from each other. The nuclear family—father, mother, and children—is now the rule. There are not only fewer adults, but fewer children too: 2.1 is the average reflected in the current birth rate. The social, economic, and emotional needs once filled by family, kin, and community must now be met by this small social unit. The task is enormous—it is almost impossible. Everyone feels the strain.

Children who are entirely dependent on one family are often isolated, confined to playpens and shopping carts, put in front of televisions, or simply sent out on the streets for long periods of time. And if they don't have a nuclear family to call their own, children can be branded illegitimate or feel abandoned and not know to what, where, or whom they belong. Men are kept busy trying to support their families at jobs that seem less rewarding—in real ways—each year. And if there is work available, many men—rather than have their wives go out to work—will take a second job, leaving them with even less time for their families. There are also 20 million people in this country who live in families where there is no adult male at all. The responsibility for child care has been falling more and more to the woman. She is left trying to keep the pieces from exploding in every direction.

The answer is not to abolish the nuclear family. We all want certain things from it. But we have to find ways of separating and defining the family's different functions. Instead of putting all the burden on this inadequate institution, we have to find better ways to fulfill our needs. Alternatives for child care will not make the family work, just as they will not destroy it. But they can help us transform the family into what many of us are really looking for: a group of people who support, comfort, nurture, and cooperate with each other.

Yet, this country has generally had a negative attitude toward alternative child care, largely influenced by the nonchoices available to most of us. With child care, as with most things in our society, there is a double standard. For those who can afford it, there are education-oriented nursery schools, or private in-home arrangements that simply shift the burden from one woman to another. These solutions are never thought to damage the child. Yet when women who can't afford these arrangements—the majority—seek child care, they are accused of neglecting their children. Well-to-do women are never asked about their reasons for wanting alternative child care; other women are told that it is available only in desperate situations.

Sue Negrin, Times Change Press

The family—then and now.

The idea that alternatives should be provided only if the woman fails to do—or cannot do—her job, has left us with a limited number of day care services most mothers can afford. Public, free, or low-cost child care is seen as a welfare service for "unfortunate" families, and the programs usually reflect this. They admit children of working mothers only ("work" being defined as a job outside the home), or other "hardship cases," and offer the child little more than food and shelter.

But things are changing. The poor—women and men—are no longer willing to be controlled by others. And women—poor and middle-class—are no longer willing to let others define their lives for them. In this country, women are beginning to destroy the guilt and fear that has kept them from developing their full potential. Women are no longer willing to be defined primarily as "mother" and are searching for alternatives that can enable them to share child rearing so that it can be satisfying for all those involved.

It is not only the image of child care that is changing. People in communities throughout the country are changing the reality as well. They are struggling against the institutions that determine how, by whom, and for whom child care programs are run. They are creating their own child care alternatives that give children as much free space to grow in as possible; child care that provides an atmosphere in which each person can develop to be the person she or he wants to be. These new child care alternatives are the basis for building new communities, based on cooperation rather than competition, on self-determination rather than exploitation, and on struggle for what can be, rather than adjustment to what is.

Communal living is one way adults are trying to transform the nuclear family and to change the ways they relate to each other and to children; the child care center is another. Not "adult-centered" child care centers where the working mother is accommodated with no thought to the well-being of the child, or where there is an arbitrary set of adult standards imposed on children; not child care centers that are "child-centered," at least not in the way it is too often defined in this society, where children are isolated from the adult world and given no genuine responsibilities, where they are overprotected and overindulged in situations that are closed to parents and the community; but the child care centers that are *person-centered,* where the rights of both adults and children are respected as part of a learning and growing community.

The child care alternatives we create in this country will depend on how we feel about our own families, what we think about the child care alternatives that already exist, and what our vision of the future may be—but a lot depends on what we are going to do about it.

Many people, like myself, have been dissatisfied with their relationships or nonrelationships with children, but it was not until we began to join together that frustration turned into understanding, understanding into anger, anger into strategies for change. This book was written in the hope that more people will become interested in getting together to create child care alternatives; to discover the infinite ways of developing our human potential; to reshape our society into one that truly cares for its children.

The book was not, *could not* have been written in isolation. With a young child of "my own" (we need alternatives in our language as well), I needed to share child care just to have the time to write a book on child care. It certainly would have been easier to write this after my "child-rearing years," but I have found that my involvement in child care has expanded my understanding, which in turn has forced constant revisions in my writing. And it has worked the other way, too. I feel I have lived what I have written, and writing it has made the emotions, the fears, the doubts, and the dreams that much more intense.

My ideas developed as I talked and worked with others, and I have tried to incorporate this into the form of the book. At every possible point, I have included people's writing about their experiences with children and child care to give a sense of the collective effort necessary for creating alternatives. Each voice, each idea, each attempt to change is part of a growing movement to build a future that we want today, to make all this society's children *our* children. This book is part of that movement; I hope it is useful, I hope it reflects some of our common concerns; I hope this book becomes *our* book. And I dedicate it to all of us.

Vicki Breitbart

PART 1

Why People-Controlled Day Care?

Chapter 1

Child Care Begins at Home

"Why have children if you don't want to take care of them?" I can't count the number of times I've heard that statement when I talk about alternative forms of child care. It implies, of course, that women have children only when they want to, that every woman knows exactly what it means to take care of a child before she has one—and that care must be given by the biological mother twenty-four hours a day, every day. In this society, we are made to feel that the exclusive mother-child relationship is the best possible form of child care, but many women find this arrangement a limiting and frustrating experience for themselves and their children.

In order to learn and grow, children need space to move in and materials to explore. They need to be with people who are aware and part of a community of thought and action, people who have the time to be constantly available for questions and answers and who are alert to the children's physical, emotional, and intellectual needs. Yet they are growing up in apartments and homes full of restrictions with the most overworked and socially isolated adults in our society—their mothers.

Most of us with children enjoy taking care of them, but the exclusive and total responsibility makes us feel alone and angry too much of the time. As one woman with two children under six put it:

> *When the kids were younger, it was fine, you know, they're small and they don't do much; but as they started to get older and started talking back and wanting you to do things with them, you don't have the patience and they get carried away. It's just that I want them to behave because it drives me crazy. I'm always yelling at them and I feel bad because I don't like to. I just have no alternative to the way I live.*

Exclusive mother-child care can make a woman's children, and her relationship with them, the sole achievement in life; any attempt on the child's part not to conform becomes a threat to the woman's entire existence. Juliet Mitchell, in her book *Woman's Estate*, describes the problem this way:

> *Parenthood becomes a kind of substitute for work, an activity in which the child is seen as an object created by the mother in the same way a commodity is created by the worker. . . . The child as an autonomous person . . . threatens the activity which claims to create it continually merely as a possession of the parent. Possessions are felt as extensions of*

the self. The child as a possession is supremely this. Anything the child does is therefore a threat to the mother herself. . . . There are few more precarious ventures on which to base a life.[1]

As we grew up many of us saw what happened when *our* mothers tried to give us everything while their own lives were limited by a lack of alternatives and a surplus of myths; when in reaction to their own lack of power they tried to make decisions for others. Many of us vowed never to wind up in this situation. We wanted something different for ourselves and for our children. We may even have felt our own childhoods were "good" ones, but we never planned to spend our lives simply repeating the patterns of the last generation. Yet here we are.

Why do we hesitate to see child care alternatives as something desirable for ourselves and our children, even when the lack of them often makes us feel frustrated, dissatisfied, and hemmed in? In large part our attitude about child care has been shaped by the definition of our role and the prevailing philosophy of child rearing.

1. Juliet Mitchell, *Woman's Estate* (New York: Pantheon, 1972), p. 109.

Woman's Role

This society sees women primarily as mothers and begins to prepare us for motherhood the moment we are born female. Everything we read and see on television and in the movies trains us to want a family and to expect that our satisfactions will come first from a man and then from children. Each institution that affected our lives—the media, school, church, the government, and the most powerful models we know, our own families—combined to perpetuate these beliefs.

If a woman has a problem fulfilling these expectations, she is made to feel it is her fault: what is wrong is wrong with her. We have been told that no matter how bad things may get, if we challenge the way things are, they could get worse. If a woman is dissatisfied with her role, she had better keep it to herself. Women who have resisted the isolation and limits of their lives have too often been singled out, ostracized, called "neurotic" and "unstable."

If a woman can't or doesn't want to have children, she is considered a "freak"; if she has children, she should definitely be married. If she is married and does go to work for the economic survival of her family, she is too often made to feel guilty for not having a man who is able to support them all. If she is among those women who work outside the home because they want to, she is made to question why she can't find fulfillment within the family.

Being conditioned to think of ourselves "naturally" as mothers also lowers our expectations about being trained for anything else. We never think of ourselves as workers or what we do in the home as work.

The Myth of the Working Mother

As a black child growing up in the Depression South, I used to watch my mother straining at the ironing board as she struggled to keep the white man's shirt from becoming sooted by her primitive, charcoal-heated iron, and wondered why she had to work so hard for so little.

That was long ago, yet I still see work-worn women of all races and colors, struggling to keep body and soul together with their meager salaries grudgingly doled out by a male-dominated society, and I know why we have to work so hard for so little. We are unorganized, brainwashed, despised females in a world that has always worshiped the male.

And the myth of the "working mother" is one of the most insidious tools which man uses to keep us wasting away in our inferior, caste-bound hell. Yet strangely enough, although it must be evident to most women that all *mothers work and work themselves half to death unless they are wealthy, most of us have been so brainwashed for so long until we've passively accepted man's self-serving definition that housework is really no work at all.*[2]

Our economic background determines whatever training we do get. Poor and working-class women may or may not want to go to college, but they don't *expect* to be sent there. Thoughts about careers are affected by the pressures of everyday realities, and soon one's major career becomes the engaging of a man's interest for one's own future security and social acceptance. And many college-educated women don't really take the idea of a career seriously; it may perhaps add to being a more desirable wife, it won't interfere with becoming a mother, and it is something to go back to after the children are grown. It rarely has anything to do with one's own capabilities and interests.

We have been taught to view any situation in which we do not function as a wife and mother as short-term; on-the-job realities reinforce this view. The Labor Department's Women's Bureau reports that in 1955 a woman

2. Anita Cornwell, "The Myth of the Working Mother," *Woman: A Journal of Liberation,* Vol. 2, No. 3, p. 58.

A girl may love her mother,
but does that mean she wants to be just like her?
1. 2.

A girl sees her mother working hard and taking care of the children,
but who wants to take care of children all the time?

A girl sees her mother get angry at her kids ... she says "You can't go out" "stay at home", but who wants to stay at home getting yelled at?

Maybe her mother wishes underneath that she could go out, and that she didn't have to take care of kids all the time.
Shouldn't this be possible?

In babysitting, taking care of her brothers, a girl has to act like a mother. She has to yell at them just like her mother yells at her.
Is this good? Doesn't it have to stop somewhere?

Bread and Roses, Boston

Housework through the ages.

working full-time made on the average 64 percent of a man's income. In 1970 (the most recent figures), she was making 57 percent as much as a man.

All women are paid as "secondary bread winners," whether or not they are married. The boss believes that eventually you will marry (if you're under 21); that you should be married (if you're over 21); that if you have children you therefore have a man to support you. And anyway, it's not the boss's worry if you don't have enough to eat—it is the responsibility of the man you are supposed to be living with.[3]

The kinds of jobs available to women make home and family seem that much more appealing.

It is certainly hypocritical that the homage (in words) society pays to motherhood as "the noblest career" is the justification for tracking women into the kind of work that is the least interesting and lowest paying. It is frightening to think that the primary role of our lives is predetermined; that it is prescribed before we are born.

Keeping women focused on motherhood has benefitted others at our expense. While we can be manipulated in and out of the work force, we continue to produce the most valuable product in this society—not the well-typed letter or the well-scrubbed floor, but the children who will be tomorrow's workers. While sectioned off into our family units busy raising future workers to fill the same roles we have now, we remain available for work in times of social or family need. And this we do because we are prepared and taught that this is the normal thing: to be primarily mothers, not workers, not persons, and never to be all three at the same time.

The Prevailing Philosophy of Child Rearing

Still, no matter how strong our conditioning, no matter how little training we have for any other role, and no matter how bleak the prospects for meaningful and rewarding employment, the most pervasive reason for wanting to stay at home is that we are made to feel it is best for the child. Mothers try to put their children's interest first, despite the direct conflict it may create with their desires for themselves. In a study[4] of women who were asked how having children had changed their lives, the most common responses were "less freedom" and "they tie you down." There were four times as many totally negative responses as totally positive ones, and barely half gave responses that in any way could be considered positive. These women felt that caring for young children was a "frustrating time," that it was a time when you were supposed to "hold back impulses, defer gratifications, and, above all, remain physically in the home." But women will continue to make these sacrifices as long as they feel that their children's development depends on it.

The work of many experts is used to substantiate the belief that the child must constantly have available her or his biological mother. Among the most often cited of such

3. Vicki Breitbart and Beverly Leman, "Women Who Take Care of Children: Why Child Care," *Up from Under* (January/February 1971), p. 11.

4. Lois Wladis Hoffman, "The Decision to Work," Chap. 2 in Ivan F. Nye and Lois W. Hoffman, eds., *The Employed Mother in America* (Chicago: Rand McNally and Co., 1963).

authorities are René Spitz and John Bowlby. Spitz's work in the 1940's found that children permanently separated from their mothers were "severely retarded, prone to disease, and incapable of human relationships." Watching Spitz's film *Grief* can be a devastating experience. It shows children from twelve to eighteen months who were without their mothers from the time they were about four months. They lie in their cribs, listless and in despair, or they rock endlessly back and forth, sometimes hitting their heads on the bars of their cribs.

John Bowlby's report, *Maternal Care and Mental Health,* published by the World Health Organization over twenty years ago, studied children reared in institutions, hospitals, and foundling homes and comes to conclusions similar to those made graphic in Spitz's film. He found that these children seemed not only less intelligent than others raised in their own families, but they often displayed physical and emotional problems as well. More specifically, his report has been used to conclude (1) that the child's development is threatened by the lack of maternal care for even short-term experience; (2) that while separation after five years of age may still have its negative effects, the younger the child, the more serious the consequences; and (3) that group care *per se* is detrimental to the child's growth.

There is also the prevalent fear that even part-time separations will "diminish both parental authority and parental involvement with children."[5]

It has been argued that for a wife and mother to work outside the home—to earn money independently of her husband and to have non-domestic, non-familial interests . . . would lessen women's femininity and maternal feelings and create dissatisfactions with the roles of wife and mother; that it would deprive children of maternal love and guidance and create confusion in sex-role identification. Theorists who [see] the rise of maternal employment in a negative light [feel] that it carr[ies] in its wake emotional conflict, divorce, delinquency.[6]

Beyond Theory

In recent years the entire theory of maternal deprivation has been seriously challenged. It is now recognized that the institutions that Spitz and Bowlby studied were overcrowded, and children were deprived of environmental stimulation as well as human contact. It is now believed that the detrimental effects were probably caused by the lack of toys and playthings, and infrequent and inadequate human interaction. It was the lack of *mothering,* and not the lack of mother, that caused the negative effects.

At present, the specific biological situation of the continuing relationship of the child tc its biological mother and its need for care by human beings is hopelessly confused in the growing insistence that child and biological mother, or mother surrogate, must never be separated, that all separation even for a few days is inevitably damaging, and that if long enough it does irreversible damage. This . . . is a new aud subtle form of antifeminism, in which men—under the guise of exalting the

5. From Richard Nixon's veto message of the Comprehensive Child Care Bill, December 9, 1971.

6. Florence Ruderman, *Child Care and Working Mothers* (New York: Child Welfare League of America, 1968) p. 7.

importance of maternity—are tying women more tightly to their children than has been thought necessary since the invention of bottle feeding and baby carriages.[7]

There are now several studies of children whose mothers work, and none of these reveals damage or defects. Ivan Nye and Lois Hoffman in their book, *The Employed Mother in America,* have compiled studies that compare children from families that are alike in almost every way—size, race, age composition, intactness, income—except for the fact that in one group the mother has worked. They have shown that there are no significant differences in physical fitness or social or emotional behavior. And one study cited by Nye and Hoffman,[8] which showed no difference between children whose mothers worked when they were infants and those whose mothers worked when they were school age, seems to refute the argument that partial separation is more harmful at an earlier age.

Researchers have also found that "a working mother is not one who typically rejects children emotionally or neglects their needs,"[9] and that "employment of mothers may actually have good consequences."[10] For daughters, "maternal employment may contribute to a greater admiration of the mother, a concept of the female role which includes less restrictions and a wider range of activities, and a self-concept which incorporated these aspects of the female role."[11] The fear that maternal employment or alternative forms of child care are the causes of our social ills is an oversimplification and a distortion of the problems that exist in this society today.

And what about the role of the father? While there has been much research into the effects of separation from the mother, little has been studied about the presence or absence of the father in child care.

Particularly absent from the psychological literature is an analysis of infants' responses to their father, or to men in general. We do not know the effects of masculine attention and male child-rearing. Nobody seems to want to know either. How can we assume the natural superiority of women as socializers of children when we do not know the effects—and think of how positive they might be—of male interaction with the infant at all levels of the socialization process?[12]

. . . If the underevaluation of women in society is to end, we must begin at the beginning by a more equitable distribution of labor around child-rearing and the home. . . . Men can and should begin to take a more active part in the affective and cognitive interaction with infants than they have done until now.[13]

There is little doubt that a child needs love, affection, consistent care, guidance, and physical and intellectual stimulation. The controversy is not around what the child needs as much as how, where, and by whom she or he is going to get it. As Margaret Mead has pointed out:

Actually, anthropological evidence gives no support at present to the value of such an accentuation of the tie between mother and child. . . . On the contrary, cross-cultural studies suggest that adjustment is most fa-

7. Margaret Mead, Some Theoretical Considerations on the Problem of Mother-Child Separation, *American Journal of Orthopsychiatry,* Vol. 24, No. 3 (1954), p. 477.

8. Lee G. Burchinal, Personality Characteristics of Children, in *The Employed Mother in America* (Chicago: Rand McNally, 1963).

9. Ivan Nye and Lois Hoffman, *The Employed Mother in America* (Chicago: Rand McNally, 1963), p. 92.

10. Florence Ruderman, *Child Care and Working Mothers* (New York: Child Welfare League of America, 1968), p. 7.

11. *The Employed Mother in America,* p. 201.

12. Sheli Nortis, Child-Rearing and Women's Liberation, a publication of the Boston Area Child Care Action Group, 1970, p. 4.

13. Ibid., p. 6.

$ACRED MOTHERHOOD

Like father . . .

cilitated if the child is cared for by many warm, friendly people.[14]

The Shape of Alternatives

What, then, are the virtues of alternative child care? *For the child,* time spent exploring a rich and stimulating environment with a balance between activity and quiet, between individual and group contact, can be a valuable experience. Recent studies of children thirty months old who had been in a day care center from the time they were one year showed that the strength of their attachment to their mothers was no different from that of home-raised children but that they had attained measurably higher "IQ levels" than the home-reared group.[15]

There can also be positive effects on the social and emotional development of the child. If she or he spends part of the day with other children and adults, a child can learn to depend on other people besides her or his parents. For the child, time spent in an alternative form of care can be a relief from the narrowness of an exclusive relationship. It can be a larger view of the world than the one seen through the eyes of one—possibly two—parents. Child care where both men and women are caring, sensitive, resourceful people can help the child expand her or his definition of adult roles. Child care controlled by the adults

14. Margaret Mead, "Some Theoretical Considerations on the Problem of Mother-Child Separation," *American Journal of Orthopsychiatry,* Vol. 24, No. 3 (1954), p. 477.

15. B. M. Caldwell, C. M. Wright, A. S. Honig, and J. Tannenbaum, "Infant Day Care and Attachment," *American Journal of Orthopsychiatry,* Vol. 40, No. 3 (1970), pp. 397–412.

who are important to the child can strengthen her or his self-image. Child care where there are people from other races and economic backgrounds can have a lasting positive effect.

For the mother engaged in full-time one-to-one child care, alternatives are not just a welcome relief, and they can be more than a cold necessity for women working outside the home. Sharing child care can bring new insights into the causes for our frustrations and can help us realize how many of our problems come from the narrow definition of our role. Alternative forms of child care can awaken dreams and help us fill the gap between our duties to our children and our desires for ourselves. For mothers and fathers who are part of a group of people who determine the kind of care their children receive, it can be an opportunity to develop a new understanding of the way they are relating to their children. They can question child-rearing practices and develop those that best suit them and their children, for their community today, and for what it may become.

Changing our feelings about ourselves and our relationships to children is frightening. It's difficult to break through the myths and attitudes about child care that have lasted for generations. Giving up old images is painful, especially when the alternatives are not clear. It's not going to be easy to build something new, but it's harder watching ourselves and our children fall into destructive old patterns. It's those times that we find ourselves saying those things we hated our parents for saying, it's those times we see our children doing the same things we hated ourselves for doing, that make us yell, STOP!

. . like son.

Marilyn Mulford

Wanting alternative child care is the first step. But, as this woman found, seeking is not necessarily finding.

"Well, I passed the park today . . ."

Lucille Abbot

How does the single mother stay sane and productive through all the hassles she consistently finds herself living through? There was a time, not too long ago, when I took in typing jobs to be free of semi-monthly welfare checks from the City of New York. I typed like mad to finish dissertations and theses by the deadlines given me. I remember once when my son came down with a severe throat infection that I finished a thesis within the deadline and myself in the process. Next, I baked cakes, watched other people's children, anything you can think of to make ends meet, and, becoming terribly insecure in the process, found myself back on public assistance. It's an experience everyone should live through. Perhaps they would empathize with the women who are widowed or left with five or six little ones and, having no skills to their name, have to live year in and year out on the pittance that the State of New York sanctions. Having lived through it for a time was like reliving the Depression years of the 1930's. If I had to remain on it indefinitely, I would probably pick up the aimless walking of these women, the trip to nowhere attitude that prevails when there is no way out of a problem.

There is one incident that is crystal clear in my memory and that is the one of the elderly lady in the surplus food depot on Fifth Street and FDR Drive, where welfare clients could pick up their rations, depending on their family size . . . small family, bi-monthly; large family, monthly. We were all lined up with our shopping carts, which the Department of Social Services gives to its clients on Aid to Dependent Children, and as we progressed slowly from stall to stall to receive butter, powdered eggs, dried beans, etc., I heard a conversation that immediately caught my attention. An old woman was trying to bargain with the young boy who was dispensing boxes of raisins. She was obviously the guardian of her five-year-old granddaughter and was trying to exchange a can of peanut butter for an extra box of raisins. The young boy, obviously delighting in his power, said no to the woman. When she explained that raisins were the only sweets she could afford for the child and didn't he realize how much children liked to have something sweet, her plea fell on deaf ears. I followed her and her young one outside and offered her my box of raisins as my son was still too young to eat them. She smiled and then begged me to take some canned milk for the baby. I cried all the way home about this incident, and in the future, whenever I gave anything away on my cart, I made it a point that it was an exchange, not "charity." That is the last thing a welfare recipient wants . . . taking instead of giving.

After living this life for a time, I made up my

mind that as soon as I could toilet train my son, I would go back to work on a full-time basis. In the meantime, I had heard of a sitter around the corner from me and decided to take my child to her for the care and attention that I understood she offered, and proceeded to take a part-time job at an Institute nearby and trundled off to work every morning. I was, at that time, receiving partial assistance, but felt that I was fulfilling half my ambition to become economically independent once more. Well, between the sitter's $15 a week and earning only $50 *before taxes* I realized that I was fooling no one but myself. I had even less money.

Next comes the experience which every mother who is alone is familiar with, and that is the one of the nursery school or day care center.

When my son was two and a half, I requested a booklet from the Board of Health listing all child care centers in the five boroughs of New York. It is free, published bi-annually, and can be obtained if you write or call them. Well, the fun just begins now, doesn't it? You eagerly pick up the phone and are confident that you can now take a full-time job, but are told by the schools that the "new" law—nobody knows when it came into effect, but it's "new"—states that they can only interview mothers a month in advance of the child's third birthday. Secondly, you must be working or have the promise of a job. Being a logical creature you question this with, "Well, how can I plan on accepting full-time employment if I'm not sure that you can accept my child?" The answer is, "We can't answer that, because we have a long waiting list." Again you venture, becoming more and more anxious, "Couldn't you put my name on the list and I'll come in a month before the child is three." Again . . . impasse: "Sorry, but we cannot take names over the phone, you must come in personally a month before the child is three . . . you understand, don't you?" You hang up realizing that you have learned nothing except that you must be there precisely a month before your child is three, club in hand and tears streaming down your face, in order to put your name on a list! You begin to live for your child's approaching third birthday; everything in your life suddenly rotates around this monumental date. Meanwhile the anxiety and poverty are so unbearable that you grit your teeth and tell yourself that the babysitter who takes your money and does little else will have to do since Nixon is busy dispensing war and mayhem, instead of nursery schools and job programs for people in this country. After all, she has to take in six or eight children to earn enough money to live on and she doesn't have the facilities or the time to really watch and play with all of them like she might want to.

When you finally become anxious enough about the pallor in your child's cheek, you say something about when she takes the child out. Her reply is the classic, "Well, I passed the park today, but it was too cold to go in." Why must we be afraid to open our mouths when we see how our children spend their idle days? You know the answer as well as I: not enough money for schools for our children. Plenty of private schools for those who can afford them, and blacks are starting to get together and demand day care, but what about the woman in the middle, who does not qualify for either? We should learn from the blacks and demand day care for our children also. You shudder at the thought of all the mothers who have yet to go through this frustrating and disheartening experience. But you are over a barrel and there you will remain inertly draped until the cry for schools becomes so loud and the moaning so dreadful that we will actually start breaking the ground with our bare hands, instead of waiting for senators and congressmen who promise to "have something done about it."

In the meantime, you prepare yourself to find a permanent 9 to 5 job. You apply and are asked if you have children. If you say yes, no job. The children might become ill. Word must be spreading that all working mothers have sickly children. I know of women who have denied the existence of their offspring and when found out, have been fired because they were "trying to get away with something." What is it they were getting away with? Is it "getting away with something" if to buy a piece of edible meat for your child, your shoes will have to suffer, and the child's as well till the Welfare check the following month? Or just maybe it could be the fact that a woman's self-esteem is at stake and she wants to produce her own earned money, instead of cringing when it is found out that she is on public assistance and thereby looked upon as a leech in this society? If that's what she is "trying to get away with," I think it should be rephrased to state that it is what she is trying to get away *from!*

My "big opportunity" came to me via a friend. It seemed there was this "research professor" at a leading medical college who was looking for someone who knew how to deal with people as well as having the necessary skills. After much interviewing and red tape, I landed this position. It was clearly understood at the outset that should my child become ill, I would remain home with him. He agreed, and stated that if, after the three-month probationary period, I was unable to locate my child in a day care center, I could take a leave of absence and come back when I was able. The Department of Welfare agreed to this and everybody was seemingly happy with the arrangement. The Department of Social Services said I could keep my Medicaid until I could secure hospitalization through my job. I felt fine about the whole thing, until my son came down with severe croup in late October. I called my job and explained that I would be home with him at least a week. Not wanting to jeopardize my position I suggested that I be docked for the week and that a temporary office worker be hired to get the work done. Ethical enough? Fair enough? Not for my boss. He called me at 10 p.m. the second day I was home to inform me that he had an idea. I should get a visiting nurse to watch my child, come to work, and therefore not lose any money. The College would even pay for the nurse. It sounds practical enough to a person who deals in theories, I suppose, but I wanted to stay home with my son, not leave him with a stranger, especially when he was ill. All that week he vacillated between concern for my health and my child's, and the fact that the work was piling up and he was most upset. Finally he offered me a choice (if I wanted to be paid for the week I was *taking off*). I could make up *forty hours.* I laughed hysterically, and he attributed this to lack of sleep on my part. Things naturally went downhill after that. Finally, I asked for a transfer to another department.

Marilyn Mulford

Between the onset of the croup, however, and my ultimate departure from that position, there were the daily trips to the day care center. When I say daily, believe daily. Now I know why the popular belief that all women are born actresses prevails. I found myself crying, wringing handkerchiefs, prostrating myself before the staff of the center in order to have my child accepted. I began to feel as though I were prostituting myself to obtain something that my taxes should have been doing for me. I must say, here, that day care personnel are probably the nicest and most sympathetic people around. They understand the crying need for more centers but can do nothing but relentlessly petition, but to no promising outcome. They take the neediest people first. Anyone who has a mother, sister, aunt, cousin, best friend, cub scout, or anyone else who can care for their child while they work is dropped from the top of the list. I qualified as neediest, as I have no one. That reality, difficult to come to grips with, had me again walking around for weeks with my chin on my sneakers. Anyway, I was pushed to the top of the list because of being a "have-not." Right before Christmas I was advised that my child would be accepted the next month, but my joy was tempered by the fact that I had to transfer to a new department, or I would go mad with frustration.

My experience with the other departments was just as disillusioning. No one wanted a woman with a dependent child. I could understand this from Radiology, Urology, Psychiatry, Pharmacy, etc., but when Pediatrics said thumbs down, you know what I said to myself, besides questioning the humanity of these "dedicated robots."

So, Christmas Eve left me jobless. I had no spirit left at all, much less the holiday kind.

I worked part-time until the week arrived that my son was to enter the day care center. While he was going through his adjustment period, I had two hours to spend between leaving and picking him up. So, I walked up and down the streets nearby asking if anyone needed a secretary. It was something I had always thought of doing, since I have a disgust for people who run employment agencies and take a percentage of your money just so that you can have the privilege of earning a living. Finally, one kind receptionist bothered to call the business manager to talk to me. I explained that I had a child and if that would be a handicap to tell me right off. She understood the problem and then I realized that I had applied to Big Brothers, Inc., a social service agency, whose aim was to help fatherless young boys to achieve fruitful lives through the implementation of volunteer Big Brothers. Their secondary goal was to service the families of these boys, should there be a need for it. After I filled out an application, took a test and had my references checked, I was asked if I could come back about 11:30 to meet the men I would be working for. When I explained that it was inconvenient since I had to pick up my child at that time, she smiled and said very matter of factly that I should bring him

Marilyn Mulford

along and someone would watch him for me. I couldn't believe it! I have been there almost a year now and if I state that my child or I do not feel well, there is no hanging at dawn from the nearest tree. Both my bosses treat me as an adult who can make sensible decisions and, being a mother myself, they realize what an asset I can be when a mother of a Little Brother calls, upset about a particular problem she is having.

I have found a position where the people are humane. They don't expound on what people "should" do, they live it. They're not the kind of people who hire you, promise you nursery school placement on their premises, and work you to death for every little crumb they throw your way because they know you are in a peculiar spot. I'm speaking of people who deal with day-to-day misery, and would be horrified if it occurred with one of their staff. I'm happy with my work and with the people there. Maybe if employers would begin to realize that the hardest worker is someone who has children dependent on her, they will have dedicated and conscientious workers.

I know that there are very few jobs such as the one I have . . . but why? Maybe if all the single women with children, women on welfare, all women were to band together and demand free child care, perhaps then we will be more content with our lives and that of our children. There is something wrong with a society that exalts the position of motherhood and then downgrades it by not allowing "motherhood" its due in the total scheme of things.

M.S.R.

Chapter 2

The Reality of Day Care

Since its inception, day care has been seen as a charitable service for the helpless, penniless, or familyless child. The first day care centers in this country were established in New York City in the middle of the nineteenth century for immigrant women, often separated from their families, who had to support themselves and their children in the sweatshops of the time. The class bias that motivated the origins of these services is clear in this statement written over a hundred years ago:

> *What shall we do with these children? . . . Born by no fault of their own, [they have been cast] into the very arms of ignorance, sin, and even in infancy into the seething Ganges of our streets. [Centers are to prepare children] for their station in life. All children of suitable age are employed . . . in performing . . . housework under the eye of a matron, thus affording them an excellent opportunity of becoming fitted for servants or future housekeepers. [Sewing is taught to the girls] as a suitable occupation for poor females.*[1]

1. "Historical Sketch of the Day Nursery Movement," an unpublished paper prepared by the National Association of Day Nurseries, Inc.

Social-work consciousness has developed far more sophistication, but the image that day care is for children who are deprived—socially or emotionally—is still locked into the minds of too many people. More than a hundred years later the prejudices still remain. It is still a popular belief that alternative forms of child care (for other than the children of the rich) should only be necessary because of the breakdown of families or the failure of individuals. The following statement is typical of this attitude among professionals and social-welfare agencies responsible for establishing and running child care services:

> *The purpose of [day care services] is to protect children by providing part time care, supervision and guidance when families are unable to meet their needs without some assistance from the community.*[2]

Or, from the Children's Bureau, a government agency:

> *The child who needs day care has a family problem which makes it impossible for his*

2. Child Welfare League of America, *Standard for Day Care Services*, 1960.

parents to fulfill their parental responsibility without supplementary help.[3]

Not until recently have some agencies added "education" or "child development" to the descriptions of their child care programs. Day care is strictly regulated by the state Departments of Welfare and/or Health; very rarely is the Department of Education involved.

In her extensive study for the Child Welfare League, Florence Ruderman concluded that in this country "there is the absence of a comprehensive philosophy of supplementary child care services, within which day care could be developed as a good, attractive form of supplementary care, rather than as either a social-work service to troubled families or a commercialized form of custodial care." The negative attitude toward day care has affected not only its desirability but its availability as well. In the same study, Ruderman asked over two thousand representatives of major philanthropic agencies that administer day care programs what they thought of the service. Almost all saw it as a custodial service for poor and troubled families and were against its expansion. As the following article shows, the only time child care services were provided on a large scale in this country was when the national economy demanded it.

3. *Guides to State Welfare Agencies for the Development of Day Care Services*, Children's Bureau, U.S. Department of Health, Education and Welfare, 1963.

Public Child Care: Our Hidden History

Judy Kleinberg

Many people are questioning the feasibility of establishing public child care centers on a large-scale basis in the United States. Where will the money come from? Who will administer the programs? How long will it take until large numbers of children can be enrolled? They are usually unaware that this country experienced in the past one of the most massive, innovative, and far-reaching child care programs ever attempted. Looking back at this earlier period should prove helpful in answering some of the questions posed.

Until the Depression, the United States was the only major industrial country that did not provide some type of federally funded child care program. On October 23, 1933, the administrator of the Federal Emergency Relief Administration (FERA) authorized funds to provide wages for unemployed teachers and other workers on relief. Within three months, thirty states had organized systems of emergency nursery schools to make use of these funds. Some nursery schools were open for five hours a day, some for nine hours, and in several cases the schools functioned twenty-four hours around the clock.

From 1933 to 1940, the federal government spent $3,141,000 on child care and provided services to 300,000 children. Because three-quarters of these nurseries were housed in public-school buildings, many people began to feel that it was desirable and possible for the public schools to provide care and education for children under five years of age. The administrator of the FERA even declared that the emergency nursery schools should become "a permanent and integral part of the regularly established public school programs."

The second phase of public child care begins with the entry of the United States into World War II. Between January 1941 and January 1944 the number of employed women increased by 4 million. In August 1942, the War Manpower Commission directed the Office of Defense, Health, and Welfare to set up a program of federally supported child care centers for children of working mothers in war-related industries. $400,000 was made available by the President from emergency funds. Almost at the same time, Congress passed a Community Facilities Bill (known as the Lanham Act), which provided an initial $150 million for facilities, including child care centers, in recently expanded war-industry areas.

By June 1943, less than a year later, thirty-nine states had fully operating extended school services administered by state and local education authorities, and thirty states had similar services administered by welfare agencies. At the peak, July 1945, approximately 1.6 million children were enrolled in nursery schools and

JOBS FOR ALL
AFTER THE WAR

child care centers receiving federal funds.

How did the states respond during this period? Within three years, sixteen states lowered school age admission to provide for children below six years, thirteen states passed laws for the establishment of nursery schools, ten states gave authority to local schools to use local funds for nursery schools, and five states provided funds for emergency "child-care programs for children 2–14 years old."

The Kaiser Child Service Centers provide a good example for federally supported centers established during World War II. On November 8, 1943, the Kaiser Shipbuilding Corporation opened two child care centers at the entrances to its shipyards in Portland, Oregon. During the twenty-two months the centers were in operation they served 4,014 children, from eighteen months to six years of age, seven days a week, twenty-four hours a day, 364 days a year. The United States Maritime Commission provided buildings and equipment.

Besides the program for preschool children, the centers were opened to older children after school, weekends, holidays, or whenever necessary; to nonenrolled children whose regular child care arrangements broke down; and to children who needed to stay on an extra shift because of their parents, overtime work, union meetings, or recreational needs. Other extras included an infirmary, immunizations, home service food which could be picked up by parents after work, a mending service, a shopping service, barbers, a lending library of books and toys, booklets for parents on child development and child care, a newsletter for parents, and a store for shoelaces and other necessities. Most of these additional services were suggested by parents and subsequently implemented by the staff.

On September 1, 1945, at the end of the war, the Kaiser Child Service Centers were shut down as quickly as they had opened. Within months, federal funds were withdrawn from all child care programs across the country. Although several states passed laws to provide state funding for child care, only California has retained its public centers on a large-scale basis. Today, Southern California has more child care centers than any other urban area in the country.

Are the needs of working mothers and their children any less urgent today than during the earlier period? Between 1940 and 1964 the number of working mothers with children under eighteen increased more than sixfold. By 1965 more than one-third of all mothers in the United States worked. These 9.5 million working mothers had a total of 4.2 million children under the age of six, 11 million under age eighteen. For these children there were places for fewer than 350,000 children in licensed child care facilities, that is, one-fifth the number of places for children in public child care centers twenty years earlier.

Child care centers during the Depression and World War II were established to meet the needs of the government and not the needs of children, parents, and teachers, whose lives were affected by them. When the government no longer needed to provide jobs for teachers on relief or to employ women in the defense industries, it closed down the centers. Although many women struggled to keep the centers open, their movement was not organized or powerful enough to change government policy.

If the federal government was able to set up, finance, and maintain such an extensive child care program twenty-five years ago, it can do so again today. Public child care centers must not open and close in response to the needs of government, but must respond to the needs of women and children. Only if the centers are controlled by those who use them can parents and children be guaranteed that they will remain in existence and provide the quality care necessary.

What Exists Now

At present, statistics on the need for child care services only count those mothers with paying jobs, and do not include women at home who are interested in alternative care. Yet the information that is available shows an enormous and growing need for services. In 1965 there were 4.2 million children under the age of six with working mothers; in 1970, 5 million, and the figure is steadily rising. Yet according to the Day Care and Child Development Council of America, there are fewer than 700,000 children in licensed day care facilities.

The shortage of free or low cost organized day care programs has created a desperate situation in this country. Thousands of children under the age of six have to take care of themselves while their mothers are at work. There is evidence that many children spend the day walking the streets with their house keys around their necks. A recent study by the Chicago Housing Authority found that in one housing project alone there were four hundred of these so-called latch-key children.

There are thousands—perhaps hundreds of thousands—of infants and toddlers who are cared for by siblings under the age of eighteen, and in this situation the desires and demands of the teen-agers are forced to compete with the care of the young child. Then, there are the families in which the father takes care of his children, often because the mother and father must work different shifts, or the father is unemployed. In these cases, the child care arrangements add tensions to an already complicated home life. Other members of the family may also care for the child, but those mothers who can't find a relative must look for pay-as-you-go arrangements, which drain the limited family resources even further. And what they find is sadly inadequate.

Family Day Care

Babysitting for a group of children in someone else's home is often referred to as Family Day Care. It is estimated that as many as 2 million children may be receiving this type of care. The women who provide Family Day Care usually have young children of their own and take a few more into their homes for the extra money. They do this either because they are unable to find other work or because the jobs open to them are unappealing. The Ruderman study for the Child Welfare League of America found that 33 percent of the women running Family Day Care homes said that they would rather do something else but were not trained for any other job. These women may wish to offer children a rich and stimulating environment but are themselves poor, isolated, underpaid, and overworked.

In these Family Day Care homes that Representative Shirley Chisholm has called "children's parking lots," the child's day most often consists of breakfast, television, lunch, a nap, and then more television. A study conducted by the Medical and Health Research Association of New York City showed that 34 percent of these homes lacked play materials of any kind, in 25 percent the children were never taken out of doors, and 84 percent were rated inadequate largely because they violated the Health Code. This is an indictment not of the individual woman but of a society that forces the poor—with their limited resources and limited possibilities to develop their own abilities—to take care of the poor.

Very few of these Family Day Care homes are licensed—somewhere between 5 and 10 percent—but licensing does not necessarily mean better care. Licensing does nothing to break down the isolation of this type of care, it does not pay for substitute care when the "provider" mother or her children are sick. It doesn't create more stability for the "provider mother." It doesn't give her a budget for supplies and equipment. And, it *does* mean more paper work, more investigation, and a medical checkup at her expense.

In licensed Family Day Care in New York City, parents pay from $15 to $35 a week to a woman who can legally take care of a maximum of six children (including her own). If

Work of the
Children's Aid Society.

Motherhood for the rich . . . and the poor.

Family Day Care is publicly subsidized, the "provider" receives a $75 a month stipend for each child and $14 a month per child for food. This is usually calculated on a daily basis for other than her own children, and there is no guarantee how much she will earn each month. The New York City Task Force that was formed to look into the availability and quality of child care services described this form of day care as having "no educational component." And no wonder. How can a woman afford any education equipment out of a meager and unstable budget? If she alone is caring for six children, where will she find the time and energy to provide activities? And if she is in a small apartment (which is usually the case), where is the space needed for children's play?

This is not to say there aren't some Family Day Care programs that do more than babysit. In small demonstration projects in New York City, in Massachusetts, and California, women do get a chance to discuss child development, curriculum, and the problems that arise in this form of child care. But in most cases the women who do this work are burdened by the isolation and the lack of resources that every mother feels. For the "provider" mother, all the problems of a one-to-one relationship are now multiplied to one-to-six.

Group Care

"Group day care," "child care center," and "children's center" all describe a full day's care for a group of at least twelve children. There are very few centers—only 17,500 nationally—and they provide care for approximately 575,000 children. In the Ruderman study and in more recent studies by Westinghouse Learning Corporation (1970) and the National Council of Jewish Women (1973), parents said that of all child care arrangements, they had the least dissatisfaction with centers. More parents who used centers expected an educational experience in addition to care and supervision of their children. They felt that centers were the most "secure" and "stable" of all arrangements both for adults and children. Many of those who used centers wanted better care but preferred an improved group program rather than another type of arrangement.

Why, then, are many of the child care centers that exist underenrolled? In some cases the fees are too high, or the centers are too far from the people who could use them. Inflexible schedules are also a drawback. They usually provide care only between the hours of eight and six for children three to five years old. Most centers are not available for women who must work part-time, nights, or irregularly. But another and more basic reason for their underenrollment is the lack of quality service. Although women who are not working outside the home and not using child care facilities have indicated they want group child care centers, in many cases they are put off by the negative image of a service intended for "problem families" or, more vividly, "by the picture of overcrowded, understaffed, juvenile halls where disturbed children . . . were indiscriminately dumped." With the prevailing ideology that maintains that any substitute for mother bringing up her children is bound to be inferior, and that group care is most harmful, little attention has been paid to the programs that *are* available; the belief that group care is not beneficial to the child has become a self-perpetuating myth.

For-Profit Programs

Most child care centers (60 percent) are run as profitmaking enterprises with average fees of $18.50 a week, and this is far from what comprehensive child care costs. After a thorough analysis of several cost studies, economic consultant Mary P. Rowe reported to the Senate Finance Committee that "*good* [emphasis added] child care costs at least $2,000 per child" or nearly $40 weekly. Able to charge only a "going rate" ($18.50), most programs and facilities exist at the minimum possible level. The proprietors of private centers may be well-meaning; many work in the center and try to provide a friendly home-like atmosphere for the children. But in order to make a profit, many of these programs have large classes, a high teacher-child ratio, little equipment, and poor food, if any at all. The staff is often overworked, underpaid, and offered few benefits and little job-development training. The profit is clearly at the expense of everyone but the owner. Joseph Featherstone in his article "Kentucky Fried Children" writes about his observations in a for-profit day care center:

> *Scarcely any adult I saw even talked to a child. The children are universally bored to stupefaction. At 2, 3, 4, and 5—all incredibly active years—they have the inert look of children in the later years in elementary school. Even when they are made to sit still, they remain for the most part inactive and passive.*[1]

A similar feeling of boredom and despair pervaded one for-profit center I observed in New York City. Some children were wandering around glassy-eyed; a few more were crying. I was told there were five staff members; I saw two. One elderly woman was tying a boy's shoe but found the time to whack another on the arm when he came up and touched the child she was helping. The other staff member was consoling a crying child: "You're not supposed to cry. You should be happy."

I was shown one room and told it was the art room. There were easels along one wall that looked used, although no one was in the room that afternoon. In the middle of the room was a large adult-sized table with benches around it—an incongruous piece of equipment for a center where most children are two or three years old. There were no children's paintings on the walls; the walls were, in fact, totally bare.

In the next room there was a television, and about ten of the twenty children there for the day were in front of it. A third room—empty—had mattresses and a playpen. There was also a kitchen and another large play room. Here is where I saw most of the other children, all of them battling for a turn on an expensive piece of climbing equipment. Besides this, there were a few toys in cardboard boxes in the corner. And on one wall a poster which very colorfully—but very sadly—said: LOVE.

A center like this one costs parents a lot—a dollar an hour, or roughly Mary Rowe's $40 a week—but money alone does not make the difference. While the fee is higher than average, the program is typical of proprietary day care. In the study of day care by the National Council of Jewish Women, they rated only 1 percent of the for-profit centers as superior, 15 percent as good, 35 percent as fair "in the sense of meeting basic physical needs with very little, if anything, in the way of developmental services," and the rest were poor or worse.

Franchise Day Care

Franchise day care is profit day care but with an added dimension—a blueprint for a day care program that can be used over and over again in any city at any time at a lower pro-rated cost. This mass-produced child care only means more profits for the owners and less responsive programs for parents and children.

In a 1971 article in *Barron's* entitled "Fleecing the Pre-school Sheep," Kirby Westheimer, President of Learning Development Corporation, claimed that day care centers cannot run profitably *except* at the sacrifice of quality. But this doesn't seem to be stopping many investors. Several large franchise programs, operating throughout the country, are already successful. A number of companies once in the nursing home business are now concentrating on day care, and other large companies, like Singer, who have already created a positive image in the minds of working women, are branching out into day care. As the Westheimer article points out, "Seldom in the annals of American education has the opportunity seemed

1. *New Republic,* Sept. 12, 1970.

to beckon venture capital in quite the same way it does these days in the pre-school field."

Franchises are sold as package deals which can't be altered; the system is thus neither responsive nor accountable to its workers or its "customers." This profit-model simply aims to further exploit the day care scene. Where day care is a "product" in a market where the demand is greater than the supply, what control can the customer have? The parents will not determine the program for their children, and in most instances decisions will ultimately be made on the basis of the profit motive alone. The following article, published in 1970, describes this situation.

M.S.R.

The Day Care Business

"Which comes first—the child or the dollar?"

Alice Lake

Everybody wants day care centers, and businessmen are rushing to supply them. But can you serve children the same way you serve Kentucky Fried Chicken? . . .

Already over forty corporations are splashing around millions of dollars to create a profitable new industry. Children will be its products.

Brand new a year ago, the large-scale day care business is rapidly gathering steam. A dozen of the biggest companies already operate over a hundred child centers in twenty-one states. But the reality is nothing compared with the promise. Half a dozen companies expect to serve close to 50,000 children by the end of 1971. One outfit alone plans to open 1,000 centers in the next few years, with close to 100,000 preschoolers eventually under a single corporate wing. . . .

A few of the companies intend to run child care centers like a chain of look-alike grocery stores, but a majority want to franchise them—to lease their name and know-how to local owner-operators exactly the way Howard Johnson licenses restaurants and Colonel Harland Sanders leases Kentucky-fried-chicken stands. The names they have chosen give a hint of what's in store, for although a few are sober (American Child Centers, in Nashville), some are pretentious (Les Petites Académies, in Kansas City), and many are downright cute (Mary Moppet's, in Arizona; Little Shaver's, in Florida and Rhode Island; Kay's Kiddie Kollege, in Florida).

The business of young children is growth and development, and the business of corporations is making money. If you mix the two, can the needs of both be satisfied? Will look-alike child centers inevitably turn out look-alike children?

Experts in early-childhood education say they are willing to give business a chance. They hope it can prove its contention that corporate efficiency will permit both quality and a profit. Privately, they wonder how it can be pulled off.

Some businessmen are equally skeptical. They are not against commercial day care, but they believe franchising is the wrong way to go about it. Conformity to a pat formula is the secret of successful franchising. "You can train anyone to produce a hamburger that tastes the same in California and New York," one business consultant says, "but there isn't any rule book for running a day care center. It's too complex."

If any company can combine quality with profits, it's likely to be American Child Centers. Headed by Edward T. Breathitt, former governor of Kentucky, the company has hired as its educational director Dr. Richard Hinze, recently dean of the graduate school of the Bank Street College of Education, in New York. It has substantial financial backing—more than $1 million from its parent company, Performance Systems, owner of the Minnie Pearl chicken franchises. (Company executives wince when wags refer to the new venture as "Chicken Little.") Four centers are now in operation: the pilot plant in Nashville, a franchised center in Frankfort, Kentucky, and two wholly owned centers, one in Atlanta, the other in an apartment complex in Kansas City. The company plans to open 50 centers by 1971 and 350 by 1973.

The Nashville center looks good. Planned for 130 youngsters aged three to six, it is bright with vivid primary colors. Equipment is generous: blocks, parallel bars, doll corners with tiny rockers and toy stoves, books, records. The outdoor play area has a large tree house for climbing and a drainage pipe for crawling.

Although the center is open eleven hours a day, a third of its youngsters attend only morning nursery school. The charge for them is $14.50 a week; full day care costs $21.75 weekly. Drop-ins, whose mothers want a few hours free to go shopping, are accepted for a Saturday play program and pay 75 cents an hour.

The staff, mostly college graduates, is organized into teams—a lead teacher, an assistant, and a couple of aides for each group of 40 children—with a ratio of one adult to every 10 youngsters. Dr. Hinze wanted one teacher for each eight children. Joseph A. Lane, Jr., his alter-ego on the business side, fought for a ratio of 1 to 12. "We split the difference," Dr. Hinze says. It is a significant compromise, because teachers represent the major expense in a day care budget. They are also the heart of its program.

Other compromises are also significant. To concentrate its staff in the hours of peak activity, the Nashville center pays them by the hour and hires the majority for a four-hour day. This saves money, but raises some questions. A part-time staff means fragmentation for children, half a dozen adult faces each day. ("When there is a rotation of teachers through the child's day, no one of them really knows how he is growing," the Child Welfare League of America warns.)

Educators who have visited the Nashville center praise its program as imaginative. What I found significant in a two-day visit was the running battle between the balance sheet, represented by Joseph Lane, and the children's needs, represented by Dr. Hinze. Other day care entrepreneurs have no Dr. Hinze. With one exception (Romper Room Schools, in Rumford, Rhode Island), none has hired a full-time educator approaching his stature. Without a strong voice to plead for children, isn't business likely —as much out of ignorance as greed—to trample on their needs?

I received an answer at the next center I visited, located in a Middle Western city and franchised by Mary Moppet's Day Care Schools, a Scottsdale, Arizona, corporation, which is currently the largest in the day care business. Seventeen Mary Moppet's schools are now operating in eight states, and the company president, Gerald Spresser, a real-estate operator, expects to have eleven more before the end of this year. Most are managed by their owners, three-fourths of whom have no background in education.

Although brochures for potential customers describe a Mary Moppet's program—science, phonics, modern math—a steady stream of material for franchisers explains what it's really all about: making money. The way to do it? Cater to the convenience of the customer—not the child but to his parents. Accept tiny children, even infants, unless state law forbids it. Remain open as long as there's revenue.

The Moppet's center I visited remains open from 6:30 a.m. until 1:30 a.m. six days a week. It is licensed for fifty children aged two to six, and they come and go constantly. The children don't know one another, and the teachers don't know them.

When I arrived at 9:00 a.m., the two teachers caring for thirty children appeared frenzied. They swept the floor, picked up broken crayons, lugged around a wailing child, rushed a toddler to the toilet. A few youngsters, thumbs in mouth, watched television. Others played desultorily with toys stocked in half-empty cupboards. A few toyed with the buckle on my shoe. One two-year-old just whimpered.

By mid-morning, with the group swollen to forty-three children and three teachers, the semblance of a program started. In one room, a teacher read to the twos and threes, but she stood instead of squatting, and they could not see the pictures in the book. The threes listened, but the two-year-olds—a third of a lifetime younger—paid scant attention.

In the next room, the fours and fives colored in outlined figures, with the teacher telling them which colors to use. "I try to teach them to write their own names," the teacher explained, "but it's discouraging when they come so irregularly."

The paucity of equipment was enough to discourage anyone. The two rooms were pleasant and bright. Small toys were available, but the typical play subdivisions—an area for block building, for water play and paints, for dramatic play—were missing. The only large blocks were piled in a plastic garbage pail, so high that a small child could not reach inside. Outdoor equipment was no better or worse than in any park playground: four hobbyhorses for the younger children, swings and a slide, a sandbox, and one climbing toy.

By lunchtime, the center was at capacity, but there were still only three teachers. This made the owner, a kindly housewife whom we'll call Mrs. Brown, visibly nervous. She explained that state law required her to have a staff of five for forty children, but that two teachers were out sick. "It's just so hard to find substitutes," she said.

Mrs. Brown's teachers are housewives in their thirties and forties; most have no training in preschool education. She herself was once a home-economics teacher, but retired twenty-one years ago. She pays the staff $1.30 to $1.60 an hour, less than many domestic workers earn, and most work four hours a day. Like their employer, they mean well, but they simply do not know how to handle small children en masse.

The Moppet's home office supplies all franchisers with a manual containing program suggestions, and Mrs. Brown keeps her single copy in the office. "I've told the teachers it's here, but they don't seem to use it much," she says. The home office also requires all operators to attend a two-week training course in Arizona, but even

Mrs. Brown admits she found the program disappointing.

In business only four months, the Browns believe they have already passed the break-even point. For day care, they charge $19.50 a week: $2.25 for a morning, 65 cents an hour for drop-ins. Their cost per child, according to Mr. Brown's estimate, is $2.30 a day. They are optimistic about the future: franchise headquarters has told them that another Moppet's school has netted $20,000 in a year.

The day care franchisers claim that they have it all over the lady down the street who takes in kids. In one sense, they are right. Their new buildings are bright and clean, more attractive than a refurbished basement in a private home. But with a few exceptions, they strike me as Mom and Pop (individually owned for profit centers) all over again, merely on a grander scale.

One exception is certainly American Child Centers. This company seems to know what a small child is all about, although it has not yet answered the pertinent questions: Can it be duplicated? Can it turn a profit? Observers believe that several other new companies may also prove above average. One of these is the Romper Room Schools, backed by the money of Hasbro Industries, the toy manufacturers who also produce the Romper Room television program. Another is Little Shaver's, in Cranston, Rhode Island, directed by a former state welfare official.

Yet the scale of the enterprises makes them different from a down-the-street operation, and this difference is significant for children. A substantial investment demands a substantial financial return. A franchiser needs about $25,000 to start a center, and he must cut the parent company in for 6 percent of his receipts before counting his own profit. He expects what he has been promised—$15,000 to $40,000 a year. Compared to this, a Mom and Pop venture is peanuts. It is typically run by a housewife who is content to net $5,000 after charging off to the business the cost of running her car, paying her real-estate taxes, and improving the value of her home. The businessman can't operate on so modest a scale, leading inevitably to these hazards:

Size: A Mom and Pop center usually houses about forty children, but businessmen believe that they need between seventy-five and one hundred fifty children to make a profit. Impersonality and restraint are necessary by-products of a large child center.

The size of the individual group is even more significant for a child. Federal standards allow no preschool group to be larger than twenty children, but Kay's Kiddie Kollege, which now has eleven centers in three states, has designed a three-classroom building to house up to eighty youngsters. Moreover, when children turn up for a day or two or an hour or two, the temptation to shove in an extra child or so is hard to resist.

Staff: A small teacher-pupil ratio is the only means of assuring individual attention. Federal standards call for a one-to-five ratio when youngsters are three to four years old, and one-to-seven for those age four to six. No franchiser approaches this standard.

Program: Franchisers spell education with a giant E and assure parents there will be plenty of it. Most intend, however, to limit it to the morning, when nursery-school children are also present. "I want to hire a high-powered teacher for two hours a day," one company manager told me. "Then I'll bring in a mother with one year of college to work for the balance."

"Such a scheme shows a gross misunderstanding of the process of education," says Dr. James L. Hymes, Jr. "A child learns continually, no matter from whom he's learning. The children who are away from home all day—they're the ones who need the best teachers."

Parents: The franchisers are quite aware who pays the bill, and they equip their centers with gimmicky toys to impress the grownups, not the children. One school, for example, features a model cow that moos and numbered squares that light in sequence as a child steps on them. Almost all have wall-to-wall carpeting, guaranteed to produce the admonition I heard from one teacher: "Anyone who gets his shoes muddy outdoors is going to get in trouble."

To impress parents, promotional literature is rich in hyperbole and half-truth. Take Les Petites Académies, a Kansas City company, which has nine schools in Illinois and one hundred planned for next year. It describes itself as "the most respected educator of young children in the world" and promises "individualized" education, including math, science, and a second language (French or Spanish). Its master schedule includes a twenty-minute "Dialogue (one child–one adult)." Director Gail Richardson could not explain how he implements this ambitious program when for each 84-child center, he hires one teacher-director and also 13 or 14 part-time aides.

Licensing: All states but two (North Carolina and Mississippi) set standards for day care centers and require that they be licensed. Most standards are minimal and enforcement staffs minuscule, but some franchisers intend to use their economic muscle to weaken them still further. The manager of one well-heeled corporation said to me, "The laws in some states make it too expensive for us to do a job. We're going to warn these states that if they keep us out, they'll be responsible for throwing on the welfare rolls a bunch of women who want to work. I expect that state people will end up playing ball with us."

For a young mother who has a job or plans to take one, the picture looks discouraging. Yet there *are* alternatives to proprietary day care, and if she yells hard enough, there will be more.

DAY CARE, WHO CARES?

by Vicki Breitbart, Member of New York Women's Liberation Child Care Collective

From "Day Care, Who Cares?" by Vicki Breitbart. *Leviathan*, June 1970.

Vicki Breitbart

The next article takes us from the single issue of franchise day care to the larger picture of business' relationship to the human services and the over-all goals of education in this society.

Business in Education: The Discovery Center Hustle

Ann Cook and Herbert Mack

If the 1960's were years of growing involvement with school problems, of concern and frustration over poor student achievement, of Head Start and compensatory education, the 1970's seem destined to be the decade of educational commercialism and hard-sell gimmickry, of day care franchisers and Sesame Street.

Mounting evidence indicates that the businessman may well become our new educational trend-setter.

Child care, like hamburgers, fried chicken, and ice cream, is now being packaged and franchised across the country. While most companies initially train their sights on the middle-class consumer market, many also hope for large-scale government contracts. Though concern for education may have come slowly to many companies now involved, President Nixon's pronouncements over the past eight months have provided ample incentive for investment and planning. According to the Department of Health, Education and Welfare, some 4 million working mothers and 1 million on welfare have a total of 24 million pre-school-aged youngsters. Nixon's proposal to put welfare mothers into the labor market (approximately 150,000 of them, anyway) means that some 450,000 preschoolers would need day care. As one businessman stated, "When the Government is ready to pay for it, we will be set up to provide it."

Such prospects are very real. At least three major bills are pending before Congress—all calling for considerable federal funding to be made available for preschool facilities. And, given the attitude of at least one Congressman, John Brademas (D-Ind.), that "the major thrust should come from the business community, not government," the investors can look not only to the middle-class parent but most likely to large-scale government expenditures for the urban poor as well. According to *The New York Times* (December 27, 1969), some franchise sellers and purchasers are *already* collecting government funds, either federal or state, or "are courting" federal agencies for additional support.

Kinder Care Nursery (football player Bart Starr is physical fitness director) is big in the South, with 68 franchises; American Child Centers (board member Edward T. Breathitt was former Governor of Kentucky), some 40 franchises sold, 130 more anticipated; We Sit Better, projected 2,000 centers in the U.S. and Canada; Mary Moppet, 12 centers already and 64 franchises concentrated in the Southwest; The Institute for Contemporary Education, Pied Piper Schools, Town Carousel Day Schools, the Green

Acres Day Care Center, Les Petites Académies, the Season Franchise Center, Universal Education Corporation (9 centers operating on the East Coast)—all are cashing in on the baby business.

Most companies have established prototype operations on which to fashion the franchise centers. For a price ranging from $18,000 to $30,000 (plus a continuing fee of about 6 percent of gross sales) one can buy into the investment, with construction charges additional. Geography is no limitation; franchises are available in almost every section of the country, particularly the South, Southwest, and Midwest.

Few question the efficiency of the corporate move into the child-minding market; however, some officials and educators do doubt the ability of profit-making corporations to provide quality day care. Several who have had contact with staff personnel seem unimpressed and assert that educational objectives are severely limited. As one day care trainer put it: "There just isn't a profit to be made. If a center is making money, that means it is overcrowded or the staff is inadequate and only doing a baby-sitting job."

Eric Breitbart

Child psychologist James Hymes states that to have no program is sometimes better than to take what is offered. He observes: "Maybe no one [tries] to teach children anything" in some child-minding operations, "but this doesn't keep them from learning a lot: conformity, submissiveness, passivity and hostility."

Considering the criticisms as well as the implications of such programs, it would seem important to examine one of the operations more closely to find just what "service" is being offered to the parent and what educational value it has for the child. According to recent reports in *Edubusiness,* the Universal Education Corporation is a leading competitor in the field. While not as large as some of the other franchise operations, it has recently attracted a great deal of attention through advertising and the mass media generally and has been praised by Governor William Cahill of New Jersey.

A New Concept of Preschool Education?

UEC, as described in its multicolored, illustrated brochure, is "a new concept of preschool education." A "private corporation founded by educators and psychologists," it aims "to facilitate early learning and to help each child develop to his maximum potential" by offering preschool learning and personal development experiences and educational materials through centers that will eventually be located in over 500 communities. To date, "discovery centers" can be found in middle-class communities in Springfield, Massachusetts; East Hartford, Connecticut; Highland Park, New Jersey; New York City, and six other Eastern seaboard locations.

Basically the company is interested in the parent market. For from $36 to $45 a month (depending on whether or not the customer signs up for the six-month package), the parent is able to bring his child for two hours a week to the "discovery center." The customer receives an initial assessment of the child's level in the "43 basic-skill areas," one free take-home toy per session with an instruction sheet, an evaluation form to fill in, a monthly report on the child's progress, and a few other services. Also available are appointments with the educational psychologist (at $25 per hour), learning materials ("These make excellent gifts for any occasion; ask for your catalogue"), books ("discovery books offered for sale as a supplement to the Discovery Program" also "make excellent gifts"), and Home Learning Corners ("a home-sized version of the Center's Learning Corner—with or without accessories").

At first glance, such services might appear credible, perhaps even reasonable. The PR is slick, bright, and appealing; graphically attractive, it speaks to the education-conscious parent in phrases such as "evaluation," "consultation," "child development," "professional staff," "learning experience," and "basic skills." One might feel pangs of alarm on reading the ad copy in one full-page spread in *The New York Times:*

Evaluating children in the 43 basic skills is part of what the Discovery Center can do for your child. The 43 skills embrace all the hundreds of things your child has to learn before he reaches school age. Fortunately preschoolers have a special genius for learning. But it disappears at the age of seven. During this short-lived period of genius, the Discovery Center helps your child develop his skills to the Advanced Level. . . . You owe it to your child to take him to the Discovery Center today.

But, over-all, many absorb the message, see the three-year-old planted in front of the TV screen, grab a coat (and checkbook), and head for the nearest center.

A trip through a center was illuminating. The New York center visited was bright, cheerful, full of children and their moms, with a sprinkling of fathers. While waiting to enter the discovery room, we were allowed a view of the class in progress by means of closed-circuit TV. Conversations ranged from how other programs in the area were "waiting-list only" to "Johnny didn't seem to get along too well with other children." When we were ushered into the children's room, the immediate impact was startling: brightly painted walls, the newest equipment in preschool furniture design, a TV screen with attached video recorder, an electric typewriter that could be "programmed for games," and an assortment of letter cards designed for the "chatterbox"—a device to "teach reading."

The guide delivered a prepared talk at rapid speed. The group viewed the "science discovery corner" (a display of small insects and rodents encased in plastic blocks), the "chatterbox" table, the video-tape circle (which can photograph the children "doing tasks" and beam prerecorded puppet shows prepared by UEC, etc.), and the electric typewriter. Most in the group seemed satisfied, filled out application forms, and left.

Those with extensive queries were referred to the "educational consultant." His answers were quick, low-key, and polite. His language was professional, sprinkled with key words such as *discovery, inquiry, learning styles, individualistic, readiness.* However, when interrupted at one point by a staff member, he needed prompting to begin again. Despite the rhetoric and the over-all physical design, some qualities were absent. There were no blocks to speak of, no dollhouse, no water-play area, no sand, no live animals—in short, one might question the richness of the environment.

The children in the afternoon session were led in a group through a series of predetermined activities by a "teacher" who made certain that they paid attention to the task at hand while a second "teacher" recorded observations of their responses on a UEC form. While children theoretically were free to roam, to explore, "teachers" seemed at ease only when the entire group was together, following the lesson plan programmed for that particular week. Those lesson plans dictate precisely what activities the teacher is to "teach." Should children attempt to opt out of group activities, the teacher is instructed to "sell the children on participating in a planned activity by your own enthusiasm and sense of enjoyment." Visitors to the center, however, are told that what the children do is up to them.

The educational consultant's role seems to be a key to understanding the operation of the Discovery Center. Of all those in contact with the public, he seems the smoothest and most accomplished. He is the legitimizer, the mark of respectability and the company's symbol of educational commitment.

"The educational consultant is a specialist in learning, personality, counseling, testing and education." This quotation and those which follow are taken from an internal investor's brief prepared by UEC. The educational consultant

. . . periodically evaluates the educational development of the children much as the family physician gives checkups.

He relieves parents of the bewilderment, worry and frustration which they feel concerning their children's educational development, and provides them with the guidance they need. He reassures them that they are doing right by their children and that by following his counsel, they are preparing their children for the world of tomorrow.

Unlike the "family physician,"

He develops . . . prescriptions jointly with the parents . . . thereby securing the parent's commitment to the prescriptions.

While the educational consultant himself does not sell products, the "UEC also has *educational materials specialists,* who would be analogous to the pharmacist who fills the prescription." In this way, UEC's "family doctor" and UEC's "pharmacist" enjoy a cozy relationship.

The educational consultant will . . . suggest or arrange a meeting with the UEC "Educational Materials Specialist" who is a salesman.

Once the loyalty of the parent to the "physician," the educational consultant, is established, this "professional" then exploits this trust indirectly to boost product sales.

After the prescription has been completed either in response to an inquiry by the parent or spontaneously, the Educational Consultant offers to put the parent in touch with the UEC materials specialist. If the salesman [*emphasis added*] *is on the premises at the time, he calls him in and introduces him, for the purpose of scheduling a visit to the home. . . . Or he offers to give the materials specialist the parent's phone number. In any event the parent is later contacted by a salesman.*

Education by Prescription

The consultant (projected salary: $32,-000), on his own (and UEC's initiative), will seek out the parent, if that parent hasn't contacted him. However, reporting sessions once a month are standard practice. The salesman, the "educational materials specialist" (projected salary: $19,000 in commissions), comes to the home of the parent "armed with the prescription" and, presumably, a catalogue of available products.

From that point on, the selling technique is similar to that used for sales calls based on direct mail prospects, except that it is somewhat lower-key, less high-pressured, and makes more use of the Educational Consultant's authority.

Those in the medical profession may shudder at the collusion between the "family doctor" and the "pharmacist"; however, according to UEC, today's parent is no longer competent to raise his child:

. . . whether or not . . . parents foresee the characteristics of the world of the future, they can't help their children. They can't help their children to cope with that world because they themselves have never lived in it, and therefore never had the opportunity to learn to cope with it.

Dan Brown

Parents cannot develop (the important) traits in their children because they cannot teach roles they themselves do not know, nor can they instill attitudes and personality traits which they themselves do not value highly.

UEC believes it has the answer and, according to their projections, they are a few years ahead of the nearest competitors. Educationally, they seem to have reached some definite answers:

. . . the critical phase of education occurs before the age of five. . . . Not even the most dramatic improvement of the schools could significantly improve their ability to produce brilliant, inquiring and creative individuals.

They believe that

. . . few companies ever formed have UEC's potential for direct and far-reaching socio-cultural impact. UEC will influence, perhaps significantly, the long-term quality of life in this country and the general direction our society will take during the next few generations.

It is projected that UEC's agent for impact and dissemination will establish "strong relationships of loyalty and trust" between himself and the parent. "This type of long-term professional relationship is the principal basis for the resistance to competition . . . and the follow-on for new products and services to be introduced in the future." Thus:

. . . it goes without saying that the consultant who has the family's trust in matters of education and child rearing will also have their trust in matters not pertaining to education directly.

If UEC offered other products and services, such as travel agency services, home furnishings, hobby products, household products, special food products, life and other insurance, etc., it would be in an excellent position to sell these to its clients. The opportunities for horizontal integration at the product level are fairly staggering.

It seems abundantly clear that regardless of claims to "social conscience and idealism," the UEC "discovery center" concept is nothing more or less than a very clever selling campaign, immensely more skillful than the traditional door-to-door technique, for in UEC's setup it is the consumer who pays to receive advertisements. Anxious parents contract for the two-hour weekly session that opens the door to the toy salesman, the "family doctor" and the "pharmacist." Such operations should be investigated by such groups as Nader's Raiders.

Many reputable figures in the field of education have lent their names to this venture. Included on UEC's national advisory board are Wilbur Cohen, former secretary of HEW; Norman Cousins, editor-in-chief of *World*; Martin Deutsch, director of the Institute for Developmental Studies, New York University; Robert Glaser, director of the Learning Research and Development Center, University of Pittsburgh; Theodore Kheel, labor arbitrator; and Bayard Rustin, executive director of the A. Phillip Randolph Institute; along with psychologist-businessman Francis Mechner, Ph.D., as president. Their roles are unclear. Are they aware of the company's practices? If not, how do they justify the use of their names in its promotion? If their presence is thought to have a moderating influence, the evidence would indicate they have been woefully ineffective.

But enough of the fascinating details of UEC's operation. What about programs? Few seem to have considered just what an educational experience ought to be. Where should the focus be placed and why? What should be the educational goals and objectives of the materials or programs? What are the priorities?

If we consider the concept of school as a "force in developing the total person," as does child psychologist Barbara Biber, then new programs are falling far short of the objective. We have built program on top of program, funded panacea after panacea, put our trust in instant success and short-term results, while losing sight of basic goals.

What seems to emerge as a pattern in the preschool explosion is an overwhelming emphasis on cognition, on the tools, or academic-skill aspects, of learning, rather than on the thinking processes or on social development. What is really being sold to parents in the name of "discovery center," "learning center," or "school" is in fact nothing more than compensatory programs for the middle- and upper-income parent. They are compensatory because they offer programs that suggest "making-up" existing deficiencies, or anticipating deficiencies. However, apparent gains related to experiences in "readiness centers" or "prep" schools, according to several studies, are not sustained in regular school.

More serious, the concern, expressed by many psychologists, that such gains may be achieved at the expense of adequate social development, is forgotten. The fact that "the developmental process takes place from birth to death," not simply within some magical period of one's life, has been greatly misunderstood. As a member of the original Head Start steering committee observed: "Misapplied thinking can overemphasize intelligence and has caused us to crucify the deprived child on the cross of I.Q. This thinking presents a simplistic view of intellect."

While such emphasis may be rooted in the recent federally funded compensatory programs for the so-called deprived child and in research studies on sensory and language deprivation, it runs counter to much that we understand about child development. Fundamentally, it is grounded in a reliance on measurements in skill-oriented tasks that have characterized the middle-class school for so long.

The post-Sputnik alarm, the scandal over "Why Johnny can't read," the increasing emphasis on competition for jobs, colleges, careers—all contributed to the demand for teaching "marketable skills." By the time Head Start appeared, the groundwork had been established. Parents believed that test scores in skill areas were the critical features of education; ghetto residents were persuaded that this should be the prime focus of their children's schooling.

The prestige of the cognitivists and the considerable federal funding for research reinforced the trend and extended it. Children of four and five were to be taught numbers, letters, and language exercises. The child's developmental pattern was de-emphasized and his natural curiosity only minimally recognized. Those who pressed for the skills approach seemed unaware of the lessons learned by high-quality private preschools and in early childhood educational practice in England.

Vicki Breitbart

Today the limited, skill-oriented approach is increasingly criticized, with many finding it shortsighted. It primes children for a year, only to find achievement results erased by experiences in poor-quality classrooms in following years. It becomes evident that, as Kenneth Clark has noted, "compensatory education . . . is no substitute for change in the structure of education itself."

The Basic Aims of Education

Yet we find ourselves arguing about programs while ignoring this structure. An evaluation of educational objectives is long overdue. Perhaps in analyzing the programs described here, we should start to deal with basic aims. We ought to question whether emphasis on skills and mechanical response should *ever* be allowed to dominate a child's educational experiences. We must examine the relationship between our educational institutions and conditions in our society.

It isn't because children can't read that our country is torn by internal conflict. It isn't because our children can't add that we elect politicians who campaign on personality, not program, that the country is embroiled in a divisive war, that consumers purchase defective merchandise, that television is a wasteland and our environment polluted. These conditions are not due to deficiencies in reading and math. It is rather that our population is not being educated in critical areas: how to judge, to ask questions, to seek information, to analyze, and to evaluate.

It is not sufficient to concentrate on reading and math skills. We must look beyond the "decoding" process that most programs are designed to teach. What is the purpose of learning such skills? Does teaching a child to discern between the *a* in cat and the *a* in fate mean automatically that the child will *want* to read, make meaningful use of his knowledge, broaden his vision or satisfy his curiosity? Learning to read is really a lifetime activity based fundamentally on one's attitude about books and is generated by curiosity and by an eagerness to explore and find enjoyment. It is critically important that children learn to question their world, to deal with the ambiguity in their environment, and to realize that not every issue has a "correct" answer.

Teachers, parents, and students are beginning to seek help in order to create schools that are relevant, challenging, and productive. They look for consultants, for innovators, hoping to find creative minds to assist them in their quest for alternatives. Do such innovators exist? What chance is there for new educational techniques to gain acceptance? If Sesame Street, a highly acclaimed preschool educational TV production is any example, the prospects are discouraging.

There is little question that the National Educational Television program, now beamed as many as six times daily to large viewing audiences, provides a visually exciting and technically superior production. Nor is there doubt that children around the country find the "cookie monster" winning and amusing. Equally impressive is the number of public figures who lend dramatic quality to the program; it is fun to watch James Earl Jones recite his alphabet.

The Sesame Street media specialists did their jobs well. However, the most imaginative communications capabilities and sophisticated technical know-how have been united with conventional, outmoded educational practices. One wonders what the educational advisers did with their time: $8,000,000 of "experimental" capabilities were committed to prove that Johnny can learn his ABC's in preschool—a dubious accomplishment when judged by what could (and should) have been included in the package.

Within the limited goals of the program, it is batting better than average. One might be persuaded that, at last, educational TV has won the hearts and minds of the young viewer. But one must ask: where is the "experiment"? What makes this program different—except in the most McLuhanesque terms—from what schools and teachers have been trying to do for years?

Perhaps, some may argue, it is enough that they succeed with their limited objectives. Perhaps it is sufficient that they manage to get children to mouth the right responses to predetermined questions and to recite letters and numbers. Perhaps this is all we can hope for. If so, the producers are to be congratulated. They have sugarcoated the essentials so that even people who should question the underlying assumptions are enthralled. Yet one does not minimize learning skills by asking if this should be all there is to education. Should this be the primary emphasis of our educational system—and of Sesame Street or other programs beamed to the mass audience? Can it be really accurate to call this program "education," to let it slip by with such limited objectives?

These objectives seem critical in the light of the program's impact. Schools may be failing, but one has come to accept (not without criticism) their shortcomings, their problems, their inefficiencies. Here is where the Sesame Streets of the 1970's have special responsibility: to broaden our vision of what education can be, to redirect our thinking or pose new questions to the mass viewing audience. Here for the first time, perhaps, we have parents, teachers, as well as children, tuned in and looking for direction, receptive to new challenge. The potentialities of such a venture are enormous as well as frightening. For if the new "experimental," "innovative" efforts do nothing more than provide

Dr. Brown's Patent Baby Tender.

THE greatest invention in the world for the comfort and convenience of Mothers and Children. By a few simple changes the child has a Hobby Horse Baby Jumper, Sleeping Couch, Ottoman, high or low Chair and Crib. Prices for the Ottoman style, from $12 to $25. Standard $8 to $12. Send to J. S. BROWN CO., 544 Broadway, for descriptive Circulars. 000

a restatement of past assumptions, where do we go for broader understanding, for alternatives? Where do parents learn to understand the uniqueness of their own child's personality and interests? Where do they find support for encouraging children to experiment and question? Where do teachers come to understand the concepts of developing a child's excitement about his world?

The children of Sesame Street perform as they are expected. They give the "right" number, the "correct" word, the proper response. In a fill-in-the-missing-word exercise, the only creative member of the cast is Bird, an ostrich-like, befeathered animal who supplies the "wrong" word to a rhymed jingle almost every time. He is a fool, to be laughed at and corrected. All the characters have been packaged into a fast-paced format that minimizes individuality and devalues creativity. Little attention is paid to the spontaneous, and low priority given to the open-ended. Neither the children on Sesame Street nor the viewing preschoolers are encouraged to extend their imagination, tap their curiosity, explore their ideas, or confront the ambiguous.

Having children draw and talk about what they see and think about in a painting (not whether it is good or bad art), discuss the various ways in which different people view the same things, experiment with items around the house to see how variously they can be used, ask what people think about places they have seen or might visit—endless possibilities exist for inviting participation and open-ended inquiry. One would feel more hopeful if the program provided a balance—some mesh, some variety—handled with the dedication and concern for quality that characterizes the limited format today. If what we seek for our children is relevancy and challenge, we won't get it by continuing to project only one aspect of the educational agenda.

Sesame Street must be understood, therefore, as yet one more example of the trend we have been documenting. UEC-type operations, and the preschool industry in general, tend to take a one-dimensional approach to education. Skills, not children, are emphasized; how the child *performs,* not who he is, or how he thinks, becomes the focus. Symptoms, not causes, are treated. This should be no surprise, for only by playing on popular guilts and fears can such firms as UEC hope to succeed in the educational market. If educational options of quality were publicly available, most profit-making ventures would find it difficult to survive.

On the other hand, with programs such as Sesame Street there is additional cause for alarm. They indicate the severe problems to be faced if basic change is to be achieved in our educational structures. The lack of imagination evident in the counsel provided by key educational consultants, from the prestigious universities, who participated in the creation of Sesame Street will certainly stifle creative efforts to revitalize our educational institutions.

That we must be prepared to respond to the actions of profit-oriented corporations with strong ties to governmental agencies is cause enough for serious concern. If, at the same time, we must fight educational "experts," our task is vastly more complex.

Non-Profit Day Care

In the coming years the only large-scale alternative to franchising will be publicly funded, non-profit programs. There are already many non-profit programs run by churches and philanthropic agencies. Some are jointly financed by private and public sources, but the largest group (30 percent) are wholly supported by government money.

In these publicly funded centers, the fee—if any—is low, and the "cost per child" (which is the total budget of the center divided by the number of children) runs on the average $1,500 and can go as high as $4,000 a year. In most cases this can guarantee more equipment, more staff, better food, etc. than the private model. But "cost per child" is a cold way to describe what the service offers the families involved. If publicly funded centers comply with the guidelines for day care programs receiving federal funds,[1] they *can* offer a comprehensive program with an education component, health care, social services, and parent education. But what *do* they offer?

Admission policies for public centers are usually controlled by local departments of welfare, who offer the service only to children from families they feel are in desperate need of care. Caseworkers are required to make inquiries into the family's personal life and to give day care only to the "deserving." Even Head Start, by far the most popular and highly acclaimed publicly funded preschool program in this country, is labeled as "compensatory education for the disadvantaged"—which patronizes the very people it claims to serve. As with other forms of public assistance, public day care in America is most often provided as a last resort, and exercised with disrespect, cynicism, and caution—or out of a pity that erodes human dignity, a kindness that treats adults like children who will never reach the age of reason. Given these attitudes, it is no surprise that so many families see public day care as a demeaning handout rather than their right.

Too often the programs in the public centers reinforce the negative images fostered by the admissions policies. Many centers are impersonal, sterile, and forbidding structures. They are built like other institutions—hospitals, welfare offices—or, as the *Guide for Establishing and Operating Day Care Centers* states, "sometimes a barracks-type building makes a simple low-cost suitable day care center." The outside of the building would not be important if inside there was a creative use of space, a rich and stimulating program with warm and sensitive adults to greet the child. But too often there is not.

In many centers children are regimented

1. Federal Interagency Day Care Requirements.

and programmed through a day of eating, napping, and group activities with little time left over for choice, creativity, or active involvement. The educational program for each center is usually left up to the individual staff members, yet on the whole they look surprisingly the same. While there is a great deal of freedom in ordering equipment, it is pretty standard. And while most of the toys in these centers are exciting for the children, they are used only certain times of the day.

After observing in one room of a publicly funded center in Connecticut, I walked around and noticed expensive equipment that had not been touched. I had seen the entire group of children color in a mimeographed American flag, but I had not seen anyone use the dolls, puzzles, blocks, and table games. I then saw a daily schedule posted on the back of the door: "free activity time" was from 8:30 A.M. to 9:00 A.M., when the children were arriving in the morning. I realized I had missed the entire "free choice" time for the day.

In another center using space in a church in New Jersey, the equipment was kept locked in storage cabinets while children sat in chairs in front of the television. When I asked about this, one staff member replied, "It's too much trouble to take the toys out when you just have to put them back at the end of the day."

It's clear that the relationship of child-to-materials, child-to-child, and child-to-adults cannot be ensured by governmental subsidy; it cannot be legislated by any guidelines or requirements.

There is a growing belief that only when the people directly involved make all the decisions will they have high-quality care; only when the staff is accountable to parents and the day care center is part of the community it serves, only when parents, staff, and members of the community are together developing the program they want will it be a meaningful experience for everyone involved—and only then will the effects be positive and far-reaching. The extent to which a program helps children deal with the real world and reflects the current forces of our time depends to a large extent on the goals of the people involved, the way decisions get made, and whether the people in the group are determined to get what they want.

The agencies that usually run public day care—philanthropic groups, civic and church organizations, governmental units, etc.—may be concerned with the problems of day care, but are often too far away from the community to know the needs of the families involved. Parents and staff within existing day care centers have therefore begun to demand that programs be more responsive to their needs; in some cases active groups of parents have taken control of programs. In other cases, community groups have become involved in organizing their own child care centers.

The Licensing Nightmare

Funding requirements have made it difficult—almost impossible—for local groups to organize and run publicly funded child care centers. Every state has laws and regulations for operating a child care program, and if a group wants funding it must meet state licensing requirements. This is often a cumbersome process. A recent government-sponsored study found that 50 to 75 tasks are required and approximately 185 days involved in the time-consuming ordeal of licensing.[2] Government requirements supposedly exist to protect the children, and no one disagrees with any rules that ensure the health and safety of the child, but some of the rules are unduly complicated and some government agencies are unreasonably strict in their application. And there are some regulations that don't face up to the reality of what exists in most communities, or the reality of what resources a founding group has. For example, in New York, before people worked to change the rules, in order to be licensed, a group needed a site that was "suitable"; in order to make it suitable, a group needed money. One Brooklyn group, Faith, Hope and Charity, found what it considered a safe place and ran a program for 50 children daily. They wanted to improve their space and wanted some professional assistance, but they needed money to get it. So they went to the Department of Health for a temporary license —a prerequisite for getting funds. The Department of Health told them they couldn't license the group because they did not have the professionals or a source of funds.

2. *A Survey of State Day Care Licensing Requirements,* 1972, prepared for O.E.O. by the Social Administrative Services and Systems Assoc./Consulting Services Inc.

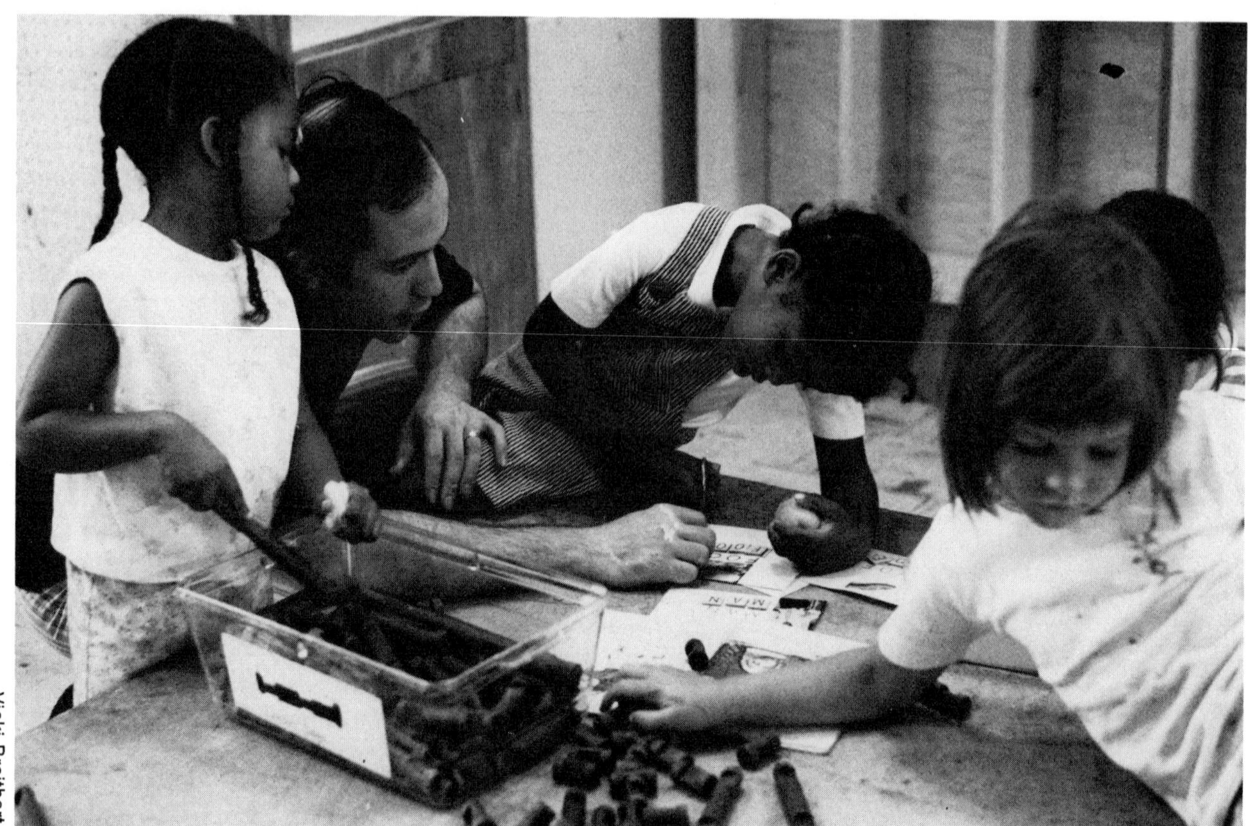

Vicki Breitbart

The physical characteristics required by the Department of Health in New York City are light, spaciousness, and cleanliness. What we all want. Yet what grass-roots organization can give the required "evidence of reasonably secure financial position to permit compliance with the provisions of the (Department of Health) Code (Sec. 47.05)" before it receives public money? This may be reasonable for do-good agencies with wealthy board members, but not for most community groups.

And even when a group gets funds, there are some regulations that are contrary to the idea of local control. Why should eligibility for service be determined by some state, city, or federal standards that require information on income? Why should families be investigated at all? Why can't we assume that subsidized day care is a universal right? Why should guidelines in some states require a college education for teachers? Why can't the people directly affected by the program decide who is competent to work with their children?

In order to create a child care center that is publicly funded and run by the local community, where parents are not investigated to determine their need for child care, where income or class background does not determine the kind of care children receive, where there is a respect for the right of all parents to determine when and how they want to be with their children and the right of every child to a group experience that is designed to meet her or his physical, social, emotional, and intellectual needs at any age—in order to guarantee these things, one must be prepared to fight the local agencies every step along the way. Yet it has been done. West Eightieth Street Child Day Care Center and Manhattan Valley Day Care Center—both in New York—are two examples.

Public Money and Local Control

The West Eightieth Street center is a locally run, publicly funded center founded by a particularly aware and active group of people. As Dorothy Pitman Hughes, a parent and the original director of the center, put it, they had to "break every rule in the book" to get what they wanted. Parents in this center were not content with "involvement" or "participation" on some advisory board, as is the case with many publicly funded centers; from the beginning they wanted control over all aspects of the program.

They started in a storefront, but with perseverance and determination, they now have a center designed and planned by the parents and the community in consultation with architects of their own choosing. The center reflects their courage to speak for the rights of children. From the outside of the center, which is painted in bold strokes of red, yellow, and blue, the visitor can tell something exciting is happening there. Another unique feature of their design is a Plexiglas tube that runs up and down the entire front of the building. On each floor the tube becomes a window on the street in a duplex platform that children use for dramatic play. Unlike many schools being built in big cities that are made of massive, windowless walls of brick and cinderblock, this day care center is not afraid to look out on the streets of its community—it is part of that community.

The program in the center reflects the economic and racial mix of the neighborhood. It includes infants through six-year-olds, and the staff and parents are now involved in designing their own training program to further develop their skills as leaders in the community.

Manhattan Valley is another publicly funded, locally controlled day care center in New York. It took more than two years from the time the group was first in touch with the landlord to the opening of the center. In that time the group lost some members, found some new ones, and engaged in what seemed like endless demonstrations and sit-ins at city offices, but by the time they began their program the group that emerged had a great deal of know-how in dealing with the city and a strong sense of confidence in what they wanted for their children.

HELP SUPPORT COMMUNITY CONTROLLED DAYCARE

COME TO A ★ BENEFIT ★ PARTY AT RED PAINT DAYCARE CENTER ★ NOV. 10 ★ 38 west 88th. st.

LIVE MUSIC ★ FOOD ★ WINE ★ 8 .P.M. Friday $2,50

I could tell a lot about their program from my visits to the center. The walls were covered with stories dictated by the children, written down by the teachers. They were about the children's homes, about people in the community, and about walks they had taken around the block. Some of the older children had written their names and a few key words. There were collages and paintings displayed on the walls—the work from previous days. Instead of the standard cubbies for possessions, there were large rural mailboxes for the children to keep their work in, and each displayed names and individual photographs.

Each classroom at Manhattan Valley had about 15 children within an age range of about two years (two to four, three to five). In one classroom, I observed two children—one about four, the other two years old—looking at a book together. Over by the tables a teacher was working with a small group of children, matching numerals to groups of objects. One child was hooked under the teacher's arm, watching. Another teacher was helping a group of children set up paints and paper on the floor for a large mural, while a third teacher was helping a child in the bathroom. Independent of the adults, a small group of children were building with blocks. There were several things happening simultaneously, everyone was involved, and I sensed that children and adults were learning in a comfortable atmosphere.

The parents and staff of Manhattan Valley have a program that tries to integrate the varied points of view in the area. They are developing a bilingual curriculum, and they have hired a racially mixed staff of men and women. In hiring the staff, Manhattan Valley used the city guidelines only as a basis for recruiting; they did not disregard formal school, but they stressed competence, experience, and caring for children over degrees, certification, and diplomas. They looked for staff who could work well together, without the divisions of "me teacher, you aide" that is found in so many centers, and who would work *with* the parents and not *for* them.

In creating a Board of Directors, Manhattan Valley developed its own guidelines. The city's policy prohibits staff who are also parents from serving on the board, because they believe this creates conflict. On the other hand, this division can cause conflicts and resentment between staff who are parents, parents who are not staff, and staff who are not parents. As the original Director of Manhattan Valley put it, "We want to create a community of interest, instead of a conflict of interest," and they decided that all parents *and* staff should be part of the Board. Together, they run a center that is publicly funded and meets *their* needs.

M.S.R.

Chapter 3

Government and Industry Move In

At the same time community groups are becoming more and more interested in organizing and running their own programs, industry and government (not simply as a funding source, but as a managing and policy-making entity) are becoming increasingly involved in providing these services. It is one thing to make money available for citizen use, but it is another to use it for citizen control—and that is the direction of large-scale government and industry planning. They are in the process of making child care outside the home more of a privilege for those who can afford it and a lure into low-paying jobs for those who cannot. Instead of helping community groups to set up their own centers, they are formulating programs that will work against the development of real control at the local level. Instead of helping to change women's feelings about alternative child care, they will reinforce our worst fears. Now, as in the past, it seems day care programs are being provided in response to the needs of the economy and will not necessarily benefit the families directly involved.

In the sixties, this country's heavy armed services commitments, new job categories in the electronics industries, and the growing need for clerical help in this "paper age," created new demands for women workers. As Vera Perella concluded in a U.S. Department of Labor report, "the industrial shift has been a vital force in fostering the growth of the female labor force." Women were not going into heavy industrial work as they did during World War II and not into highly skilled administrative jobs as the media would have had us believe. Women were needed as cheap labor in new semiskilled technical jobs. In response to this development in the economy, legislation was passed in the 1960's which instituted various day care programs designed to provide and/or keep women in the work force.

The government's primary focus was on families receiving public assistance. A Department of Labor survey of ten high-poverty areas found that one out of five women who wanted a regular job gave the unavailability of day care as the principal reason for not looking for work. Another study reported that more than 51 percent of women receiving Aid to Families with Dependent Children (AFDC) said that the difficulty in finding day care was the major reason for not seeking employment. So the government came up with plans that included day care and training and/or employment for the poor. Both day care and jobs are desperately needed, but the way they are being linked together may turn both into disadvantages for the people involved.

Losing with WIN, and Other Dangers

Day care for children of welfare recipients has been part of the Social Security Act since 1962. In 1967, Congress amended this act and significantly broadened the possibilities for services. The amendments provided money for families receiving AFDC where the mother was working part-time or where the Department of Welfare felt the family would benefit from day care because of medical or psychological reasons. It included "former and potential" AFDC families among the eligible; these were defined as families who couldn't afford to work if they had to pay for child care.

These amendments also created the Work Incentive Program (WIN), which was "an effort to place all appropriate adult welfare recipients in jobs or in training programs leading to employment and economic self-sufficiency." Women with young children were the last category to be referred for this program. However, since they make up an overwhelming proportion of AFDC recipients, it was expected that with this program large numbers of day care services would become available. What on the surface seemed to be a new and desirable opportunity for parents and their children turned out very differently.

In several cases the "training" was simply the channeling of mothers into unskilled, dead-end jobs. While a recipient was eligible for training in such occupations as secretary and practical nurse, a demonstration project in New York City had some 40 percent of the total working recipients holding unskilled jobs such as domestic worker. Although mothers did not have to register for jobs or training, the official government-supported Auerbach appraisal of WIN affirms that "some mothers are coerced into [this] program."

At the same time, while parents or parent groups were supposed to be consulted about the kind of care they would have liked for their children, in reality most participants were never informed about the full range of possibilities. Instead, they were told that child care was their individual responsibility. The result has been public money going to pay for baby-sitters and not for setting up comprehensive child care programs.

Another day care/training program was created in 1968 with amendments to the Economic Opportunities Act. A total of $15 million was authorized for day care services in conjunction with a work training program called CEP (Concentrated Employment Program). But here too, the day care services are far from what parents wanted. In one CEP center in Hoboken, New Jersey, children were eligible for the service for the duration of their mother's training; once the woman was working at what was inevitably a low-paying job, she had to make other more costly arrangements. Moreover, women in this program were often employed for as short a period of time as a few months.

The more recent Comprehensive Child Care Bill, which was backed, as one Congressman put it, by "the broadest coalition assembled in support of a piece of social legislation," would have drastically changed the picture of day care availability. It would have made day care possible for families of differing income and backgrounds, and while it still linked day

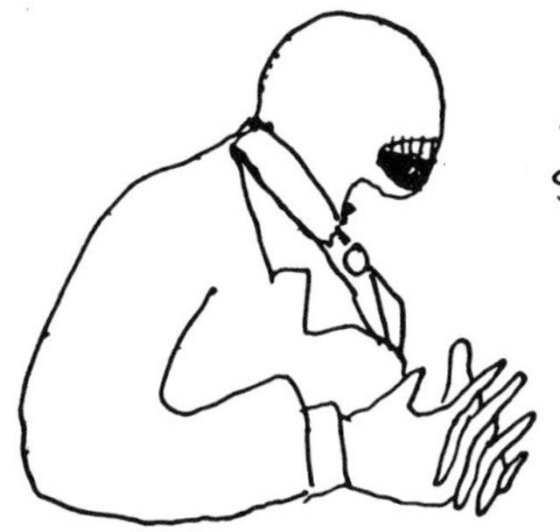

care to maternal employment it did not channel women into specific jobs. It was more open-ended and did emphasize the health, educational, and social aspects of child caring. It also would have allowed communities to have a greater say in the organization and control of day care. It was passed by Congress . . . and was killed by Presidential veto.

In the President's veto message, he called the Child Care Bill a "radical piece of legislation," "a leap into the dark." Elinor Guggenheimer responded to this in *The New York Times* of December 12, 1971:

Perhaps the most cynical part of the President's message is his reference to funds available for children of families on public assistance in H.R. 1 (his proposed plan). If President Nixon believes that day care is a poor alternative for children and that it diminishes "parental involvement," then there can be no moral reason for foisting it [H.R. 1] on the poor.

Day care is either good for children, or it is not.

Nixon presented his day care plan in 1969 as part of H.R. 1. It was similar to WIN and CEP in that it was directed to families on welfare and combined work and child care, but it went much farther than the earlier programs in its attempt to control the lives of working people while benefitting industry. Nixon asserted in his original message on the measure that he thought the Manpower effort was a "terrible tangle of confusion and waste," and he promised to "organize and suit it to business demands." His plan might have forced mothers to train for and accept jobs even at a distance from their home and at very low salaries. And day care was to be the means to this end. What had been a work incentive under WIN and CEP would have become a work requirement. While past legislation limited the possibility for community-run quality programs, H.R. 1 would have seriously affected their very existence. The plan allotted $750 per child per year for day care and this is far from adequate: it can only mean compulsory custodial care, nothing more. There was no mention of health care, social services, education, certainly no mention of parent control. It would have been the government's way of setting up "dumping grounds for the poor" so that women could be forced to work in oppressive jobs.

The administration met heavy resistance on H.R. 1, and the bill's day care plan was never passed by Congress. Yet the intent of the bill is being carried out anyway in several programs recently set up in New York City. Directed to families receiving AFDC, these programs provide employment not in industry but in city agencies; the startling feature here, however, is not the particular job, but the level of government control over people's lives. Under such names as Incentives for Independence (IFI) and Public Service Work Opportunity Project (PSWOP)—a new set of euphemisms for what many people would call slave labor—an "eligible" welfare recipient must work off her or his welfare check in a public agency. All publicly funded day care centers are told to inform the city of any vacancies, and an opening in a day care center can become a mother's ticket into a forced-work program. Even when the welfare recipient fills a job previously held by a government employee who had adequate training, a

decent salary, and union or civil service benefits, she or he receives none of these. Admittedly, in some cases the jobs offered to welfare recipients provide interesting work, but the element of choice is completely gone. Under these programs welfare recipients may also be required to receive special guidance, their teenagers may be required to work after school, and all their children are told to "behave." In short, if one doesn't do as told, part or all of the welfare check will be forfeited.

The government's latest move on day care is in the form of new rulings proposed by the Department of Health, Education and Welfare, which will severely restrict income eligibility for day care services. They will also require that assets (savings, insurance, car) be considered and that gross income and not net income be used to determine eligibility. This doesn't take into account family expenses or the present rate of inflation and jeopardizes people's chances for what is supposedly the purpose of this plan—"self-support" and "self-sufficiency." The new regulations will stipulate no payment for staff training or medical health plans in the center and will eliminate both parent involvement and parent rights. Parents will no longer be required to sit on state, city, or center level policy boards and will no longer be granted "fair hearings" before day care services are taken away from their families.

As it stands now, the government will continue to offer limited day care, which will reduce welfare rolls, generate more taxable income, and increase and help ensure the efficient flow of women into the work force, but it will be a far cry from universally available child care, or even comprehensive day care for families with mothers who are employed.

Enter Business and Industry

While legislation in the last few years has increased the possibility for day care programs that help create a more stable, and cheaper, work force, the red tape of municipal bureaucracies and the inability of states to come up with their share of the matching funds (25 percent) has hindered industry's use of woman power. In 1969 Congress allocated $22.6 million nationwide for day care; the states used only $4 million. Private companies have, therefore, become more active in providing day care themselves.

In New York City in January 1970, a luncheon was held to discuss the ways corporations could participate in the day care scene. It was attended by representatives of Consolidated Edison, Standard Oil of New Jersey, United Fruit Co., Irving Trust Co., Bankers Trust Co., United States Steel Foundation, Squibb Beech-Nut Inc., Chase Manhattan Bank Foundation, Atlantic Richfield Co., Morgan Guaranty Trust Co., Metropolitan Life Insurance Co., and Enjay Chemical Corp.

The representatives were informed that industry could aid in the expansion of day care by providing space or by setting up a revolving fund for day care emergency underwriting that would make available the "seed money" that community groups need to cover the initial cost

Lynn Phillips

of incorporation, housing design, and renovation. So far, however, industry has made few attempts to make money available to local groups; instead, private companies are themselves beginning to establish and operate day care centers. In a report by the Women's Bureau, *Day Care Services: Industry's Involvement,* it shows that several industries are already involved—In textiles: Curlee Clothing, Mr. Apparel, Skyland Textile, Tioga Sportswear, and Vanderbilt; in food processing: Tyson Food and Wintergarden Freezing; and others: Arco Printing, Control Data Corp., and BroDart Industries.

Under the Social Security Act amendments of 1967 (the same that created WIN), private employers are listed as "eligible operators." In some instances industry has taken advantage of this option; in others, they foot the entire bill for day care—but in all cases, the benefits to the corporation are very real.

A report on industry and day care by the Social Administration Research Institute states that with day care "an employer may be able to tap new sources of workers particularly if his production process involves repetitive procedures of *the type that can be serviced best by females.* Usually these employee skills . . . require a short time to learn and do not necessarily require a high level of education. Such jobs are often *the only kind that disadvantaged parents can cope with and hold under current conditions*" (italics added). KLH Research and Development Corporation, one of the first companies to become involved in day care, is a case in point. At KLH, where work is generally assembly line work for stereo equipment, 50 percent of all employees are women (65 percent are black and Latin women). Most are employed at the lowest level jobs, which pay $1.90 an hour, or $3,900 a year. Industry-related day care can be a way to track women, especially black and Latin women, into low-paying occupations.

In those industries (such as light manufacturing and the needle trades) that have traditionally hired women in low-echelon jobs, as well as in those service areas where mostly women are expected to work (i.e., hospital aides),[1] day care is seen as the kind of "fringe benefit" that will attract women into these jobs and keep them there.

There are other ways in which industry-provided day care can make the employers seem like benevolent protectors when they are actually acting out of simple self-interest. The report by the Social Administration Institute states that industry benefits because employee turnover, absenteeism, and tardiness may be diminished.

All of which, of course, have direct cost savings for the employer. At the Vanderbilt Shirt Company it was found that the $12,000 cost of providing day care was returned to them through the retention of workers and the reduction in absenteeism, which was much less common among parents of day care center children than parents of children not in the

1. A recent survey by the Women's Bureau showed ninety-eight hospitals were operating day care centers for their personnel; most of them were established within the last five years.

center. The company found that termination of employment on the part of employees because of "lack of babysitter" and employee absence because of failure of the babysitter to show up were practically eliminated. The company also found that their plans for expansion were greatly accelerated because of the center, as "many additional employees were attracted to the company by the existence of the day care center."[2]

To be sure, the fact that the employer benefits from industry-provided day care doesn't make it necessarily bad: in several instances it has been a worthwhile experience for the children, and it has definitely proved to be better than no day care at all. But when there is such a desperate need for day care, and when the need is fulfilled with a well-controlled trickle of services, the real possibilities are hidden from us and the real dangers are often overlooked and obscured.

Dangers for the Workers

While industry-related day care helps provide female labor at the least possible cost, it also makes women more vulnerable and socially dependent on the workplace. When moving to a new job will also mean the loss of child care, a worker will think twice about it. It will be harder to struggle for better work conditions or higher pay or against unfair labor practices when the job is directly linked to the care of the worker's child. Furthermore, in most cases the employer administers the day care center; hires its staff; owns, equips, and designs the space in which the center is housed, and provides all maintenance. An employee strike would mean the closing of the center; any action at the center itself—for control, for better education, for better facilities—could jeopardize the worker's job or be used by management to pit workers in the plant against the hired staff of the center.

Programs provided by industry offer little opportunity for parent involvement and less chance for control. If the program uses federal funds, parents are required to make up 50 percent of the center's policy board, but this in no way guarantees that the people directly affected by the program will really have the final say. In fact it turns out to be just another way to muddle the issue of real control. A "policy board" can easily be different from a board of directors or a governing board of a center: a policy board advises, a governing board controls. And there are even more blatant ways parents can be kept from control, or even mere involvement in a center. In one case, parents asked for some time off so they could serve on the board and go to meetings, which were taking place during work hours. They were told by the management that this violated the original agreement that the day care program would not interfere with the normal work schedule and worker-employer relationships.

In short, programs may be *called* parent-controlled, but when the vital services are controlled by the management, when staff is hired by the corporate personnel department, when management can sit on the policy board and *be* the governing board, then the parents are not in control. And just as after World War II, day care services can be closed whenever the sponsoring corporation desires.

At a conference on Industry and Day Care, Judith Raup, a parent from an industry-related day care center, said: "Industry is a community, and the residential areas where people live is another community. They are two very different things. Community control may work in a residential area, but when you are talking about industry as a community you are talking about an entirely different situation. It is not a community there; it is a hierarchy of management, working people, and kids in day care." At the same conference, Andrew Jones of Honeywell, Inc., clarified it even further: "You can talk all you want about what industry should do, but business is based on profit; and if there is no profit you are not going to have any industry-based day care centers. If you go to industry and say, 'We want you to give us a day care center, and we will tell

2. *Voice for Children,* Vol. 6, No. 2, p. 7.

you how you are to run it, whom you are to hire, and we will fire whom we wish,' industry will say, 'We are not going to buy that type of thing.' No businessman in his right mind is going to get in a position where his money or the business's money is going to be spent and somebody else is going to control it, because he has to answer to the stockholders, and stockholders are not interested in people generally; they are interested in clipping coupons."[3]

3. *Industry and Day Care* (Chicago: Urban Research Corporation, 1970), p. 35.

"The Brains," by Thomas Nast, 1871.

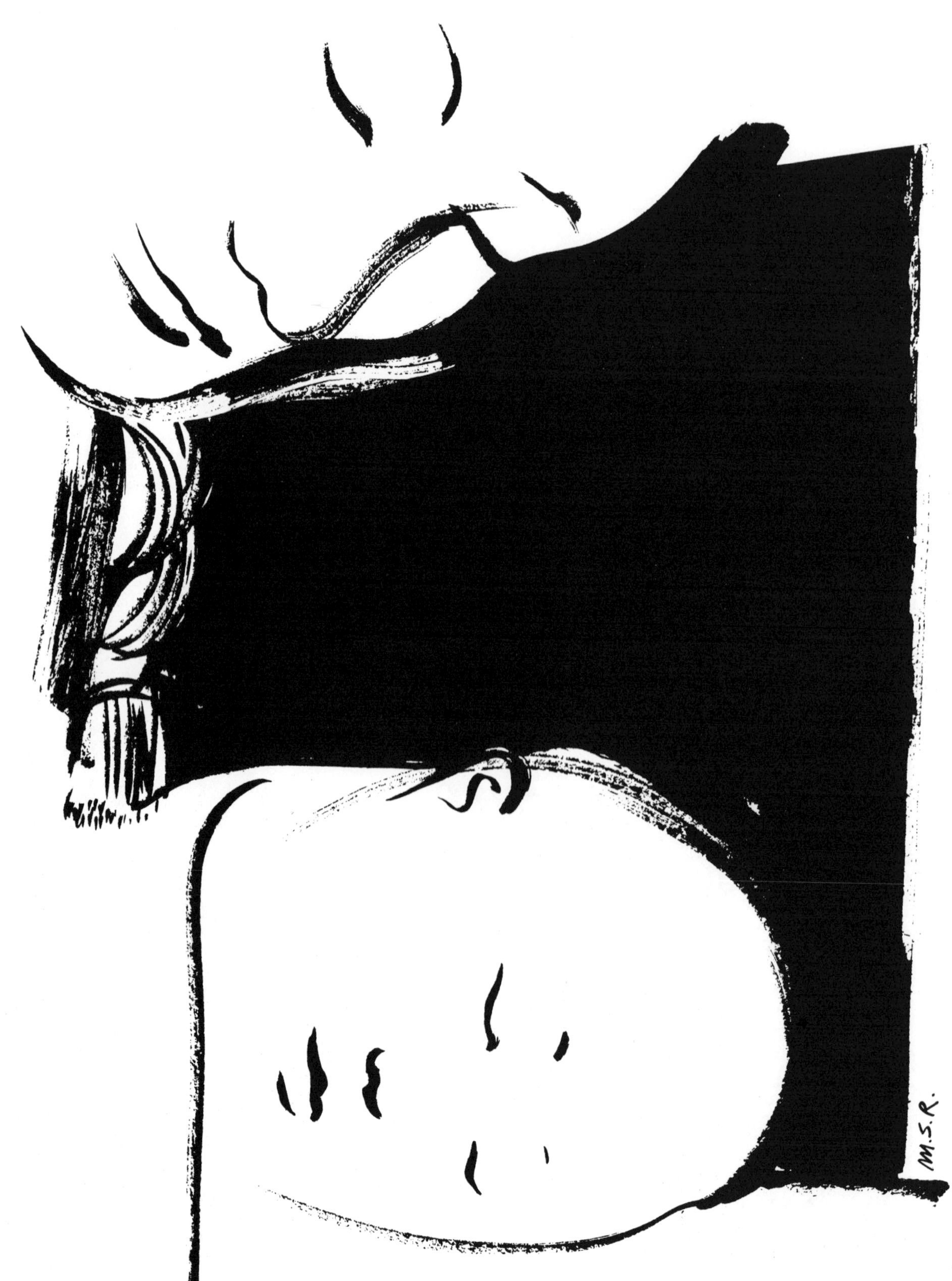

Chapter 4

Child Care in Other Countries

A look at the child care alternatives in other countries makes it clear that child care is part of a much larger picture. The kind of care provided for children is a reflection of the values of a society and affects what that society will become.

In western Europe, as in the United States, day care has traditionally been available primarily to low-income families, and this has influenced the quality of the service. The Parisian *crèches*, for children two months to three years, have been available for fifty years and are in great demand. Yet the demand is attributed more to economic necessity than to the desirability of care. Dale R. Meers, in his observation of the *crèches* in 1965, found that the quality seemed to depend largely on the attitudes of the staff and the limitations of the space, but it was generally poor. He continued:

With cribs placed close together, blankets are draped over the sides permitting the baby to observe little more than the ceiling and a few hanging toys. Such nursing practices have extended to a rejection of handling babies, on the rationalization that they might be accidentally bruised. Some nurses have rejected instructions that they turn babies on their stomachs for part of the day, out of nominal fear that the babies might suffocate. Despite strict regulations prohibiting premature toilet training, some caregivers have attempted to induce compliance by tying three month old infants on a pot.[1]

With an average staff-child ratio of 1 to 6, even the directors and the staff with the best attitudes are severely overburdened. Expansion of services consumes the available resources, and little money is left for the improvement of care.

The situation in Belgium is similar. Here, too, day care consists primarily of *crèches*, usually holding 80 children, with the same 1-to-6 staff-child ratio; their primary emphasis is on health care and supervision. Recently, however, a new definition of woman's role has changed the picture considerably. In an article on day care centers in Europe, George D. Jensen reported that whereas in the past women were discouraged from working, the general attitude now is that "if a [mother] wants to work it may be better for the whole family." This change in attitude is reflected in the development of the Pregardiennat (Pre-G), which provides a smaller home type atmosphere for groups of

1. Dale R. Meers, "International Day Care: A Selective Review and Psychoanalytic Critique," *Day Care: Resources for Decision* (Washington, D.C.: Office of Economic Opportunity), p. 15.

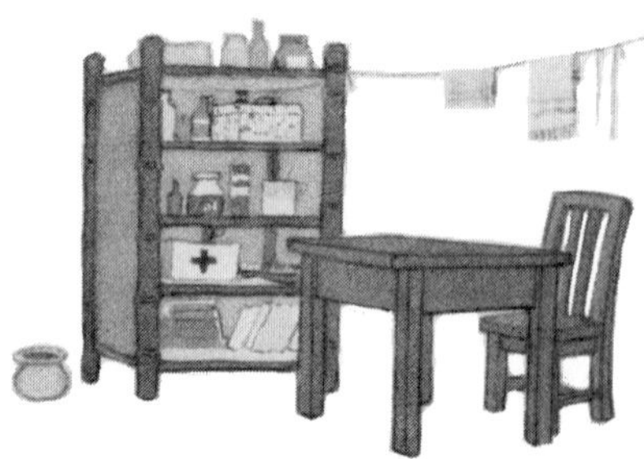

Little Ping Ping is playing doctor,
Younger sister comes carrying her doll
To find out what's wrong.

only 20 children, with less regimentation and more individual attention. In 1971, these centers were opened to all families, regardless of income.

In Denmark, day care is clearly seen as society's responsibility and is available for families of all economic backgrounds. National and local government pay 65 percent of the cost of care for infants and toddlers, and 75 percent for care of three-to-five-year-olds, with parents paying the remainder, on a sliding scale. These services are becoming available to all. American observers Marsden G. Wagner and Mary Miles Wagner believe that the Danes have evolved "the highest quality and most human services for children that we have observed anywhere."[2]

Danish child care programs are distinguished by their emphasis on freedom of exploration for children and involvement for parents. There is a low staff-child ratio (1 to 4 for infants), the staff includes an increasing number of men, and the program is one of stimulation and discovery, with both individual and group contact. There are also frequent visits between parents and staff, at the center and in their homes, and all centers have parent councils, which, among other powers, have the right to decide who will fill staff positions.

Although there are many centers in Denmark that are housed in traditional buildings, and the national, municipal, and county governments are all responsible for day care, the trend is toward small neighborhood units and decentralized administration.

New Societies, New Programs

Day care systems in western Europe have evolved over a long period of time; in the kibbutzim of Israel, and in China and Cuba, the establishment of day care services was part of a much more dramatic process. In the formation of the kibbutz and in the building of new societies in China and Cuba, child care facilities were created to free women from their primarily domestic role and to establish equality between men and women through equality of work.

The first kibbutzim were created in the early 1900's by people who immigrated to Palestine from the ghettos of Eastern Europe, where, says Bruno Bettelheim, "the essential female role . . . was one in which the wom-

2. Marsden G. Wagner and Mary Miles Wagner, "Day Care Programs in Denmark and Czechoslovakia," *Day Care: Resources for Decision* (Washington, D.C.: available through Day Care and Child Development Council, 1971), p. 29.

Mao-Chiu, from *The Little Doctor,* China Books

an's entire life was swept up in caring for husband and children and nothing else."[3] In part, the kibbutzim were created to change this role of women, and alternative child care was provided for all children. There are variations among kibbutzim, and they differ as to the involvement of parents in the care of their children, but in all kibbutzim someone other than the mother is a major figure in the child's life. Most often a child enters the nursery when he or she is four or five days old and is cared for by the *metapelet,* or trained child care worker. Generally, the mothers nurse their babies, but in some kibbutzim they also put them to bed and spend their nights with them.

Day care in China was also developed as part of a redefinition of the role of women. Before the Revolution, women were virtually slaves, married by arrangement at a young age and uneducated and unemployed outside the home. Now women are encouraged to work in all fields—in factories and as doctors, pilots, and political leaders. Fifty percent of Chinese medical students are women, and 90 percent of Chinese women work. There are now public child care facilities everywhere. When a woman returns to work (usually fifty-six days after giving birth), she can bring her baby with her. She puts her or him in a nursery, and can leave her work and breast-feed her child twice a day. There are also nursery-kindergartens for part-time care or twenty-four-hour care. Child care alternatives are provided so that women can enter all areas of work without totally relinquishing the intimacy of early child care.

In Cuba in 1961, the Federation of Cuban Women (the mass women's organization), initiated the Círculos Infantiles, which could offer six days of care a week, from 6 A.M. to 6 P.M. daily. By constructing dozens of centers and converting old structures like abandoned mansions, Cuba had a massive day care system almost overnight.

Cubans initially mistrusted the ability of the centers to respond in loving, kind ways. However, once Cuban families were convinced that the círculos provided essential services—good food, proper medical treatment, a clean wholesome atmosphere—the demand for day care started to outdistance the availability of space.[4]

3. Bruno Bettelheim. *The Children of the Dream* (New York: Macmillan Company, 1969), p. 31.

4. Marvin Leiner and Robert Ubell, "Day Care in Cuba: Children Are the Revolution," *Saturday Review,* (April 1, 1972).

At present, 50,000 children are in Cuban day care centers. Cuba spends $50 million a year on day care, which is a higher percentage of the Gross National Product than any other country in the world.[5]

In Israel, Cuba, and China, alternative services were created to have an immediate effect on women's roles in these societies, but the kind of programs they developed for children were to have a long-range effect on the people they would become and the society they would build.

In the nurseries on the kibbutzim and the child care centers in China and Cuba, children are reported to have a real sense of belonging to something larger than a family or even a particular community. In each of these situations, by integrating productive labor in the child care program, children are made to feel that their work is part of the larger collective effort. For example in the kibbutz, children eat what they grow, and the income from their livestock is applied to the group's needs. In the Chinese kindergartens, once a week there is time set aside for productive labor. In one case, a factory that packages crayons leases the work to the school, and they are paid according to the number of boxes they make. The money then goes to purchase equipment for the group.

There is a strong emphasis on collectivity in child care facilities in all three countries. Where in the kibbutz it is more in the general attitude of the adults, in the Chinese schools they have developed various activities to promote cooperation. In one nursery, two three-year-olds sit across from one another and string beads on a common string. In the winter the children wear jackets that button in the back and they are encouraged to help each other put them on; in this same school, the teacher makes a point of not running to help the child who falls down, but asks other children to help her or him up. In Cuba, collectivity is fostered in other ways. There are collective playpens that can hold six children, and collective birthday parties for children who are born in the same month.

5. Ibid.

Of course, we cannot and would not want to duplicate the development of other countries. Their history and their present values are different from ours. We may want men to take a more active role in child care than they do in most other places; we may need a different balance between the needs of the individual and the group. But the alternatives of child care that other countries have established lead us to question what the possibilities are here. In her book *Women and Child Care in China*, Ruth Sidel wrote:

> *The Chinese say that they cannot export their form of revolution. So they cannot export their form of liberation for women or their form of preschool child care. What will liberate women in their society may not be meaningful in another society; the system that provides adequate care for children in China may not work elsewhere. But some of their principles may be useful in our society.*
>
> *Like the Chinese, we must search out whatever in our past can enhance our future. We must find techniques which are consonant with our cultural heritage and mesh them with our goals for a future society. Only if we are open to change and willing to relate to each other in new ways can we assure the optimum development of each human being—man, woman and child—in our society.*[6]

6. Ruth Sidel, *Women and Child Care in China* (New York: Hill and Wang, 1972), p. 191.

Little Ping Ping is playing doctor,
She's going to answer a call.

Child Care:
Not from One Generation to the Next, but from One Social System to Another

Margaret Randall

I'm thirty-five years old and I have four young children: Gregory is now eleven, Sarah is eight, Ximena is seven, and Anna is two and a half.

Today my children are growing and learning and living very differently from the ways in which I did.

I was cared for by my middle-class parents, who loved me though I sense there was an overdependence on whatever or whomever must have been the "Dr. Spock" of their day, balanced by little intuition. They gave me space for independence (their greatest gift), had frank sexual discussions with me, and exposed me to their cultural tradition, a Middle America version of upward mobility, private property, and rugged individualism. I went to privileged schools within the public school system, privileged because my parents were able to choose the neighborhoods where such schools existed. I did typically well in school in all the arts, history, creative writing, etc., and typically bad in all the science and math—typically, I say, because this was expected from a female.

I've spent a great deal of my adult life unlearning many of the things I learned in school, especially my "role" as a woman and the idea that possessions mean satisfaction.

Since I left school—with a discipline I built by myself—I've been learning some of the things I should have learned as a child. Among them trust of other human beings and my solid identity.

So when I think about child care in relation to each of my children I realize they were/are part of my particular learning process. I experienced their care in New York (where Gregory, my oldest, was born), in Mexico, and now in revolutionary Cuba. What I say therefore is necessarily shaped by the changes my children experienced from beginning their lives and learning in a capitalist society and continuing their development in a socialist society.

I was alone when I had my first child. That was 1960, New York City. I was trying to "be a writer." I still thought the painful distance between the reality of my relationships with men and what the books and advertisements said it was going to be or should be was my individual problem. But I wanted a child. Gregory was desired from before his conception, and the love his arrival brought was a complicated mixture of "the ectasy of being two" with a lot of firmly held "ideas" and what I've since discovered has always been my strong intuition born out of practice.

How did I care for him and work to support us at the same time? First by storming the Dalton School's exclusive nursery with fast-talking determination. (Dalton School is an expensive high school that had a small day care program carried out more to teach its girl students how to care for babies than to serve any significant number of unwed mothers' needs. They only took three babies at a time! But it was free.)

And later, but not much later, when Gregory passed the Dalton School's six-month-old limit, I stormed the elegant offices of Jewish Philanthropies; I held up under the scrutiny of social workers who tried to talk me into offering my "Jewish baby" up for adoption. In fact, his acceptance in the Jewish Child Care Program resulted from my throwing a furious scene when they threatened not to consider him eligible because he hadn't had a *bris!*[1]

Public nurseries in New York only took children from 2½ years up—when you could find an opening. None of the women I knew was into child care and its few alternatives. When my son was ten months old we moved to Mexico. At least part of the reason for that move was the vague idea I had that it would be different in Mexico. Dalton School and Jewish Child Care were simply babysitters; the first had sparkling accessories but nothing more; the second had Gregory sitting before a television set in another family's home to whom Jewish Child Care paid $40 a week for his "upkeep." Never was he *taught* anything in either program—whatever he learned came from the love, warmth and interest of many other people, including me.

1. A Jewish circumcision ceremony.

Venceremos Brigade

What happened in Mexico was different. At least on the surface. And for me, deceiving. I got married. I didn't know the phrase "male chauvinism" (*machismo,* in Mexico) yet. I married a Mexican poet who "took Gregory as his own," and two more children were born: Sarah in 1963 and Ximena in 1964. Together we began to build that particular brand of family/home life that society had been grooming me for; but no one had prepared me for the isolation and despair and all the resulting unexpressed resentments.

I seemed never to be able to really get to know my kids: look at them straight on and see them. From my present vantage point I can see that it wasn't "just me" but all the conditions and conditioning of society that made things so difficult; and the means it used—from parents to school to magazines to husbands—to make me accept it for so long; to make the fears, drudgery, and responsibilities overwhelm my senses and numb me toward the real pleasures and joys of being with children.

In Mexico, family life, even for working-class people, includes servants: we had one, then two; eventually a whole family of very poor people lived with us. Not *with* us in the sense of sharing but working *for* us. And to a great extent, those warm, abused, bitter, energetic women, often illiterate and often with many of their own children—those women were my children's child care during our years in Mexico.

For the children this meant good physical care, close contact with some really beautiful human beings, but also the idea that just about everything would be done *for* them because they/we belonged to a privileged class to be served by an oppressed class.

In Mexico, the United States exerts a lot of control over the economy, and the majority of Mexican people are very poor. The schools for their children were second cousins to the schools in East Harlem, Watts, and Birmingham. The teachers, having to hold down two or more jobs just to survive, often didn't show up for weeks. And "free" school supplies were sold to the children in the poorest neighborhoods. Not wanting that kind of education for my children and being able to make that choice, I got all three of them—one by one—into an experimental school called the Freinet School. (Freinet was a French educator, one of the initiators of "the active school.") There is no testing or grading in the conventional sense. The children learn a variety of subjects through the connections made with that which interests *them.* A great deal of emphasis is placed on manual skills (from puppetry through electronics), and they learn to read and write through using small hand presses on which they print their own words (in first grade) and their own stories (in sixth grade).

At the time I felt fortunate that my children were getting that kind of education. I understood the exclusive nature of the school—most of the other children could not go to such a school, when they could afford to go to any. But what I didn't understand was how that elitism, that exclusivity, was really affecting the children's lives; just as I didn't understand how my own elitist condition was affecting my life. I remember that once the mother of another child in the school went to the Soviet Union and wrote back that her daughter was now studying in an ordinary school with all the advantages and defects that has, but with a nation of Soviet children. Commenting on this with another friend at the time, it seemed difficult for both of us to see the merits of an "ordinary" school, even with the mixing of many children, over the Freinet school, a "progressive" school, training children to be creative, inventive, and "free" human beings—in an unfree society.

I finally separated from my husband in Mexico. Later I began to live with Robert Cohen. Then Anna, our youngest, was born. Gregory, Sarah, Ximena, and Anna came to Cuba under difficult circumstances. In 1968, after Mexican university students demonstrated against their government's policies, several hundred students were shot in the streets and the government crackdown spread to anyone considered "progressive," which included nonstudents. When the repression hit our family we were forced into hiding. After about a week, we decided to send our children out of the country; we needed to know they'd be safe, and we ourselves needed more mobility. The children arrived in Cuba in mid-1969, under the care of the Cuban Revolutionary Government.

They were taken to a mansion in Miramar (Havana), once the home of the millionaire Bacardi Rum family but now a health center within a boarding school program. The children were made to feel wanted and cared for, while the Cubans checked them out for any health problems they might have. The three older children were taken three days later to a vacation plan at Santa María Beach; little Annie (3½ months old) should have been sent to a live-in children's circle (Cuban day care centers are called children's circles, or *Círculos Infantiles*), but the women at the health center felt very close to her—especially one of the women—and asked to have her left in their charge until we arrived. This health center houses children who are in the final stages of recuperation from diseases for which they've been hospitalized—they're up, running, playing, eating a special extra diet, and generally getting back their health. So the atmosphere—big gardens and light, open rooms—is not that of a conventional clinic; it was a relatively happy place for Annie to grow. She was 3½ months old then, and she was to live in that house for seven months.

When we arrived and were given housing, we brought Annie to live with us and put her in a children's circle during the day, as we both were working. The circle takes children from forty-five days old to six years (when they enter grade school). Annie can arrive as early as 6:30 a.m. or as late as 3, and we can pick her up anytime between 5 and 7 p.m. In the circle she eats all her meals, bathes, naps, plays, and learns. The learning process begins from the start: the children are encouraged to move their muscles and imitate sounds and musical notes while still in cribs.

There are waist-high collective playpens for the younger children, with climbing and entering apparatus for all ages. The Cubans make their toys out of anything and everything. The children do as much as possible on their own from the moment they're able, from tying their shoes and brushing their teeth to growing and tending a vegetable patch. The children's circles are completely free of charge.

The three older children undoubtedly felt more painfully the circumstances of their move. They were aware of what had happened in Mexico in 1968, and when the repression hit, Gregory (who was nine) had been arrested and had spent thirty-six hours in a Mexican adult jail. They were anxious about us—still in Mexico—and the culture shock of sudden socialism wasn't easy for them.

The vacation plan they were sent to hosted lots of children whose parents were involved in struggles in different Third World countries. Latin American children, African children. Gregory later talked a lot about Agna, a boy from the Congo whose mother had been killed and whose father was still fighting. Agna became one of Gregory's good friends and helped him to understand what this was all about: this big family of comrades that often has to take over when the smaller nuclear family broke down in the struggle for liberation.

When school started in September, and we still weren't reunited, the older children were sent to a boarding school in the Miramar section of Havana, where many of the mansions left by the rich in 1959 have been turned into schools for the hundreds of thousands of children who never before had any access to education.

In the schools the children learn a collective rather individual learning process and a great respect for workers, who are held as examples to be proud of and emulated.

In this, a socialist society, emulation is fostered in place of the individual competition that is encouraged in a capitalist, free-enterprise system. Children in Cuba begin to understand emulation from preschool on up. A group of children may compete with another group to attain or surpass goals which both groups have decided upon collectively, in open discussion beforehand. Individual competition is involved, of course, in that each child wants to do his or her best, but it's more important to help a classmate understand a problem or do better in order that the goals of the whole collective be reached than it is to win as an individual. In short, emulation means to do the best that one can in any undertaking, not in order to beat the other person but for the good of all.

Another relevant aspect is the profound connection made between classroom, factory, and farm: Cuban children intimately link their lives with production, with the workers who make their education possible.

From the very beginning of the Cuban Revolution an extraordinary literacy campaign was carried out. Thousands of young people went to the most remote areas of the country—where peasants live who had never even seen a school—in order to teach people of all ages how to read and write and accomplished their task in one year. But with the idea of an "elitist education for the elite" becoming a "mass education for the masses," thousands of teachers had to be trained—and fast. The first child care centers were staffed by women who had previously been the maids and nannies for the children of the rich. Many of the grade school and junior high school teachers are themselves students, teaching the lower grades during the day and continuing their own studies at night. When Gregory was nine, one of his teachers was fourteen. These student teachers still need a lot of training, but what they lack in experience they make up for in not being burdened with old ideas; they're as young and as much a part of the tremendous wave of revolutionary vitality as the children they teach.

The process of adaptation wasn't quick or easy for our children. In Mexico they had seen a police-run country, but in school they learned

PRIMER FESTIVAL NACIONAL DE TEATRO INFANTIL Y DE LA JUVENTUD set. 15/66

centro cubano del ITI / consejo nacional de cultura

Poster for the First National Festival of the Childhood and Youth Theatre, Cuba

Venceremos Brigade

about "freedom." In Cuba, the army is "the people in uniform," and acquiring military discipline and skills is simply the minimal requirement for learning how to participate in the defense of a country constantly under the threat of aggression. In Mexico Gregory was a little "hippie" with shoulder-length hair. Here his hair is short. All three kids bought more or less whatever they wanted whenever they wanted at the nearest neighborhood store in Mexico; in Cuba they got a few toys a year at the beginning of January. They had to *learn* to get joy not from a chest full of toys but from the knowledge that *every* child in Cuba also receives these toys. Last year the children, although actively involved, were still not totally convinced that the boarding school was where they wanted to be. This year they feel completely convinced that it is *their* community.

How have they changed? They are much more independent. They lost most of the childhood fears that used to hold them back. Most important, they understand that they have a methodology for dealing with things like fear, and that it *works.* They know a comradeship and community they never knew before. They are growing up in a society where children *always* come first: when they feel an interest in something, they just find out where they can learn something about it and they go and say, "Here I am." That way Gregory was apprenticed to the National Puppet Theatre and learned about puppetry last year. More recently he went out to the Academy of Science's Astronomical Institute and made friends with Cuba's only astronomer (a thirty-two-year-old woman who was a door-to-door saleswoman before the Revolution). Now he has his own cot there and frequently spends the night in order to use the telescope.

Sarah and Ximena take their little sister to the movies or the zoo; they have no qualms about running and stopping a bus mid-block or making friends with a militiaman and going to his house for a treat. Last year, during a huge, spontaneous demonstration in protest against the United States' capture of eleven Cuban fishermen, Sarah suddenly jumped up on a TV sound truck, grabbed the mike, and "spoke in the name of all the children of Cuba," demanding the fishermen's release!

Ximena, in a recent hospital experience that included a serious operation and a month away from home, was able to set an example of courage, serenity, and joy for all the other patients, most of them adults. After the first night, she didn't even need mommy to spend the night; one of us simply visited her for a short period daily. She was secure.

All the children are growing up with a deep respect for work and a nonseparatist idea about physical and intellectual labor. They are acquiring a profound sensitivity to other people and their problems.

Unlike me, in my own childhood years, they are growing up in a society where there is no contradiction between what they learn and what they see and do in their daily lives.

Havana
December 1971

Mao-Chiu, from *The Little Doctor,* China Books

The little doctor
Listens to Dolly's lungs,
Listens to her heart;
Then smiles as she says:
"Dolly is perfectly well,
She doesn't need either medicine or injections."
Younger sister is happy to hear this.

PART 2

Other Ways of Getting There

M.S.R.

Chapter 5

Sharing Child Care

It is impossible to suggest one immediate solution for all our child care problems. We are all living different lives. Some of us are in crowded cities where hundreds of children live in just a few buildings; others of us are in places where children are far away from one another. We also have different needs. A single woman with children who works full-time, a woman at home with children who wants a paying job, a woman living at home with her children who needs some relief from their care but doesn't need or want a paying job, someone with children who works part-time or at night—all these people need very different child care alternatives, different options and possibilities for change. We clearly need a government that supports—financially and in every other way—a variety of quality child care services for everyone, with enough flexibility for parents to determine the kind and quality of care. While many people are working toward this end, some are creating alternatives that best suit the way they live now.

A Variety of Alternatives

The existing alternatives for child care differ to the extent to which they challenge the isolation of the nuclear family and the roles of it members.

Fathers have been involved in child care arrangements before, but they have often been made to feel negative about this role and their wives are left with their share of child care as well as all the other household chores. Now, couples are sharing child care with a new consciousness about the division of labor—and are feeling good about it. Where it is possible, some couples take turns working—six months or a year at a time—or find part-time work. But with the kinds of work available to most of us, and with women's earning potential likely to be less than their husbands', this arrangement is limited to small numbers of people. It does relieve the biological mother from the total responsibility for child care and does allow the child to relate to two caring adults on a consistent basis, but unless couples are part of some form of group child care, the child is still at home and isolated from her or his peers.

Group Living Arrangements

Communes, group marriages, collectives—sometimes called second-chance families—are an extension of couple-sharing alternatives. Each group living arrangement looks different—the ages of the members vary, their work, their political and social style. Some live in separate apartments in a large house, sharing responsibilities only; others live communally in one unsubdivided house. Each person in a group living arrangement comes to it with different needs and expectations, but there are a great many people who are motivated to live with others because of their relationship or nonrelationship with children. Many people without children of their own don't want to be deprived totally of the joy or the work involved in caring for them; people with children of their own want to break down the possessive one-to-one full-time relationship without destroying the fun or the responsibility for their children's care.

The organization of communes can be as different as the people in them. In some, there are weekly meetings and rigid schedules of work, house care, and child care responsibilities; others are more fluid, more informal. But in any such setting, a child can learn to relate—more than that, to love—other adults besides her or his parents. And if there is more than one child in the group, close relationships can develop between the children.

Eric Breitbart

Some Thoughts on Communal Child Rearing

Louise Gross

As I think about my experiences in collective child rearing, it is always difficult deciding which of my "hats" to wear. In my first communal experience I was involved in helping raise a three-year-old child, Justy. The collective I live in now includes my nine-month-old daughter, Jeannette. These two perspectives have given different insights into both the values and problems of collective child rearing. Helping me to evaluate the children's experiences as well as my own has been a background in child development—as a graduate student I received an M.Ed. degree in early childhood education. The biases and prejudices each of these three roles traditionally holds toward group child care have certainly been intertwined in me, and I would like to begin to unravel them here.

I have found that in American society a childless person has extreme difficulty in having responsible and meaningful interactions with children. It seems to me that this condition partially comes from a concept of children as the property of their parents and partially from the way jobs tend to define whom people relate to. For the four years that my husband and I lived together as a separate nuclear family, my relationships with children revolved around my teaching and our friends' children. Because of my job I had considerably more contact with children than most childless people do; but still this contact was limited to classroom activities, curriculum planning, home visits, parent conferences, babysitting, present-buying, and the like. If I wanted to relate more closely to a child, why did I remain childless? A number of reasons come to mind: lack of money, desire for a career, adjustment to married life, and real uncertainty about what it meant to raise a child. Behind all lay the ambivalence of wanting to be part of raising children—knowing that I had a lot to offer children and they had a lot to offer me.

My first communal living experience was able to fulfill a number of these needs, as well as offer "our" three-year-old Justy some unique and meaningful experiences. I became part of a seventeen-person family involved in helping make decisions that affected all of us. While not feeling singly responsible for a child, I was intimately involved in Justy's life—her good and bad moods, her achievements, and her regressions. As a group we worked over a number of months to develop a child care plan that met both Justy's and the adults' needs. At first we cared for Justy in three-hour shifts. Soon we realized that this plan made Justy's day too choppy and gave her too many people to relate to. She was having a difficult time switching caretakers, and we were having a hard time planning a good day for her. Eventually we developed a system of a day shift and an evening shift, with an overlap period to provide both the adults and Justy with enough time to enjoy each other and still allow for space apart.

Child care, or more specifically Justy care, was an important part of our group's weekly meetings. We would discuss different ways people related to Justy, how Justy was interacting with individual adults and the group as a whole, what kinds of emotional and physical changes seemed to be taking place, etc. It was partially through these discussions that we all became people responsible for Justy—not babysitters.

My experiences with Justy reinforced already strong feelings that I would want my own child raised in a commune. The family we now live as is made up of seven adults, five dogs, one cat, and our nine-month-old daughter, Jenny. I see our commune as a family that has developed from a set of shared values, rather than from blood or marriage ties. We share some values—not always fully carried out in practice—which led to our decision to try communal living. One of the most important shared values is that collective child rearing offers a necessary alternative to nuclear family life.

As in our previous commune, child care discussions are an important part of weekly meetings; but for me their function has changed. Whereas as a childless adult I once gained a sense of responsibility for these discussions, as a mother I now get support and reassurance. People whose judgment I trust are discussing and carrying out a plan for raising Jenny. We discuss, for example, what it means to say that we want Jenny's early childhood experiences to reflect our shared attitudes about sex roles. Women and men spend equal amounts of time with Jenny, and she sees us sharing other daily tasks. Both sexes bake bread, patch clothes, repair cars, and have outside employment. Our jobs are diverse: two teachers, a typist, a school bus driver, a stage hand, an auto mechanic, and a service station attendant. Through this variety of role models, we hope that as in a nuclear family Jenny will see and absorb some of our basic values.

Communal Jenny care also allows me time and space to do a number of things I want to do. I'm able to teach a half-day nursery class, as well as have time for interests such as karate and music without feeling as if Jenny is constantly being left behind. The group follows a schedule: one person for the 6 a.m. feeding, a morning person, an afternoon person, and an evening person. In contrast to Justy's needs, these shifts seem to make sense for Jenny's age—especially inasmuch as having fewer people involved in her over-all care means she is cared for by each of us fairly frequently. Also, the schedule is not rigid. People who feel like being with Jenny at a particular time do so; and as Jenny reaches out to individuals, they respond.

My experiences with Justy and Jenny have provided me some observations regarding communal child rearing and child development. After living in the commune for two weeks, Jenny could clearly distinguish between "us" and strangers. At eight months, she became upset by strangers and would seek out any one of the seven of us for comfort. By nine months, she became able to accept strangers if they approached her in a quiet, slow manner; but at the same time she clearly related more comfortably and positively to her seven communards. One week when a number of communal people were on a trip and visitors were around a good deal of the time, Jenny was crabby and irritable. As soon as the visitors left and the communal group returned, Jenny's usually cheerful nature reemerged. In effect, Jenny's development of trust has been generalized to include seven people. I believe the phenomenon of fear of strangers has not been eradicated, but rather altered by communal living.

Much of the time I lived with Justy she was busy developing her sense of autonomy. This process became a struggle, which involved more than the usual two adults and one child; the increased number of adults seemed to significantly diffuse some of the traditional battles. Toilet training was a long process, but not a particularly tense one. Justy's periods of "no" to every suggestion were shared by a number of people, and thus were easier for all of us to put up with. Also, since Justy was growing up in a

Vicki Breitbart

household composed predominantly of adults, we were all concerned about her relationships with other children. We made conscious efforts for her to spend time with children her age, but frequently felt that the lack of opportunity for her to do so was a problem. Yet when Justy at three years participated in a parent cooperative nursery, she made a rapid, easy, and joyful adjustment.

From these and my more general observations of communal children, I have been most impressed by how the necessity of relating to a variety of adults has lessened the intensity of some traditional child-rearing battles. The traditional developmental issues have remained, but their intensity seems diffused. A partial explanation may be that these children have a variety of models to relate to and do not have all of their emotions tied up in one or two intense relationships. I believe that by watching and participating with a group of adults in daily living situations, communal children also learn to see adults in ways that lessen many of the childhood fantasies of parents as omnipotent human beings.

At the same time, it would be foolish of me to suggest that communal child rearing *per se* is "the answer" for all children or all adults. Just as there are successful nuclear families, there can also be problems with communal families. In forming or evaluating a commune that included children, I would be concerned with questions such as: How do the people feel about children in general? These children in particular? How do *I* feel about the way the other adults relate to children? What are the children's relationships like with these adults? With each other? From these and other general questions about individuals come more specific questions about the group as a whole: What kinds of stability does this child need, and will this specific group be able to fill these needs? Can the child feel secure and accepted in this group? Will the child or children feel overwhelmed by adults or vice versa?

In general, I feel it essential that people feel they have choices to make in determining their living situations. In deciding life styles, we must think about the above questions as well as many others. No one living situation suits everyone, and each has its own advantages and disadvantages. What is crucial is that people's lives deal with the issues *they* see as important and in ways they find satisfying. For me, the problems and joys of communal life in general, and communal child rearing in particular, are exciting and fulfilling to deal with.

Children in Communes

Virginia Rankin

From October 1970, to October 1971, I lived in a commune with eight other adults and six children—three pairs of siblings. When we began, the children's ages were three and a half, four, four and a half, six, six and a half, and eight. The four youngest were boys, the two oldest girls. Only one pair of siblings moved into the commune with both parents; the others had lived with just their mothers for quite some time (I was one of the mothers). The kids had all known each other before; four had traveled cross-country together for six weeks. They had all seemed to get along well.

The three of us who were mothers had been in the same women's consciousness-raising group for a year. As we talked about our lives and our families, we were drawn to the conclusion that a radical change in our life styles was what we needed and desired. We would talk of a problem—our lack of freedom, or our loneliness, or the jealousy and competitiveness in our children's sibling relations. As our understanding grew, we looked for practical solutions and often ended by saying wistfully: "Well, communal living . . ." Finally we grew frustrated with this and began holding meetings to start a commune.

As we anticipated problems, in our meetings prior to moving in, care of the kids was not one of them. We felt that it would be much better for them to be living together. In their nuclear families, they competed with one other sibling for the limited attention of a parent or parents. In the commune there would be lots of other kids to relate to, lots of other adults to respond to them. The breaking down of the nuclear family looked pretty simple. We all felt that we would be much better off once we eliminated family units.

We had two sorts of communal child care goals. Some were on a very practical level. We wanted life to be easier for all, not so tiring, not so confining. This seemed an automatic blessing we would attain when we moved in together. Our practical goals led us very quickly to our visionary ones. We were designing a new way for adults and children to live together. We would knock down the walls of dependency, jealousy, competitiveness; we would break through to freedom, trust, and a community of support. Ultimately, we would eliminate the causes of problems our society accepts as part of growing up: sibling rivalry, Oedipal conflicts. Although we did not assume that this would be simple or automatic, we probably underestimated how hard we would have to struggle.

In the adult group, people who were not parents outnumbered people who were. This seemed a very positive asset. Because they did not have to break out of old patterns and responses, they could bring us a fresh perspective. Because kids would not perceive them as "belonging" to any other kid, it would be easier for them to trust them.

This was the model we started out with: every kid should trust every adult equally. Every adult should try to share equally in the task of rearing them. Upon moving in we would all become the kids' parents, and even before that move the kids seemed to understand this. Sometimes one would do something like refer to all the men who would be living with us as "all my Daddies." When we went on outings together the kids generally responded to whichever adult was caring for them.

We saw what we were doing as important for adults, too. We were developing a new way for people to be involved with and responsible for children. It would provide an alternative to establishing one's own family and biologically reproducing.

When we finally moved in, after six months of planning, the kids, quite simply, freaked out. Most of them became very dependent, each wanted *everything* done for her or him by his or her mommy. They couldn't get along together. They fought—loudly, constantly, and brutally.

Adults who were not parents were disappointed and ultimately angered by the kids' seeming rejection of them. Sometimes they placed the blame on the mothers for being overresponsive to the kids. Mothers were disappointed and angered by their kids' extreme dependency. Sometimes they blamed the nonparents for not trying hard enough to build relationships with the kids.

We embarked on a process of growth and change. At the beginning it was hard to see it this way. Not only were we disappointed in terms of our visionary goals, but on a practical level, the child care was harder rather than easier.

Our biggest initial problem was that what was happening bore little resemblance to our expectations. As I wrote in my journal, "Our prime desire really does seem to be that our children 'be good.' This is the only thing we are really attending to. Perhaps that's wrong. We *think* about other things. We talk about how they might be happier; we get analytical about that question. But our actions are mainly devoted to helping them 'behave' as we think they should. This leads us into a lot of moral imperatives:

Vicki Breitbart

'Don't ask for your Mommy! I'll do just as well.' 'Don't bother us now, we're busy.' We have an ideal of how children in a commune should be, and we constantly hold it up to them."

This is similar to what happens in a nuclear family. We have an ideal for our kids. It focuses on "goodness" and it profoundly influences how we adults relate to them. We are product-oriented. We keep referring them to the end, to the person they will be. This keeps us from acknowledging and dealing with the process from the kids' side.

Seeing it from the kids' side means that we communicate to them that we do acknowledge their own very real feelings about what is happening. What does this mean? Often something as simple as saying: "You're really sad now because you miss your mommy," or perhaps talking about why a child of our time might well miss her or his mommy.

I felt that our failure to see it from the "kids' side" only made it harder for them to change. Understanding and accepting where they were at that moment would help.

It is an overwhelming thing, no matter what your age, to be informed that your current behavior simply isn't satisfactory, that something else is required. The larger and more total the change required, the more overwhelmed the person is likely to feel. "But I don't know how." "I can't." It makes it hard to accept criticism at all. Even if criticism is accepted, you are likely to feel pretty hopeless about changing, and therefore pretty bad about yourself. And a vicious circle starts because guilt and self-disgust only put further barriers in the way of change.

It can be really helpful and supportive to build bridges to change by pointing out ways that the desired behavior already exists in a person's life.

One night I went in to say goodnight to my son Dylan, three and a half, after he had spent the evening complaining to the people helping him to get ready for bed that he would prefer me. Now he was being particularly charming. I told him, "Mm—hugs and smiles—I really like them. Remember how you gave Allan hugs and smiles at dinner? That made him very happy." The information about Allan seemed to surprise and please him. It seemed right at the time to give him feedback on the ways he was making progress relating to other adults, rather than to berate him for ways that he was lagging.

As with so many other things, the "problem of the ideal" was not just a kid's problem. From my journal: "I think that people in the house are hassling each other about not being good enough, about not living up to an ideal of collective living."

When I wrote that, I was trying to figure out different causes of tension in the adult group. Kids were one. "What their presence means is jangled nerves and constant interruptions for adults. On a weekend or a holiday we tend to flee to separate outside pursuits because the option of being together in a relaxed sort of way just isn't open to us. It's as hard for us all to do something together without the kids as it is for a married couple."

Different ideas of how to relate to the kids also increased tension. At first we expected that every kid would trust, and respond to, every adult. When this proved not to be the case, we tried to make them trust everybody by arguing them into it. As we began to realize that it was foolish to expect the kids to trust all the adults just because we told them they should, we began to think about how we could build that trust.

Initially there had been a great emphasis on spontaneity in the commune. In terms of the children, this meant that the absolutely essential tasks of getting the kids up and off to school, and bedding them down at night, were the only tasks to be assigned. During the week most of the kids were away at school for the better part of the day; for the remaining part of the weekdays and all weekend long they were basically expected to fend for themselves. Obviously our kids didn't need and would have been greatly hindered by a lot of adult supervision. But what seemed to be happening was that the major way adults related to kids was through maintenance and by mediating crisis situations. It's hard to build up any kind of trust or understanding in such unrelaxed, goal-oriented situations. Though certainly the way we behave influences how we feel about the kids, and how they feel about us, the kids' perception of the adults gets skewed if these are the only data they have to go on.

The balance between assigned tasks and spontaneity in adult-child relationships became an important issue in the commune. For a while the house seemed split into two factions. Nonparents felt they could not relate well unless they could always spontaneously choose when they would relate to a child. In practice, in the early weeks, nonparents seldom did choose to be with kids. Partly, this was because the kids were pretty freaked out. But even when nonparents did want to be with kids, they weren't sure exactly how to do this. Most of them had never lived with kids before.

Parents felt less free to choose not to respond to the children. They felt that other people's insistence on spontaneity trapped them in their old roles.

Once we had seen collective child rearing as an answer to many of our needs. Now we were realizing that we weren't so sure we knew what collective child rearing meant. First we had found that it was not all that simple for the kids to trust all the adults. Now it was becoming apparent that neither was it all that easy for all the adults to be responsive to and responsible for the kids.

Everyone was concerned about the quality of the children's lives in the commune. Those of us who had lived with any of the children before felt that their lives were not as pleasant, or their needs as well met, as when we resided in nuclear family units. It is not enough to say that this will happen because there are more people to assume responsibility for the children. It is a larger question of *how* nine or ten people assume responsibility for a child.

Here is an example of a problem we weren't organized to deal with. When I picked up Sammy from school, his teacher informed me that he'd had a hard day and was pretty cranky. That's standard teacher procedure—they give you information like that so you can act on it. A mother then can do her best to make the rest of the child's day easy. But what was I to do? Spend the rest of the day with him because I felt responsible? Okay, maybe once in a while, but I get data like this on the kids a lot, and sometimes I have plans for my time. Or I can run around telling every adult what I know in the hope that someone might want to deal with him (take him off for music or a story), or at least they could bear his emotional state in mind should they have contact with him. Often in the late afternoon, however, the only person one finds around is the cook for the evening, who's already too distracted to bear anything in mind.

Sometimes the problem with child care in the commune is that when responsibility is divided up among so many individuals, no one is responsible, and chaos ensues. A single parent may be overburdened by meeting all the child's needs, but at least she generally knows what they are. With large groups of both parents and children, it's hard to keep communication flowing so that all are aware of individual wants, problems, and enthusiasms.

Another serious communication problem relates to actions rather than knowledge. I tell the kids to do something only to discover they've been forbidden to do it by someone else. This can include four or five people in a short space of time, telling kids conflicting things about what they can or cannot do.

It became clear that life was none too good for the kids, but everyone did not immediately feel that the way to improve things was to end spontaneity. However, other ways of coping either didn't work, or failed to materialize. Finally, we reached a consensus. We would have a single individual in charge in the late afternoon on schooldays, and two people responsible for a whole weekend day.

Things were immediately better for the kids with this new system. As the adults in the house began to arrive home that first afternoon and evening, we were struck by how quiet the house was. Usually we were greeted with shouts, screams, and the pounding of footsteps. Often it seemed the kids spent most of their time purposelessly galloping from one end of the house to the other and trampling each other on the way. But if one person is watching out for the

Jane Melnick

kids, a number of different things happen. Simple immediate needs like Band-Aids and untied shoes will be attended to. Situations that if unnoticed would develop into crises can be redirected. If certain children are not getting along they can be distracted from each other, or an activity can be initiated which makes it possible for them to relate again. Often, right before dinner, when everyone starts to get hyperactive, reading a story can quickly restore calm.

One doesn't have to act in high gear all the time, directing kids' energies and initiating activities. The important thing seems to be that somebody is *aware* of what is happening to the kids and ready to respond if necessary.

The first weekend we operated on this system was pleasant and low-key. Because there were two people in charge, the kids usually had some basic choices: whether to be inside or out, whether to go bike riding or to the playground. We planned several different projects and trips, but the children never had to get carted off anywhere as a herd.

A person not on duty all weekend is freer to spend an hour or two with one of the kids, freer to really attend to the particular child he or she is with, because the adult knows there's plenty of time left for her or his own wants and needs to be met. Freer, too, because of the knowledge that the wants and needs of other children won't intrude. Here's where spontaneous relating can be good. It's fine for adults and kids to spend time together just because it seems like a good idea to them.

At our house, things definitely improved after the "end of spontaneity." But our initial feelings that we'd ushered in the millennium were short lived. We'd taken a step. The quality of the kids' lives was improved, and in its improvement we saw our vision beginning to come true.

Play Groups and Co-ops

Play groups and cooperatives are other forms of alternative child care that challenge the exclusive mother-child relationship, provide the child with a consistent relationship to a group of her or his peers, and are controlled by the people directly involved. The play group describes an arrangement that is half a day in duration, small and informal in feeling. It usually involves a group of about 5 to 8 children who meet regularly in different people's homes or apartments, with parents taking turns supervising the group. Many groups have found it preferable to use space out of the home (if they can find one for free or little rent). When the group of children meets outside the home and the parents hire a teacher, it has been traditionally called a cooperative, but the terms "play group" and "cooperative" can be used to describe any group alternative where parents work with children and are responsible for the over-all direction of the program. Because these programs are usually part-time and rely on the energy and resources of the members, they have almost exclusively been formed by middle-class families where the mother did not have a full-time job outside the home. Recently, however, with the growing demand among students that universities and colleges provide space for child care services, cooperatives have been set up on many campuses. And by recruiting volunteer staff, and finding other ways for parents to help run the center, some community groups have also been able to set up cooperative child care that can include people from a variety of economic backgrounds and parents who work at full-time jobs and therefore cannot work with the children in the center. Groups have also formed cooperatives on a temporary basis while working for public funding.

Play groups and cooperatives have been around for a long time, but it is not the form of the group child care that makes them alternatives to what has existed in the past. They are alternatives because they involve groups of people never before part of parent-run child care programs. They are alternatives because many of the people involved are attempting to liberate themselves from traditional sex-role stereotypes, race prejudices, and class bias and to undermine the traditional power relationships in this society (male/female, white/non-white, rich/poor, schooled/without-formal-schooling, etc.); and they are different because they are part of a growing movement of people who want to change all the institutions that affect our lives.

Starting a Play Group

Georgene Gardner

When I was still pregnant with my first child, I began to realize how necessary it was for mothers to organize neighborhood child care centers. I began to wonder why play groups weren't everywhere, so that mothers could take turns watching each other's children and then have some free time each week for themselves. I didn't look forward to years of taking care of my baby all by myself, cut off from other mothers, existing only between my apartment, the supermarket, and the park. It would be so much more interesting, and less isolating, to share some of this time with other young women like myself.

When my son was eight months old, I could begin to see why play groups weren't everywhere. I could see some of the difficulties more clearly. The idea of organizing with other mothers and actually committing myself to a project that might fail was overwhelming, and I couldn't get started. I was made to feel guilty that I wanted to be away from my child, and was told a play group would just be a place "to dump him." Some of the other women were asked by their husbands what they were going to do "with all that free time." On the whole, our husbands weren't too cooperative. So I vacillated between commitment to the project and withdrawal until I happened to meet two women who had already overcome these hurdles and started to set up a play group. They were definite about what they wanted, and were looking for a suitable location in downtown Manhattan. Several other women had chipped in with them to pay a month's rent and had begun cleaning the floors and cupboards and getting donations of display toys from local stores. It was a reality all of a sudden, and the simple difference between the reality and wishful thinking was that these women had said "I can" instead of "maybe I could."

Once a definite commitment had been made, the play group quickly got off the ground. We found a low-rent apartment near the park. It wasn't large enough so children taking naps could be separated from the children who were playing, but it was the best we could find. The youngest child was six months old and the oldest was two and a half. Both caused some problems: the youngest needed to be held more than was convenient, and the oldest was bored. We have found that it works better to have children who are at least old enough to crawl. The oldest should have at least one or two children at about the same age to play with.

At first, we set up a schedule to be open from 10 a.m. to 2 p.m. each weekday. Each mother or father who doesn't work full-time was to work three days every two weeks. As could be expected, most of the children would cry when they were left with people who were still strangers to them, but within one or two weeks, almost all the children had made friends with each other and with the adults. The desirable ratio of adults to children depends upon the age of the children, the size of the play group center, the temperament of the children and adults. A typical afternoon in our play group might find five children with two adults.

Some of the women in our group have done some reading about nutrition for children and recommended that, instead of just cookies and milk, we have apple juice, yogurt, honey, brown rice, carrots, fruit, cheese, and spring water. We try to feed the children natural, organically grown fruits and vegetables, so they won't be eating DDT and other poisons. We also avoid popular-brand baby foods which contain salt, white sugar, bleached flour, and all sorts of chemicals the children don't need. Recently, we have been setting out some finger foods like carrot sticks and apple slices for the children to take themselves. Vitamin C tablets are given to the children when they arrive, helping (we hope) to cut down on runny noses. For each child, the cost of sharing rent, food, disposable diapers, vitamin C, and other expenses comes to $9 a month.

I would like to be able to say that the fathers share equally in taking care of their children, but it just wouldn't be true. If the women have to assume total responsibility because the men work full-time during the week, an all-day play group on Saturdays could be set up by the men. A man would have to devote probably one Saturday a month to taking care of the children; surely that's not too much to ask. Though several of the men in our group are free during the day, only one father regularly follows the same schedule as the mothers. There are other fathers who can sometimes be seen delivering or picking up their children, but seldom or never stay to share the work. If we were to do it again, we would set up a schedule committing the fathers to work on a regular basis. Even if there is resistance, it's easier to deal with at the beginning than to try to break bad habits later on.

In our group many of the mothers are on welfare and are separated from the fathers of their children. While this accounts somewhat for the lack of men, it also serves to accentuate the need for play groups for children who are being raised by single parents. The child has an opportunity to learn that there are other loving adults in addition to his or her mother and has more children to play with.

Obviously, all the women involved have more free time now and enjoy their children more. I know a few women who haven't been away from their children more than two or three hours at a time within an entire year and cannot admit their resentment even to themselves. And it is their children who have to bear the brunt of their buried resentment.

I don't claim to have been "liberated" because I have three free afternoons a week. Actually, I often use the time to do the same chores I would have done if I had the baby with me. But without him the supermarket or Laundromat is less exhausting. I feel revitalized by a few hours to myself, and then it's a pleasure to go and pick up my baby, to see with fresh eyes how beautiful he is.

The Children's House

Marcia Sprinkle and Norma Lesser

The outside needs paint and the porch tilts and sags but the front door is shocking pink. Inside is a furious amount of activity, most going on at three feet and under. The walls are covered with posters, notices, and pictures of the children. The Children's House is a fully cooperative, parent-run day care center. For most of the adults it is far more than just an adequate place to leave their children: it is a new way to care for and relate to children and each other. Two of us wrote this article to share the experience of what we are doing.

Our Past

Early in 1969, when "women's liberation" was barely a household word, a few women from women's liberation, men, and their infant children began to get together and discuss the possibility of a place where children could be looked after and loved. We read *Summerhill* by A. S. Neill and *How Children Learn* by John Holt and discussed various philosophies of child rearing.

The winter was spent discussing what the center would have to look like. We wanted a space such as a house or a church with a backyard, conveniently located for the people participating, safe, clean, and not subject to harassment by landlords. We also wanted a place where the children would have all the freedom they needed to mess around, explore, and get to know adults other than their parents.

That summer we did some communal "babysitting." We also had some devastating meetings, which left us depressed about our lack of progress or community.

The fall brought in a handful of new people primarily because of the growing popularity of women's liberation. The women and children met regularly in the basement of one of our houses. We talked to each other about the children, ourselves, and women's liberation. Soon the play group was meeting two afternoons a week. Mothers were encouraged to leave, because we were crowded with the many people who came regularly to enjoy themselves with the children in that congenial setting.

By spring, the children were getting older and beginning to walk and talk and were not so easy to backpack. We women felt the need to become an all-day, all-week play group. At the same time the few men who came were disturbed. They felt ill at ease in a group of all women but wanted to be able to spend time with children other than their own. So we decided to expand and to require equal involvement of men and women.

Jane Melnick

Since it was spring we started using friends' backyards for our all-day operation. They were generous, but it was still borrowed space and we felt restrained in what we could do. Eventually a committee was set up with the power and money to rent a house. Within a week they found a decent but ramshackle house—at last we were in business.

What's Happening Now

We have been operating full-time for eight months now and the mechanics of running a children's center have been fairly well worked out. Our group now includes 25 children from the ages of ten months to three years (most are around two) and approximately 50 adults (nineteen to thirty-five). The house is open Monday through Friday from 9 a.m. to 5 p.m.

Children are signed up for any combination of hours, but in order to simplify planning the adults must come the morning shift (9 to 1) or the afternoon shift (1 to 5). We usually maintain a 1:3 ratio of adults to children or as close to that as possible. There also must be at least two adults in the house at all times.

Every couple comes a third of the time their children are there, the man and the woman working equal time. Couples with two children spend the same amount of time as those with one child, and single parents come only a sixth of the time their children are there. We don't penalize people for having more than one child or for being a single parent. In addition there are many nonparents who also come. We can sign up ourselves and our children for different hours each week, so the center is flexible enough to meet our fluctuating needs.

How We Do It

The administrative jobs are rotated weekly through the list of adults in the group. There are four jobs that have to be done:

1. *Scheduling.* The purpose of the scheduler is to make sure there are enough adults per children. The scheduler calls anyone who has not signed up. People find their own substitutes when they can't come, and some wives feel they must substitute when their husbands are unavailable. The pnone calls help to deal with paternal reluctance to accept responsibility for child care. When there are extra people on the schedule, they are available for helping out by taking care of sick children or going on special trips. The scheduler also writes the agenda for the bi-weekly meetings and notifies people about their jobs for the coming week.

2. *Buying Supplies.* The supply person buys the food and Pampers for the week and makes up the menus so the morning people know what to prepare for lunch, including snacks for the kids and coffee for the adults. We have a continuing unresolved debate over whether to fix organic health food or supermarket variety. At this point the food person does what he or she wants each week.

3. *Laundry.* One person washes the sheets and extra clothes.

4. *Cleanup.* A thorough cleanup is done every weekend.

On a daily basis, the morning shift serves lunch, the afternoon shift cleans, and we all do small jobs.

Every family unit contributes $5 to $30 a month, depending on what they feel they can afford. People can change their pledges up or down depending on their finances. We have a standing finance committee that signs the checks, pays the bills, and keeps the records straight. So far we have had enough money to pay for rent, utilities, food, supplies, and toys.

Our House

To get started everyone donated new or used toys, furniture, and equipment. A standing equipment committee has bought some things and made others. The house is well supplied with riding vehicles, dolls, crayons, paper, pull toys, puzzles, balls, books, and other kid stuff. Toy shelves and doll beds were made out of fruit crates. Playhouses were made by putting curtains across the front of a huge open cabinet. A wonderful four-foot-wide group slide was made out of old boards and doors.

Linda Firestone

The first floor of the house has a kitchen and two rooms where most of the toys are kept. Upstairs are three bedrooms with cribs, cots, extra clothes, and linens. The basement has larger toys such as a bouncing horse, a seesaw, and the slide. At first we thought we'd have separate activities, but the kids all travel in a pack from one room to another, so everything happens everywhere. The backyard contains a wading pool in the summer, another group slide, and a playhouse but is too confining for all-day use.

Our Day

On a typical morning 13 to 16 children come. Weather permitting, many of us take trips to museums or parks and go on walks. Lunch, which is usually served around 11:30, is always a nice part of the day. Paper plates of easy finger food like cheese, apple slices, and pieces of meatloaf are put out on an old coffee table. The children just take whatever they want. They sit down or stand or walk around, coming back to get more for themselves or more for someone else. The amazing thing is how quiet it gets and how rarely they fight over the food. They all eat without being pushed and there is relatively little mess. Afternoons are generally quieter because most of the children nap.

Licensing

At this writing we are unlicensed. We aren't willing to comply with some of the objectionable laws—for example, no children under six months and boys and girls must sleep in separate rooms. Even if we were willing to be licensed, it's not likely we could find a house in the prescribed nonresidential area that would meet the extensive safety regulations. We would also be periodically investigated.

Our Common Ideas

We think it is very important for our children to have the freedom to grow, explore, learn, and be. That means providing a secure, interesting environment. It also means respecting their ideas, emotions, and business. There is little structure imposed on the children: all the toys are always available, all the space is open and free, and the children are free to do whatever they please. We try not to interfere in the relationships they have with each other. Fighting is infrequent and even the infants have the capacity to develop unique relationships. It also means ending the possessive/dependent relationship between parents and children so typical in isolated nuclear families.

It means, despite conventional wisdom, that parents are not always the only important people to a child, even an infant. It means we let our children be free to develop very special relationships with other adults and that we have the time and openness to develop the same loving concern for other children that we have for our own.

At first, some of us felt some guilt about involving young children in a day care center, since the prevailing myth is that children in that age group are insecure in large groups. But our experience has shown that it isn't true. Providing a secure environment means that for certain children we made sure there were always some familiar faces until the child got to know more people in the group. It seems that the younger the children join the group, the easier it is for them. However, parents have a problem no matter what their age. For instance, almost every parent is shocked the first few times their leavetaking goes unnoticed. The parent says three or four "goodbyes" and "I'm going now" until the kid finally cries a little so the parent can leave reassured.

Success and Failure

In place of taking votes or establishing rules, the group has tried thorough ongoing discussion to reach a consensus that is satisfactory to everyone. Issues are always considered open for more discussion and new consensus. We have always hoped to relate to each other in an open, honest way that is supportive. This involves the very difficult tasks of listening to each other, trying to understand each other, being tolerant of others, and still expressing and working for what you think is correct.

Nonparents' participation is varied. Some are as active as the parents; others are not. We have repeatedly discussed whether nonparents should be expected to carry the same responsibilities as parents at the children's house. At first we felt so grateful to nonparents for helping at the center that we asked very little of them. Then we realized that if we wanted society to be responsible for all children, we must treat all adults as parents. This meant we didn't have to be grateful or expect less of the nonparents but it also meant we couldn't continue the old possessive/dictatorial role of parents.

The center and the discussions we have there have pushed us to change our own life styles. We have challenged our work situations —Larry asking and fighting for a two-thirds-time contract at his teaching job in order to work at the center, Marcia and Lorraine asking for release time when interviewed for jobs, men cooking, washing dishes, and spending lots more time caring for their children.

Many of us want to go beyond just maintaining child care for our personal use and to take more kinds of positive action, including publicizing what we have been able to do so other people will have some knowledge and feeling about our children's house and perhaps be inspired to set up their own.

DAYCARE

M.S.R.

Chapter 6

The Struggle for Public Funds and Local Control

Many groups setting up child care centers have steered away from public funding for fear that in the end it will change their programs in ways they can't control. Often these centers survive on the time, energy, and money of their members, and most often they are left alone by the authorities. But not always. The Children's House in Washington, D.C., was closed down because it violated restrictive zoning and licensing regulations. They had been operating for twenty months; they had been able to maintain a ratio of one adult to three children and to operate what they thought was a good program. But their being closed down made a lot of things clear to them. They saw the government's position and power as well as their own vulnerability in a new light.

This sudden interruption of our normal routine [the closing of the house] caused us to rethink many of our former conclusions about child care. We realized that the government would not even let us meet our own needs. Even if we concentrated on day care for our own children only, we would have to join with other people to make our fight stronger.

But we also became much more conscious of the child care needs of other children and adults. Many people in the District can't afford even the low rent we are paying. And racism means that many of the houses our mostly white group can rent are out of reach to black groups. We maintain a ratio of one adult to three children only because most of us work part time, are students, or have jobs that allow us some time off. Men and women who must work daily at 9-to-5 jobs don't have that luxury. They must either work out whatever ad hoc arrangements they can or else send their children to custodial day care, over which they have little control.

We are determined to join the fight for quality child care facilities funded by the government and entirely controlled by the parents and the community. We no longer think that we can meet our child care needs by ourselves. We see the issue in much more of a political perspective now, in a sense that we feel there is an over-all responsibility of society to care for its children, and that the nature of that care involves questions of money, control, and power.

We see little chance that the government will respond to our needs without a large number of us organized together to force the changes we feel are necessary.

Clearly, it will take an all-out effort to change the regulations and fight for new day care legislation, but people in different cities and in different towns have to also work out their own local strategies for obtaining public funds for community-run programs. It takes a lot of organization, and even more determination.

Interim Funding

As in many cities, the desperate need for child care services in New York City motivated a growing number of groups to start their own "underground," or unlicensed centers. Many of these centers that challenged the existing regulations joined together to fight for government money. They called themselves the Committee for Community Controlled Day Care. When the committee started in 1969, it was a group of people primarily from unfunded, unlicensed programs, mostly in black and Puerto Rican communities, committed to the development of quality day care run by those directly involved. Since then the group has grown in size and strength and has won several battles with the city. Chief among them was the struggle for "interim funding."

From the beginning, the committee's meetings were primarily discussions about the city's red tape, and strategy talks about how to get funded in spite of it. One or two centers—like West Eightieth Street—that had a lot of community support and had conducted large and loud demonstrations in the office of the Department of Social Services, had gotten money without meeting many of the city regulations, and in the spring of 1970, the members of the committee demanded immediate funding for all community groups operating child care programs.

Many of the member programs had existed for a long time on the resources of parents and volunteers. Often programs were chaotic, without enough staff, equipment, or people who had experience working with children in groups. They all wanted money to fix up their centers, to run programs that would reflect the racial and economic heterogeneity of their community, to pay good salaries to those who were working in their programs or to hire staff of their own choosing, to buy equipment, materials, and supplies they selected, to provide a health care plan they would pick, to provide on-site training they would design—in short, they wanted public money to create better centers for children, while continuing to fight many of the city's rules.

In order to publicize this struggle, people from seven centers blocked traffic in the streets in front of the Children's Storefront, one of the committee's member programs. People also sat in at the office of the Mayor's Task Force on Day Care (a group the city had formed to advise on future day care policy) and demanded that the Task Force act as an advocate for funding community-run centers. There were demonstrations at the Human Resources Administration demanding that immediate funding become a policy and not a way to pick off the most militant or most visible groups. The committee knew that the city had money that wasn't being spent because of the problems with licensing (with waiting lists more than double the actual enrollment, an allocated $5 million went unspent in 1969) and was determined to get it. By the fall, the city came up with "interim funding": money given with the stipulation that the center meet the requirements for licensing within two years.

Village Co-op was one of the programs that received interim funding. It had started as soon as space was found (Congresswoman Bella Abzug had donated her campaign headquarters). The space wasn't without problems—people who were sharing the space were not primarily concerned with children—but it gave the Co-op people a chance to get started while they were looking for a permanent site and fighting for city funds. In the beginning, parents had a choice of paying $10 a week or working a full day in the center. Now, with city funds, parents who work in the center are paid for their work, and in spite of city guidelines requiring fees, no one pays a fee. With city money the Village Co-op built a special infant room, hired an experienced staff member to work with children under two, and bought

L.N.S. Women's Collective

more equipment. The center was started by a small group of white women; now it is racially and economically mixed.

Of course, there are problems with interim funding. As Roz Baxandall, a parent in one of the original centers, explained: "There unfortunately turned out to be a hitch with interim funding. We are only given funds on a month-to-month basis, which means every month we have to telephone, beg, make trips to the commissions on day care, and demonstrate for every penny to keep going. Interim funding means our funds could be cut any time, and we'll never be sure how long we will exist. We have money, but we can't guarantee we will always be around."

But interim funding has brought people together, has given them a glimpse of what their programs can be, and has allowed them the opportunity to experiment.

Public Day Care with a Difference

In the belief that programs can be more responsive to the needs of everyone when they are locally controlled, a great many of the interim-funded centers are run by the people directly affected by the service. In very few instances does local control mean that every member of the center exercises this right, but no one is closed out. In many cases, it hasn't eliminated the need for committees to take on planning and executing certain tasks, or the selection of an over-all coordinator for a definite period of time, or some structure that creates a system of accountability between members of the group. But no decision about organization, policy, administration, curriculum, money, or hiring and firing of staff is left to a small outside controlling group.

There are also attempts to break down the hierarchy that usually exists within the organization of publicly funded centers. In the Children's Storefront, teaching, cooking, maintenance, and coordinating jobs are rotated regularly. Believing that the hierarchical structure of publicly funded centers is reinforced by salaries scaled according to education and experience, Children's Storefront and Children's Mansion, another interim-funded center, have equalized all staff salaries. These experiments with nonhierarchical and democratic organizations of child care programs have grown from people's belief that everyone has something to offer the group and that the survival of the group depends on the full cooperation of all its members. These experiments come from people's past experience with authority and the inhibiting ways it has been used in this society. Initiative and leadership are crucial, but if leadership is based on past advantages, competition, or exploitation of others, it can hinder everyone's growth. On the other hand people are finding that leadership that expresses the entire group's needs will help everyone to be stronger, to make the program run smoother, and to better serve the families involved.

Although the existence of "interim-funded" centers may seem shaky, such centers continue to benefit the children and the adults involved. As René Blakkan wrote in an article about the day care struggle in New York City, "[these centers] have emerged from their battle—of organizing, getting funds, and learning to fight city rules—as a strong militant force." And what other power do we have?

On the Road to Child Care for All

Marnette O'Brien

Free twenty-four-hour community-controlled child care—one of the key issues of the women's movement—has been talked and written about extensively. Various methods of achieving this demand have been tried. The Cambridge Child Care Referendum was the first attempt to bring the question to the people and to put the responsibility for providing child care where it belongs: on the society.

In Cambridge, Massachusetts, on November 2, 1971, by an overwhelming majority of almost three to two, residents of Cambridge voted in support of free, twenty-four-hour, community-controlled child care, thus making it the policy of the City of Cambridge to provide such care for "all residents who feel they have need of this service." This victory was the culmination of a campaign that began at the Congress to Unite Women sponsored by the New England Women's Coalition in February 1971.

Women from Cambridge and surrounding towns chose Cambridge as the initial city for a child care referendum campaign because of its mix of intellectual and radical groups with a working and welfare community—all people who could respond to the child care issue. Secondly, because it was a city of 100,000, only 3,400 valid signatures of registered voters were necessary for the initiative petition. By building support for child care with an intense publicity campaign and a "Yes" vote on the Referendum, we hoped the movement to get child care ballot status would spread to other places across the country.

The first job was to create a committee. The women from the Congress to Unite Women contacted people in women's collectives and organizations, teachers, and people working in day care. Our idea was to involve as many individuals and groups as possible who agreed with the goal of the referendum. We sought endorsement from churches, social organizations, political organizations, community groups, prominent individuals, and already existing child care groups. We knew that in presenting this new concept to the public that people would want to know who else agreed with it. The Cambridge Child Care Referendum Committee was formed of people of varied backgrounds and political beliefs.

One of the dilemmas of winning child care is that women with children have difficulty working on the issue. The Cambridge Child Care Referendum Committee made arrangements with one of the better community nursery schools to use their facilities on Saturdays for children of people working on the committee. The Saturday program was set up by a committee member who is a specialist in early childhood education. It was a good experience for the children who participated, and it freed mothers who wished to work on the activities on Saturday mornings.

The committee formed subcommittees: publicity, research, fund raising, petitioning, endorsement, and child care for people working on the committee. We found a small office and chose three coordinators, who staffed the office on a volunteer basis. Educational material for the community was compiled based on the work of the research group that had turned up statistics for day care in Cambridge—which are similar more or less everywhere in the United States.

There are 9,000 children in Cambridge under five years of age. At least 1,170 of these children have mothers who work. Yet Cambridge has only 230 working-day child care places for these children. There are a total of 22,000 children under fourteen in Cambridge. About 4,620 of these children have mothers who work. Yet the grand total of part- and full-day child care openings in Cambridge is 1,000. Of these inadequate 1,000 openings for children, nearly 20 percent are reserved for those affiliated with Harvard, MIT, or Radcliffe. That leaves about 800 child places for the community. Three hundred of these places are for those eligible because of welfare status and poverty or by way of residence in a particular area or by employment at certain companies. For the remaining 500 places, a family must pay an average of $15 a week per child.

Some good child care programs were found. These usually had severe financial problems. The one infant care program run by Catholic Charities was restricted to use by welfare recipients only and had the potential for implementing the forced-work aspects of welfare "reform." Research into the major charity fund-raising organization in the Boston area, the United Fund, showed that the fund spent little on day care in line with a general pattern of sex discrimination. From their $14 million 1970 budget less than 2 percent was specifically earmarked for child care.

The committee wrote a position paper on twenty-four-hour child care with a view toward making the idea understandable to the community. Three situations were used as illustrations of the need for care that lies outside the "normal" working day: illness, a night shift, and a mother in a stressful, isolated situation. We also pointed out that twenty-four-hour child care is provided now by the state in the form of foster care, which is usually in the homes of strangers outside the community, over which parents have no control. We tried to make the concept of community control of child care real to the people. We emphasized that each area or community in Cambridge should be given sufficient child care funds completely unfettered by regulations. We believe that each community would then set up excellent facilities suited to the needs of their children.

Child care facilities must be under the direction and supervision of parents and concerned members of the community. This is the only way to ensure that the services are what we want and what we need. The community should decide how to get the money and how to use the money, where the centers should be, when the centers should be open, who will staff the centers, what programs will go on in the centers. Should black consciousness be emphasized in the curriculum? Will there be bilingual education? Should we have a curriculum designed to counteract sexual stereotypes?

Many mothers, particularly AFDC recipients, fear that public child care means their children will be taken from them and they will be forced into training programs and jobs that are unpleasant and unrewarding. A vital element in the child care referendum is that of *choice.* Women should be free to choose to work, to study, to be active in community affairs, to use child care facilities or not. Community control of child care facilities is vital to maintaining the right to choose.

We were also concerned with explaining why we felt that child care centers must be free. If a fee is charged, even on a sliding scale, it would automatically make it difficult or impossible for some children to be cared for. The wealthy already have all the child care they want. It is the poor and middle-income people

L.N.S. Women's Collective

who must leave their children with a different relative every day, with an underpaid, untrained sitter. High-quality child care is expensive, but so are schools, and they are free to all. Child care should be seen as the same kind of social responsibility.

We emphasize how child care could be provided to Cambridge residents without raising the already swollen tax rate. For example, if businesses and institutions that employ more than 100 people provided day care to employees on the same basis they provide other benefits as a deductible operating expense, many child care spaces would be available. If Senator Mondale's bill, which proposes spending $13 billion on child care programs from 1973 to 1975, passes, Cambridge would be in a position to use the allocations. Cambridge does not use Title I funds of the Elementary and Secondary Education Act for child care, as Brookline and Somerville do.

When we had put together our position based on all the facts we could unearth, the challenge was to get our story to the people so that they could decide the issue. Door-to-door and streetcorner petitioning gave us an opportunity to talk to individuals, but we wanted to reach greater numbers. We held a press conference that was well covered by the media. We held a community forum on child care that was attended by nearly 200 people. Members of the committee spoke at meetings of neighborhood groups, churches, civic organizations, and political groups.

The most successful publicity was done through radio talk shows. There are about thirty talk shows in the Boston area that invite guests to talk on controversial subjects. Ten members of the committee made themselves available to speak to the public on radio and television and at meetings. The talk shows reached many people and stimulated much discussion on the issue.

In July the committee held a Children's Fair. Forty-five people worked on the children's games, refreshments, rummage sale, balloon

Child care demonstration, England.

Sally Fraser

VOTE YES

on

NOV. 2

QUESTION OF PUBLIC POLICY No. 2

stand, ticket booth, and mural. There were musical groups, a clown, and a puppet show. More than 300 people attended. Some people found out for the first time about the concept of free twenty-four-hour community-controlled child care. Many people understood that the Cambridge Child Care Referendum Committee had made the hot and dismal city livable for several hundred kids for at least one day.

In September the committee turned in over 6,000 signatures on the petition. The remaining work of the committee was to organize an educational campaign for a "Yes" vote on the ballot in November. We wrote a brochure and went from door to door talking to people. We continued our work with committees and organizations in the city concerned with children. We had one final press conference the week before the election, which resulted in some favorable media coverage. There were several talk shows and a major television show during the last two weeks. On November 2, the referendum won with a 16,000 "Yes" vote (11,000 no, 3,000 blank). In addition three liberal women won seats on the City Council indicating the extent to which the issues of the women's movement have reached the public and the extent to which there was a "woman's vote" in Cambridge this year. It is worth remarking that there was almost no media recognition of the victory. As one member of the committee commented, "If we had lost, it would have made headlines. But when women win a victory, it is ignored."

There was much to be gained by a campaign to put child care on the ballot and then to get a majority vote. The Cambridge Child Care Referendum Committee reached many people with the hard facts of the need for child care and of the benefits for women, children, and the community. The campaign provided an opportunity to take one of the key issues of the women's movement to the voter, and to engage more people in the women's movement.

Now it is the policy of the City of Cambridge to provide free twenty-four-hour community-controlled child care, but it is not a law. Funds must be allocated. The city must actually order and arrange for the centers to be set up. In short, the referendum mandate must be implemented. The city is not going to implement this policy without pressure from the people who voted for it. The question of child care in Cambridge is not yet settled. We have another long struggle ahead with the City Council. The referendum offers a mandate to the city. We reached 16,000 voters, but there are still thousands of people in Cambridge to be reached with the message about child care.

Why a Referendum?

Defining child care was one thing. Working to get child care is another. In thinking about the future and tactics for implementing the Cambridge child care referendum policy decision, we should bear in mind the reasons we decided to have a referendum in the first place.

Lobbying in various legislatures for passage of a well-funded child care bill has proved to be totally ineffective. Year after year day care bills—almost always inadequate—slip down the drain. In Massachusetts, a bill simply to accept federal and private funds for child care has been defeated three years running despite efforts of feminists and day care associations. Even if bills were passed, continued public support would be necessary to guard against withdrawal of funds. It is clear that the legislatures are not willing to establish any child care and especially not free, twenty-four-hour, community-controlled child care.

The referendum is a tactic never before used for child care in the United States. By its nature, a referendum draws many persons together. The campaign entails educational meetings. People must sign petitions to get the referendum on the ballot. Then every voter expresses her opinion in the voting booth. Thus, a referendum turns child care into an immediate issue, not only for a small number of parents in one model child care center or to people who might like to care for their own children, but to everyone in the community. Once implemented, a referendum can fill an immediate need for stable, free, community-controlled twenty-four-hour child care.

The Cambridge Child Care Referendum Committee was in agreement on one major idea: that the responsibility for good child care should not rest with the individual family but with the community. In choosing to have a referendum we chose to bring the question of who should provide child care to the people.

PART 3

How to Start Your Own Child Care Center

Chapter 7

Starting a Child Care Center

Creating a new institution that meets the needs of your community is an exciting experience. At first, the idea of starting a child care center may seem overwhelming. But learning what others have done can make it seem possible; breaking down the enormous job into small steps can make it manageable; and becoming part of a group of people with similar concerns can make it happen. As many groups have discovered, whether or not you have money, space, or prior experience with groups of children, it *can* be done.

Getting Together

The first step is to bring together people interested in starting a child care center. The idea can start with one person, but you will need a group of about ten active people to get the job done. Everyone in the organizing group need not have children. There are a great many people who do not have children of day care age but who may be interested in volunteering their time and energy to set up and to work in the center.

Ways to bring people together:

- Contact friends or acquaintances from your building, block, or neighborhood.
- Go from door to door talking about the possibility of starting a program.
- Put up a sign in supermarkets, Laundromats, clinics, pediatricians' offices.
- Call people from waiting lists of existing programs.
- Contact other community-action groups.
- If you are at a university, or workplace, distribute leaflets or questionnaires.
- Put ads in the local newspapers.

(The terms you use to describe the proposed program are important. Remember, "play group," "nursery," "day care" all have different meanings.)

At the first meeting:

- Have people introduce themselves and talk about their particular needs—5 days a week, all day, weekends?
- Find out what the resources of the group are: Can anyone get money easily? Can anyone get space in a church, community center, workplace, etc.? Does anyone have a car? Extra toys? What are the skills of the people in the group—carpentry? nursing? experience with groups of children?
- Find out if people are aware of city, state, and federal regulations for child care. Copies

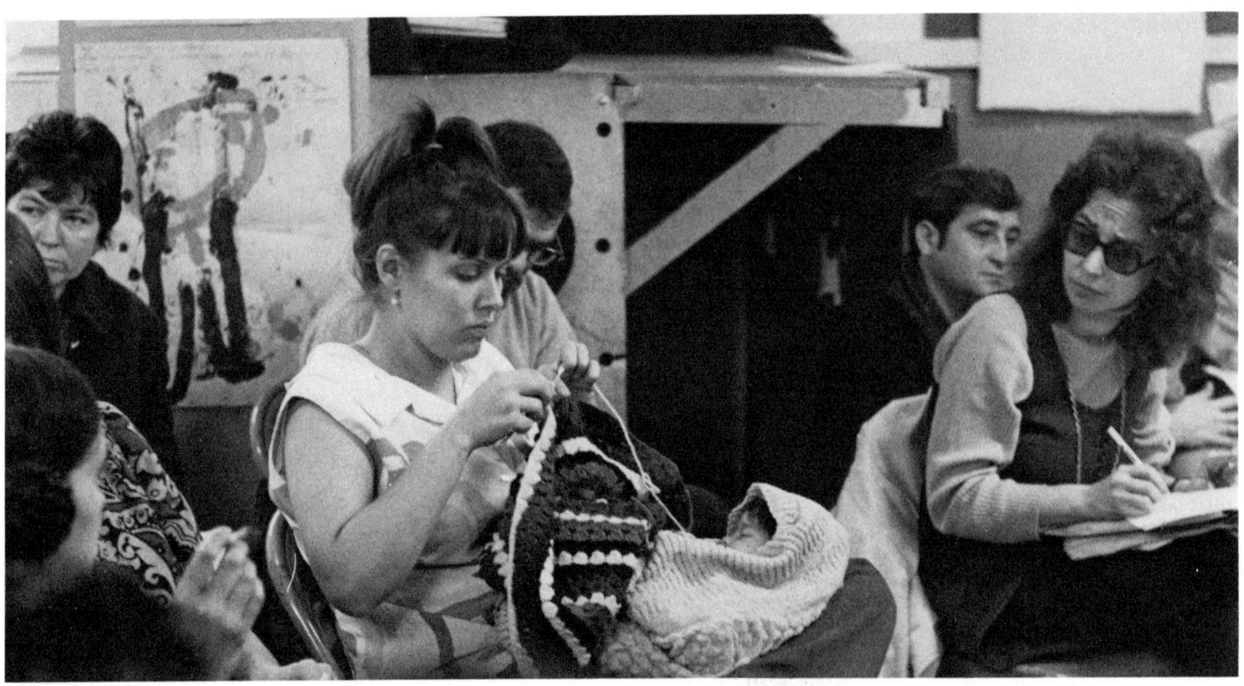
Vicki Breitbart

of regulations are available from the licensing agency in your area (see Appendix), but don't be surprised if there are some requirements you don't want to, or can't, meet.

Before you break up the first meeting, decide what needs to be done and who will do it and make a list of names, addresses, phone numbers (when available), and number and ages of children.

Plan the next meeting. If the first meeting was in someone's home, try to schedule the next one somewhere else, so as to begin sharing the responsibility. It's a good idea to have one or two people take responsibility for calling and contacting other members of the group to remind them about the next meeting. These people can also serve as contacts so other members of the group can phone in any new information or find out what's happening between meetings. By next meeting every member should get a list of names, addresses, and phone numbers of the rest of the group and you should set up some form of communication, such as a phone chain.

Early in the development of your program, certain issues will come up. You will want to open your center as soon as possible, but you should have general agreement on the following things:

What Will Be the Age Limits of the Children in Your Center?

If it doesn't get decided by the very fact of who shows up for the first meetings, you may want to establish a policy on the ages of children rather than leave it to chance. Will you accept children from birth to six? Six months to three years? Your decision should be based on the needs of your community and on the other available resources, as well as on the kind of program you want to run.

Infants need different programs and different facilities than older children. They also need adults who understand their individual nonverbal ways of communicating and who in turn can express delight over the child's developing skills. They need adults who are sensitive to the individual child's need to vacillate between dependence and independence, who can provide the appropriate materials that stimulate success rather than frustration, and who will encourage mastery of self-care. To some extent, all children need these things, but infants require more of it, more of the time. Feeding, holding, and changing diapers are daily and time-consuming tasks for adults in the center. In one center with a fair number of children under three and several volunteer staff members, it was found necessary to write a detailed handbook that described how to change a diaper, as well as some of the ins and outs of feeding and playing with infants. They also kept a chart in the playroom where workers filled in the time diapers were changed, and time children were fed. There were also some suggestions, like the most appropriate times for a nap for each child. The handbook clearly stated that the individual routines of infants had to be adapted to the child's developing and changing needs. If you do decide to have infants in your center, whether or not you have volunteer staff, you need to discuss the special means to provide for their care.

Who Is a Member of Your Group?

Another issue that will come up early is the group's concept of membership. Can anyone who hears about the program join? Will you accept children with special physical needs? Can two families share membership if they both plan to use the center part-time? What will be your policy for recruiting new people? As friends tell friends, you may wind up with a fairly homogeneous group. In order to have a group that reflects the entire community—racially and economically—priorities may need to be set, and recruiting may need to be a more deliberate process.

Early in the history of one group, when it found that most of the children were six months to three years old, a special effort was made to find three- and four-year-olds to join the program. After almost a year of operating, the same group changed its priorities—in fact, changed its entire concept of priorities. Whereas age of the children had been most important, what the group now wanted was: 1. Children from minority-group families. 2. Children from single-parent families. 3. Children whose fathers could work in the center.

Once you decide on who is a member, how will membership be defined? What is an equal share of the responsibility for each member of the group? Will it be determined by work in and/or for the center? Will each person's share be the same, or will it be based on a combination of factors, including need, ability, and other commitments and responsibilities? Will the share of the work be the same no matter how many children in the family or how many adults are caring for the child? What about parents who have full-time jobs the same hours and days the center is open? How will they participate? Some groups have tried to find ways people can contribute to the group in lieu of spending time with children during the week. Some non-open-hours work: making equipment, food shopping, fund raising, cleaning up, repairs, bookkeeping, laundry, recruiting volunteers, weekend activities . . .

Membership in one group included required attendance at three weekly meetings each month. Another group required participation in at least one of several committees, while still another based membership simply on continued demonstration of need for the service.

In deciding the question of a member's "share," the emphasis needs to be on opening the center to all people in the community. Even if you are a co-op, don't close out those with full-time jobs because of the organization of the center. The way a center is run needs to take into account people's different options in this society. Working cooperatively definitely depends on everyone's concern and commitment to the survival of the center, but everyone having an equal share doesn't mean everyone has to have the *same* work.

Whatever you decide are the requirements for membership in the group, the organization and philosophy of the program needs to be communicated fully and in detail to all new members.

How Will Decisions Get Made?

There is no doubt that community control is at the heart of what is called the child care movement, but how you define your community and the specific process of control can vary from group to group. Will the nonparent workers and the parent nonworkers have the same responsibility for decision making? What about parents who are also workers in the center? What about members of the community who are neither parents nor staff?

If the group is small, will all decisions be made at regular meetings of the entire group? Will you want to set up a coordinating committee, a small group of people who are empowered to make certain decisions? If so, how is membership on this committee determined? How often will it meet? How is the committee accountable to the group as a whole?

Instead of, or in addition to, this coordinating committee, you may want to have small groups or specific individuals responsible for certain aspects of the program. How often will these groups meet? How often will the entire group meet? Will members be required to attend a certain number of meetings? Who will be responsible for calling meetings, chairing meetings? Will the chairpersonship rotate every meeting?

Starting a center is a process with every decision affecting all other decisions you make. Who you are affects how you will set up and run the program, your program will in part determine who will join the group, who joins the group will determine the age and number of children, this in turn affects the number of staff you will need, and so on. In the first few months you will talk about all these things, but some of the initial tasks will include: finding space, finding legal help, getting insurance, finding staff, and obtaining money. These efforts usually occur simultaneously, and you will need to set up committees for each and have someone responsible for coordinating all of these tasks. Some people can also be responsible for getting in touch with other child care programs and other community groups with relevant experience.

Finding Space: What Kind? Where?

The space you look for is somewhat determined by the kind of program you want and how large you think your group will be. Guidelines for day care usually advise 35 square feet of indoor space for each child in the center (100 square feet per child is recommended for outdoor space). But if you want enough space for children to group themselves in a variety of activities, both active and quiet, then you'll need more like 50 square feet of classroom space per child. This doesn't include the kitchen and special-function rooms. If you have a choice of sites, here are some things you might consider before making a final decision.

- Does the space provide separate areas for different groupings of children, for different activities, for different age groups? If not, can it be so partitioned?
- Does it have an adjacent or nearby outdoor playground?
- Does the indoor space have easy access to the outdoors?
- Is the place well lighted, well ventilated, pleasant? In other words, is it a place in which *you* would want to spend a lot of your time?
- Is it safe (no loose wires, no lead-base paint), or can it be made safe with little additional expense?
- Do you have to share the space with another group at night or on weekends? And if so, do you have to move all your equipment before others use the space?
- Does it have kitchen facilities and toilets?
- Is the landlord friendly, or at least comparatively friendly?
- What does it cost?
- With necessary renovations, what does it cost?

Renovation can mean anything from painting, where the paint and labor can be donated and

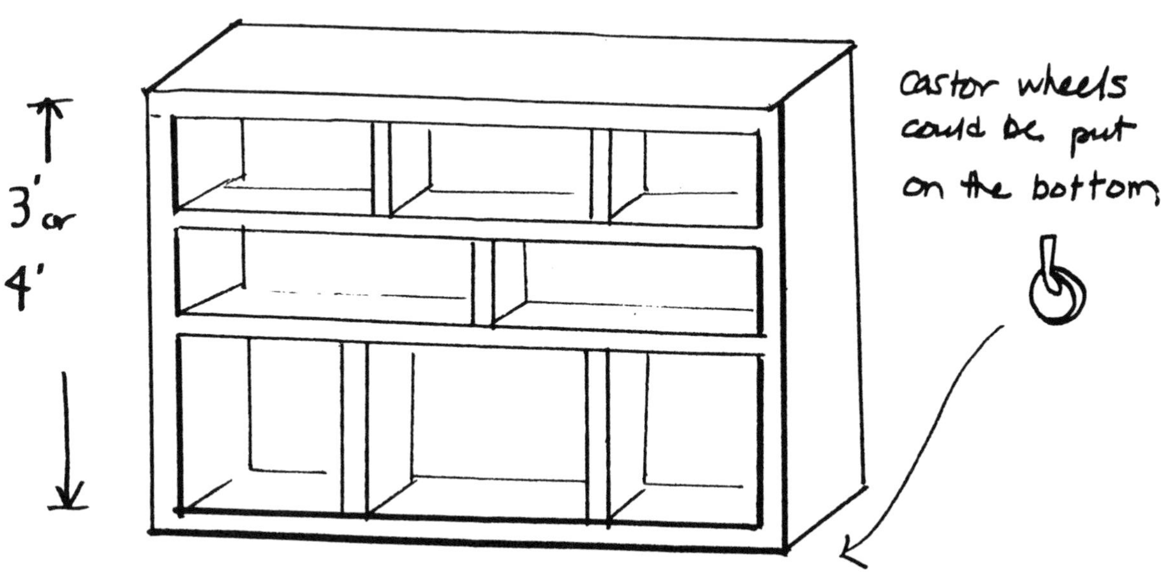

Joan Vermulen

cost you nothing, to rewiring and major plumbing, which are very expensive. If major renovations are necessary, you might be able to get the landlord to do it for a slight increase in the monthly rent, instead of having to pay it in a lump sum. The site of your center can determine:

- *The size of your group.* You may have already decided how many children will be in your group, but if you find a large community room with extra space, will you expand to include more children?
- *Who will use your center?* Who lives in the immediate area? If you are on a university or college campus, will the surrounding community be able to use the program?
- *Additional resources for your center.* A center located in a church may get donations from the congregation. If the center is on a campus, then there is the possibility of using food and medical facilities, as well as recruiting volunteers for the program. Arrangements can be made with teacher training schools, etc.
- *What the program will look like.* If there is an adjacent outdoor play area, children can flow in and out instead of having a special time for outdoor play. If there is an adequate kitchen, children can use it for supervised cooking activities. What about quiet places? What about building platforms or other semi-permanent structures?
- *How involved will you become with city, state, and federal regulations?* A center in a hospital or in a community room in a public housing project is more likely to be monitored by the authorities.

If you have to draw up your own lease for the space (and you should have legal advice for this; see page 121), it must be clear, and both you and the landlord need to know exactly who is responsible for what. Some of the things to include are: an accurate description of the space to be used and exactly when it will be used; how and when rent is to be paid; who is responsible for maintenance, repairs, insurance, extermination, garbage, and snow removal; who will pay for any increase in real-estate tax; who will obtain the certificate of occupancy, and other official permits.

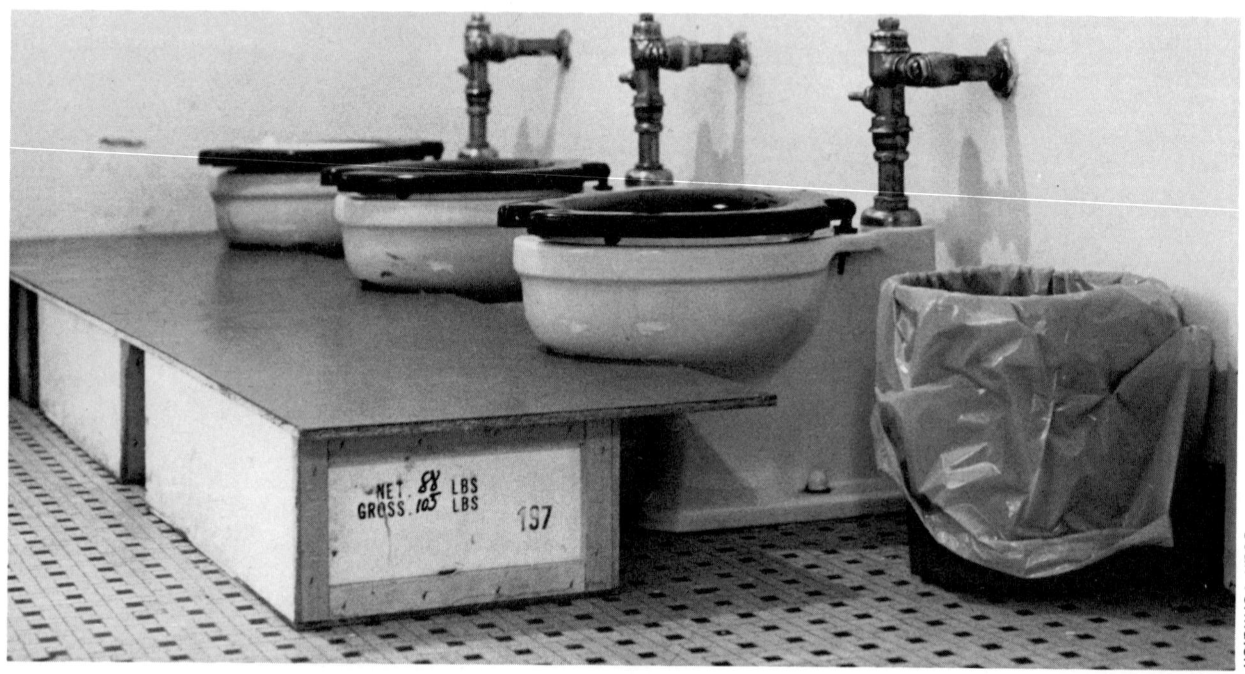

Joan Vermulen

If the group has money to rent space, then privately owned storefronts, community rooms, or even apartments and houses can be on your list. Space is also available in most churches and synagogues, but getting it for a day care center is a different problem. If a member of the group or relatives of a member are in any way connected with a religious institution in the community, it's a place to start. Many groups canvass the entire neighborhood to find the most convenient, most attractive, and in other ways most desirable space. And then they start a campaign to get it. It may be that the institution you choose is looking for a way to serve the community. But more likely you'll have to make at least one appointment to see a member of the board; make a second and third appointment; find a lawyer particularly adept at dealing with nonprofit institutions that are not at the moment serving the needs of the community (see below); get help from other community groups. Other possibilities for low-cost or free space include places where you work or study or such possibilities as: recreation buildings in parks; campaign headquarters and offices of sympathetic politicians or political groups; buildings and storefronts taken over by the city; buildings in good condition, but awaiting—although not in the too-near future—demolition.

The last way to get space is to TAKE IT. With enough community support, groups have occupied unused—or used—buildings and storefronts.

Finding Legal Help

Your group may be using rent-free space and running a very informal operation, and you might never need legal help. But if you need to draw up a lease or to incorporate, a lawyer's help becomes essential. The advantages of incorporation are that it makes it possible for a group to own property, take out insurance, and sign a lease without individuals being liable for damages, injury, or debts. You can incorporate as a not-for-profit program, and call yourselves a learning center, a school—anything. But in order to receive public money you need to be incorporated as a non-profit day care corporation. This is a time-consuming process, but it is easier to get tax-exempt status once you are a non-profit corporation. And tax-exempt status makes foundation money and individual contributions easier to come by. If you are not incorporated and/or don't have tax-exempt status, you can find a group to act as a conduit for the funds. If you are in the process of getting tax-exempt status, you can have your lawyer write a letter saying that you will send the gift-giving foundation or individual your tax-exempt number when you get it. Information on incorporation laws may be obtained by writing your state's Department of State.

If there is no lawyer in your group, see if there is a community legal-services office in your area. If you hire a private lawyer, fees have to be added to the program's budget; there will also be, in any event, a fee for use of a corporate seal (for instance, in New York it can be $100 or more, depending on the type of corporation).

A few words about bylaws. Bylaws are necessary for incorporating and getting tax-exempt status. They include the purpose of your program, the organization of the center, who is responsible for what, and how these people are chosen. When you are getting started, and things are going smoothly, bylaws will seem like just another formality without much meaning, but they should be taken seriously. Many groups have found that as time passes bylaws can hinder as much as help the smooth operation of a program. Bylaws are usually written for organizations where the board of directors is a small group with most of the power, so you will need to work closely with a lawyer if you want to write bylaws that give power to the full membership of the group.

Getting Insurance

There are three types of insurance applicable to day care programs: liability, workmen's compensation, and fire and theft. Liability is a necessity. It covers any medical and medical-related expenses for injuries to adults or children that occur in the center. The standard policy recommended to groups is $100,000–$300,000 ($100,000 for injury to any one person, $300,000 for injury to any group of people), and premiums run anywhere from about $100 to $1,000 a year, depending on the condition of your space, the size of your group, and which insurance company you use. It's worth shopping around.

The need for fire and theft insurance is obvious; different states have different requirements for workmen's compensation insurance, usually dependent on number of employees.

Finding Staff: How Many, and Whom?

How large a staff you need depends on the ages of the children, the size of the group, the ratio of adults to children you want to maintain, how much time children will spend in the center, and how many hours a day each staff member will work.

If you have infants in your center, they require more adults for their basic care and you will need a lower ratio of adults to children. Most states recommend one adult to three (1:3) for infants to three-year-olds, but 1:5 for children three to five years of age. The ratio of staff to children will affect the kind of program you can have. One study on child care[1] found the teacher-child ratio to be the most powerful influence on the quality of a program; that the "warmth" of the center (measured in terms of teacher response to children) was related to teacher-child and administrator-child ratio, and that this one factor could make the difference between "custodial" and "developmental" or "comprehensive" care.

The hours children spend in the center and the staffing pattern you want will also influence the number of workers you need. Most day care programs are open ten hours a day and if parents or volunteers work only one day a week they may be willing to work long hours (eight) on that day. But in most cases, staff who work five days a week find that six hours a day can be the limit of their energy. If staff people are hired for an eight-hour day, they might use the other two hours for planing and preparation. It is also essential that full-time staff be given fifteen-minute or half-hour breaks during the day.

An example of a staffing schedule: If you have 15 children and want a ratio of one to five, the center is open ten hours daily, and teachers work at most six hours, it might look like this:

STAFF	TIME 8–9	9–10	10–11	11–12	12–1	1–2	2–3	3–4	4–5	5–6	WORKS
A	X	X	X	X	X	X					6 hours
B							X	X	X	X	4 hours
C					X	X	X	X	X	X	6 hours
D	X	X	X	X							4 hours
E	X	X	X	X	X	X					6 hours
F							X	X	X	X	4 hours

But all the children rarely come the full ten hours and there may be few children at the center in early morning and late afternoon hours. If only one or two mothers need to be at work by 8:00 A.M. and you can't open the center till 8:00 A.M. or later, you might be able to work out an arrangement in which parents bring these children to another parent's home and that parent brings all the children later. The same would apply at the end of the day.

Similarly, if there are fewer children in the early morning and late afternoon, and you have more than one classroom, you can combine the groups and staff for this time every day. If most of the children don't come at 8:00 A.M. or stay until 6:00 P.M. but seem to cluster in the middle of the day, the staffing schedule could look like this:

1. Abt Associates, Inc., "A Study in Child Care, 1970–71," prepared for the Office of Economic Opportunity.

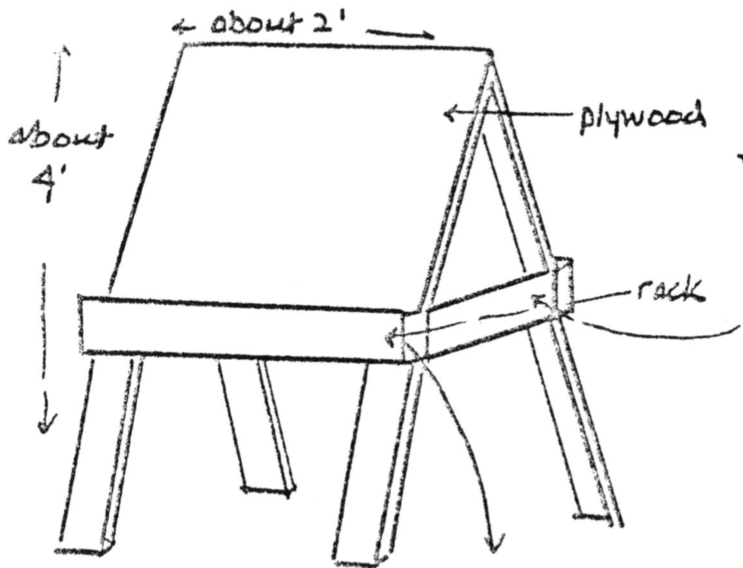

This is a double standing easel, and can be used inside or outside
To make easel collapsible, use heavy cord instead of wood here, and add hinges on top.

This paint rack is attached to the easels. Put cans of paint in it for the children to use.

Joan Vermulen

STAFF	TIME 8–9	9–10	10–11	11–12	12–1	1–2	2–3	3–4	4–5	5–6	WORKS
A	X	X	X	X	X	X					6 hours
B					X	X	X	X	X	X	6 hours
C	X	X	X	X							4 hours
D							X	X	X	X	4 hours
E		X	X	X	X						4 hours
F						X	X	X	X		4 hours

If most of the children nap from 1:00 P.M. until 3:00 P.M., you can adjust your schedule accordingly.

In the patterns shown here, adults come in for afternoon shifts, bringing a fresh supply of energy and ideas, and helping to keep the afternoons from dragging for the children. In these patterns, there is also some overlap of staff time, which eliminates a mass exodus and allows for some continuity each day. It should be noted that in none of these examples is there a time when the whole staff is together for planning and talking. In some centers where the staff work longer hours, everyone meets when all the children are resting. But if there is no time during the day when the entire staff can get together, it is essential to arrange for regular all-staff meetings at another time—for example, evening meetings once a week. Staff meetings allow for continual development of the adults' skills and talents and help keep the job from becoming static and routine. In the end this benefits the children as much as the adults.

Who will staff your center? Can it be staffed exclusively by parents and other volunteers?

Even if most of the parents can and want to work with the children, you may want to consider hiring some other people. A teacher can offer continuity and consistency to the program; she/he can be a source of ideas and insights to the other workers. Depending on the available funds, you have the choice of hiring part-time staff or full-time staff or merely finding someone who is very knowledgeable and experienced in working with groups of young children and who can run workshops for parents—someone to be, in effect, a consultant. Organizations like VISTA and other antipoverty programs should be contacted; they can provide staff (sometimes from your own community and of your own choosing) to work in programs that serve low-income families. Work/study programs in some colleges allow interested students to work in child care centers; so do teacher-training and social-work schools.

If you decide to hire outside staff, the whole group needs to be involved in the discussion of criteria and procedures for choosing staff and/or consultants. How important is it to your group to have men working with children? If there are no fathers or male volunteers working with the group, will hiring men be a priority? Will parents be given a priority?

Most states do not require formal child care training, but even in New York City where teachers are formally required to have some years of college, particularly early childhood courses, community-run programs are nonetheless determining their own criteria based on a combination of education, experience, and what could be loosely called style. Yet it is usually desirable to have people with practical knowledge and experience available to plan activities appropriate for different ages and interests. Of course, you wish your staff members to be warm, responsive, cooperative, creative people. But it must also be considered whether prospective staff people share your group's general views on child care. It is therefore necessary for the group to know precisely what its goals and attitudes are.

In most centers, a small group makes up a job description for each staff position and a list of questions that will help determine which applicants share their views; it then conducts the initial interviewing, but hiring is finally approved by all of the members of the center.

Questions for applicants should be specific but can cover a wide range of topics. You can learn more about an applicant with a few open-

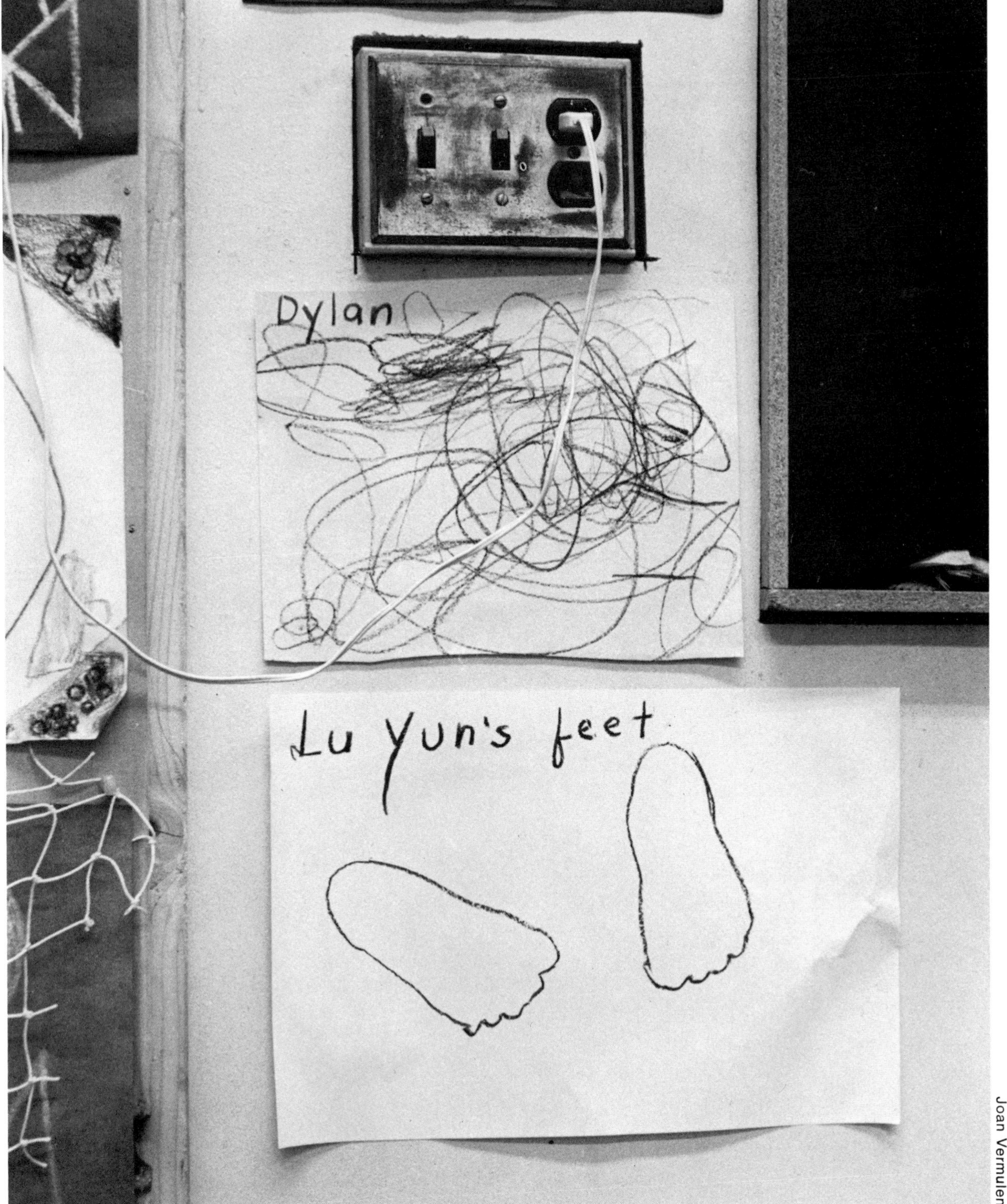

Joan Vermulen

J. J. Linsalata

ended questions (What would you do if . . . ?) than with questions that can be answered either yes or no. The following are meant only as suggestions, not as a model.

A question like . . .	*. . . might give you some idea about a person's . . .*
Why do you like to work with children?	Attitudes about children and reasons for teaching.
How did you feel about your own education?	What meant most to her or him in the learning process; values in education.
What would you do if two children were fighting over a toy one brought from home?	Ideas about discipline, violence, property, and social development of young children.
What would you do if a child who comes from a home with bare walls and only a few pieces of furniture continually runs around the room, seems overstimulated and unable to focus on any work in school?	Ideas about the relationship between home, school, and community.
How would you go about planning a trip for the children in your group three to five years of age?	Ability to plan age-appropriate and interesting activities and to what extent she or he builds on children's interest and community resources.
What would you do if a girl in the group wore only pants to school and liked to play with trucks and blocks?	Attitudes about sex roles.

Applicants (at least those you are seriously considering hiring) should observe your program if it has started and if possible be observed at work with children by some parents. Nothing will tell you more about how people relate to children and adults in a center than watching them at work.

What kind of staff development will you plan that will help staff and parents learn new skills? develop new understandings about children? about the group? about themselves?

Until recently, publicly funded centers in New York were provided with money for "in-service" training. Because of a policy decision of the city's Agency for Child Development, each center could use the money as it saw fit. In some cases this meant enrolling some staff members in local colleges, in other cases the entire staff was brought together for seminars, workshops, and open discussions. Is there money for this purpose available in your city? Are there local agencies that could do this for free? Are there people in your own group or community with special talents who could volunteer to run workshops?

Suggestions for bringing in resource people and running skill-oriented workshops are in no way meant to minimize the importance of your group's getting together in informal discussions to talk about how you feel things are going. You can pick certain topics or leave it open-ended, you can run leaderless groups, or find someone skillful in running discussions. But these times when you (parents and teachers together) evaluate your own program are essential for the smooth running of your center. There is time needed for learning skills and for gathering information, but you also need to have time set aside specifically for working at becoming a community.

Obtaining Money: From the Government, from the Group, from Others

Quality child care that includes everything you want is expensive. But your budget will be somewhere between what you want and what you can get.

While demanding and fighting for the government to pay for quality child care for all, many groups have found ingenious ways of making do. By building their own equipment, giving their own time, recruiting volunteers, and finding or making materials, people are running programs on very little money. The biggest expenses in running a center are rent and salaries (teachers' salaries range anywhere from under $6,000 to over $10,000 annually). Obviously programs without these two expenses —those with donated space and volunteer staff —will need very little, if any, outside funds to survive.

If you do need additional money, perhaps the most realistic possibility for federal funds is available under Title IVA of the Social Security Act. Under Title IVA, the federal government will pay 75 percent of the cost of day care as long as the state and/or city comes up with the other 25 percent. This used to be an open-ended appropriation, but an amendment to the Revenue Sharing Act put a limit on the federal money for social services. Under Revenue Sharing, a few states will receive considerably less than anticipated and services will probably be drastically cut back, but twenty-three states are still eligible for more special service funds. In some states, government money is available when a local welfare department purchases a "slot" in an already existing center. Therefore, starting a center without government funds becomes a strategy for getting money. Some of the drawbacks and dangers of using these funds were discussed earlier in this book, and before applying for this money, it is important to become well informed about the ways it will affect your program.

Other sources of federal money are the Child Nutrition Act, which supplies free milk, and the National Lunch Act, which will reimburse food costs plus 75 percent of the cost of kitchen equipment and its installation if your center is an area with a high concentration of working mothers or an area with generally poor economic conditions. This money is administered on a local level by Departments of Education. The regulations and requirements for getting these and other federal funds are included in *Federal Funds for Day Care*, a publication available from the U.S. Department of Labor Women's Bureau.

Joan Vermulen

Another way to support the center is to have all families involved pay a fee. The question then is whether everyone puts in the same amount, whether people pay according to their self-determined ability to pay, or whether people pay according to a fixed schedule determined by their income. The fixed schedule means getting into W2 forms and investigating people's lives, so it is best avoided. If everyone determines their own tuition fee, then people could suggest a scale which takes into account income, size of family, and major expenses. In one center in New York, parents chose a small group of parents to work out individually (and in confidence) a fee for every new member.

Fees are by no means the only source of income, and centers have also paid staff and rent from what they have raised in benefits given by local talent, children's fairs, cake sales, and other fund-raising events. These events take a lot of work, but they have kept many centers alive. Some centers have been successful with foundation grants, which is difficult but worth a try. Begin with those local foundations that take a particular interest in the life of your community and those particularly interested in education.

Starting a child care center is clearly not a job for one person—it is a group effort. And to best serve the needs of the people in your center, your group cannot work in isolation either. Child care agencies, institutions, and community-action groups in your area can help you find space, legal help, staff, and money. And these are only part of the resources available in your community.

There may be other child care centers in your area. Can they share their experience, ideas, resources? What about stores in your neighborhood? Will they donate materials or food? Are there health programs, social services, mental health programs that you can use? Is there a doctor nearby who will volunteer to be on call? Where is the nearest emergency room? Nearest clinic? What arrangements—private or public—can be made for medical and dental examination and care?

Is there a university or college in the area that can help with people and/or facilities? The Bank Street College of Education in New York City set up a Day Care Consultation Service that has proven to be an invaluable asset to community groups setting up child care services. They have provided consultants with administrative, legal, medical, and educational experience; written a manual on organizing and financing child care programs; helped to plan and run conferences; and organized free courses in curriculum, health, and administration of child care for parents involved in community-controlled centers. What is the possibility of your interesting a university or college in your area to apply for foundation money to set up a similar service?

The people who come together to start a center are rarely of one mind about styles of child rearing or the political significance of alternative child care. Everyone may agree that a center is desirable, but it may be wanted for as many different reasons as there are people in your group. Creating a child care center by the collective effort of a mixed group of people is a difficult process; it is radically different from most other things we do or have done.

In order to create a center, people must be active, passionate, committed, and concerned, but, above all, they must be able to work cooperatively. And this may be the hardest part. We may have been told to "share" and "be nice to others," but it was in conflict with what we saw around us. In this competitive and highly individualistic society, few of us have learned the skills of listening to others, of taking the time to appreciate another point of view, of developing our own strengths not for personal gain but for the collective effort, of influencing the direction of a group without controlling it. In short, learning to work together is a whole new experience for us but one which enables people to have an impact on the institutions that affect their lives, their community, their children.

M.S.R.

Chapter 8

A Center Is Not a Program

I didn't feel it was really going to happen until the night we talked about whether or not we wanted hot lunches, what would happen if one of the kids got sick, and should the children take naps. Then it was real!"

In the months before opening your center, when you are immersed in the business of finding space, working out the mechanics of incorporation, and signing a lease, you may feel you're losing sight of the children. Sometimes it seems as if there's one crisis after another, constant negotiations (read arguments) with the landlord and city officials, and endless meetings that deal only with "business." Although these tasks give you insights into the workings of society and a deeper understanding of who you are and what you want, nothing will make you feel more like a group than making decisions about the program for your center.

Some groups starting a child care center have a clear idea of how they want their program to run and what their general goals will be. Other groups develop their philosophy with each new decision—from what the children will do every day to how and whether the center becomes involved with political issues. Every decision is part of defining your group. You may start with verbal agreements on some vague phrases like "economic heterogeneity" or "permissive but not chaotic," or even "I just want a child care program for my child," but by working out the specifics of the day-to-day running of the center you develop your program.

The program is the life of the center. It is what the children do. It is everything from daily menus to your involvement in citywide child care meetings and demonstrations, from a health care program for everyone in your group to organizing and running a benefit concert, from informal rap sessions to special adult courses in child development and administration of child care centers. Your program is who you are and what you want to become.

Some issues in running a program need immediate decisions, others are continually being worked out, but every decision needs to be flexible and open for review throughout the duration of the program. As you learn from experience and as the group changes, policy will be modified, expanded, altered. What follows is only meant as a beginning discussion of the issues; they are all too complex to cover here in depth. The attitudes expressed are in no way offered as hard truth; they are, rather, suggestions offered with all due respect for the autonomy of each group. (For references on each issue see Resources in back.)

Vicki Breitbart

Will the Children Learn?

Everyone setting up a child care center wants more than a babysitting service. "We want our children to learn" is the common cry. But learn what and how? Children learn from everything; put them in boxes and they will learn about boxes and the people who put them in there. But give children an environment rich in things to do, changing often (but not too often), surround them with sensitive and resourceful human beings, and they will more likely learn that the world is a friendly and exciting place to be.

There is a danger in defining learning as the ability to order complex experiences or master a specific skill, when it can also mean developing creative and adaptive intelligence not measurable by standardized tests. There is the danger of abstracting mental growth from the entire process of child development, of isolating cognition from all other human capacities. Yet cognition "affects and is affected by the state of feeling, the degree of trust, the pattern of attention and the surge of curiosity."[1]

The child, as a human being, needs to:

- develop skills that give her or him a sense of competence.
- feel unique and able to make an impact on the world
- develop mutually supportive ways of interacting with children and adults
- gain an understanding and functioning knowledge of the environment and the people in it.

How Children Learn

There are many points of view about how we learn. Some psychologists believe that learning can be compartmentalized. They then look for the gaps and attempt to fill them in with drills, programmed learning techniques, and a system of rewards and punishments. Recently there has been a wave of high-powered adult-centered programs based on this idea and claiming to raise the IQs of "disadvantaged" children. Typical of this "pressure-cooker" approach is the Bereiter-Engelmann program, an approach aimed at developing specific skills in areas in which the poor child is supposedly "deficient." Picture a small group of children sitting in chairs arranged in a semicircle and facing an adult sitting in a big chair. While pointing to a block, the adult chants: "This is a block; this is not a car," and the phrase is mechanically echoed by the children in unison. Children are also told, "If you work hard, you get a cookie. If you don't work hard, you don't get a cookie."[2] And if you don't conform to this system you can be put in a room which the authors of the scheme describe as "a small, poorly lighted closet with a single chair."[3]

What are the side effects of this kind of approach? Children are taught specific skills, and they learn them (even though it may be for only a short period of time), but what about the cost in self-esteem, what about the implicit racism that says well-off white children can be educated but poor black children should be trained?

In opposition to this approach is the work of Jean Piaget. Very briefly, Piaget's theory of intellectual development suggests that a child's thinking goes through stages. Each stage is built on skills and information obtained in the preceding one, and the child's cognitive development depends not only on the maturation of the central nervous system—the gradual control over reflexes—but *also* on the experiences in her or his environment. Formal instruction and rote learning are therefore not the important variables; their effects are only temporary. What is important is the richness of stimuli that challenge a child and the opportunities she or he has for manipulating materials at every stage of development. The child

1. Barbara Biber, *Challenges Ahead to Early Child Education* (Washington, D.C.: National Association for the Education of Young Children, 1969), p. 15.

2. Bereiter (O.N.), Engelmann, Siegfried, *Teaching Disadvantaged Children in the Pre-School* (Englewood Cliffs, N.J.: Prentice-Hall, 1966), p. 86.

3. Ibid., p. 86.

may be able to count to ten but will not understand the abstract concept of ten or be able to independently complete formal mathematical operations unless she or he has had countless opportunities to manipulate real things in a real world. Building with blocks, moving a chair, mastering a saw, painting a picture, fitting the pieces of a puzzle together, climbing a jungle gym—these are all real things in our real world that children need and want to do.

Those who believe in this theory argue that play is not something a child does when she or he is not learning but is a child's natural method of exploring the world. Play is a child's way to experience, to touch, to feel, to try out, to question, and to *learn*. Even as adults we remember 30 percent of what we hear, 60 percent of what we see, and 90 percent of what we do. We also know that something we are interested in learning will probably be better absorbed by us and stick with us longer than something we are told to learn. Children therefore need opportunities to choose their own activities from a wide range of experiences and a variety of materials.

Creating an Environment for Learning

Your general understanding of how people learn will affect the design of your center. Most preschool programs that incorporate the ideas of play, discovery, and exploration include several "areas," each based on the child's age, abilities, and interests. In a center for three- to five-year-olds, there might be an area for:

Dramatic Play. Children learn about the world around them by trying it out. They like

J. J. Linsalata

to act like other people, and this area would contain materials that might stimulate them to assume the roles of truck driver, teacher, construction worker, plumber, hospital worker, baby, parent, etc. There would be household equipment, tools, stethoscopes, dolls, hats, shoes, coats, dresses, telephones, and other accessories that would help children play out the things they see every day. The entire area is usually designed to look like a house, but it can be a shoe store, a supermarket, a clinic, or any other place where children spend their time.

Blocks. This area includes a set of hardwood unit building blocks that are shaped in mathematical proportions to one another. For instance, the "unit" is half the length of the double unit, but it is the same width and depth. They are unpainted and sturdy and include the basic shapes of squares, triangles, and rectangles. They need to be stored on low shelves and arranged so that the differences in shape and size are apparent. The block area should be protected; it should be away from the main "traffic" of the room. At the same time, children need a lot of room so that they can work alone and in groups, exploring the many possibilities of these materials.

One group of children can be collaborating on a complex highway that includes bridges and overpasses with houses and stores along the side of the road, while another child can be working alone discovering the mathematical relationship of a small block to one twice its size, or experimenting with balancing a tower of double-unit blocks.

This area would also include toys children can use in their constructions, such as small trucks, cars, and rubber figures (about 6 inches high) of people and animals. There might also be a set of large, hollow wooden blocks or large cardboard or Styrofoam blocks that can be used to make such things as cars or fire engines for dramatic play.

Manipulative Toys and Group Games. This area would provide materials like puzzles, pegs and pegboards, stacking toys, and beads and strings, with nearby tables or rugs where children can work. There might also be games that are usually played by a small group of children—Lotto, dominoes, and the like. All these materials require quiet and concentration, and this area should therefore be enclosed and separate from active play areas.

Art. At different times the open storage shelves in this area would have clay, a supply of crayons, paint, brushes, sponges, scissors, paper (in different textures, sizes, colors, and shapes), and found objects and bits of cloth to glue onto flat surfaces for collages or on boxes and pieces of wood for constructions. There would be tables, easels, and room on the floor for children to work alone with the materials or on group projects.

Science. Children enjoy collecting, studying, sorting, observing, taking things apart, and finding out how things work. This area can provide rocks, shells, seeds, plants, magnifying glasses, microscopes, batteries, etc., for these purposes. Children also enjoy taking care of animals. Many centers find that gerbils, guinea pigs, rabbits, fish, and snails make valuable additions to this area.

Water Play. Basins of water can be provided as part of the dramatic play area, but they can also be set up in a separate place. Large baby baths or special tables built for water play can be filled with various-sized containers with different-sized openings. Food coloring and soap flakes can also be added to the water. Children can wash dolls, toys, furniture. For further experimentation you can add straws, funnels, tubes, egg beaters, squeeze bottles.

Sand. If possible, your center can have a sandbox on the floor that is big enough for three or four children to use at one time. If not, you can fill a large metal wash basin with sand, gravel, rice, or even kosher salt, for pouring. By adding strainers, shovels, and funnels, you can expand the play possibilities.

Woodworking. A sturdy table with a large piece of wood, nails, a hammer, and a piece of sandpaper can be the beginning of woodworking. But eventually you will probably add clamps and saws, pieces of leather, wire, and wheels for more complex work. A nearby peg-

J. J. Linsalata

board divider with silhouette markings of the different-shaped tools can serve as a good place to store tools when not in use. It is important that this area is isolated and that an adult be available to help children learn the proper use of the tools.

Music. In a certain area of a room, you can have drums, shakers, bells, tambourines, and horns, as well as a phonograph and records that the children can use.

Library. In this area there are rocking chairs, rugs, couches, or anything comfortable where children can read or look at books, magazines, and pictures. Lay books flat so that the covers are exposed, offer a very carefully chosen selection, and change the books as often as the children's interest changes, and this area will be an inviting, interesting place to be.

Many of the materials in your room cannot be confined to one area. Art is involved in making a tree for a road in a construction; music can be part of dramatic play, and books and pictures can be used in any project in any part of the room. Interest areas are only places to find things that stimulate ideas, to work with certain materials when you want to, and to put things back so that you can find them for the next time. You will find when planning your room arrangement that some areas will work well together; putting the blocks near the dress-up clothes can add to the play in both areas, while others need to be as far away from each other as possible; placing the library near the woodworking area or the music area would of course severely limit the activities in both areas.

All the areas have only been described briefly here; they are meant as points of departure. You may have to or want to eliminate some, and if space allows you may want to add climbing equipment, large wheel toys, and platforms to multiply the variety of experiences in dramatic play. But whatever goes into your room, make it an exciting place to be. Paint the room a color other than the institutional green or beige of most day care centers; create special crawling, climbing, playing places.

The Effects of Your Design

The way you organize your space tells children a lot about what you think about them, how you think they learn, and what you expect them to learn. Many of us remember schools where the teacher sat at a large desk in the front of the room and we all sat in smaller seats all in a row (sometimes nailed to the floor). This told us that we were to be quiet, passive recipients of knowledge from above. On the other hand, a room with child-sized furniture arranged in a flexible and creative design says to a child, "You are part of the learning process that takes place here."

Your room arrangement will communicate your expectations and will affect children's behavior. It can give children a sense of security or insecurity, create stimulation or overstimulation. For example, a room that has all the furniture lining the walls and looks like a child-sized toy cafeteria will encourage children to move around a lot (there may be a great deal of running) and children may go quickly from one activity to the next. This design may also overwhelm some children with the vast unfocused array of materials. On the other hand, grouping the materials into areas that are partitioned off with movable screens, low storage cabinets or platforms—areas that separate active from quieter activities—children may be helped to make choices; they will be encouraged to explore as well as concentrate on their work. By keeping equipment and materials in relatively the same place every day, children will get to know their way around and feel at home and secure in this new place.

The way you arrange your room and where you put the equipment and materials can foster or inhibit the child's independence. Very simply, knowing where to find things reduces the need for an adult's assistance. Do the children need to ask adults to help every time they want to paint, or is everything they may need right there—smock, paint, paper, sponges, brushes, easel (or other clearly designated surface)? Is paint put out in small manageable containers or large clumsy bottles that will inevitably spill or break? Are the block shelves marked with large tracings of each shape so children can easily put the blocks back after using them?

It's helpful to try to put yourself in the place of a child in your center. What do you see as you look around? Is it a frightening, cluttered jungle of shelves, boxes, toys, and month-old paintings, or is it a warm cozy place where you know the places to run, the places to climb, the places to sit, where you can find the hammer for the hammer-and-nail toy, and where there are five pieces to the five-piece puzzle. It is important to maintain a balance between interest on the one hand and order on the other; to have fewer good toys than a lot of unusable ones.

Of course, individuals vary as to how much stimulation and noise they can handle. That's why the behavior of the adults and children is the best guide to the success of your design. If the group is not happy with the way people are interacting with each other and with materials, it may be more effective to look at ways of changing the space than to create more rules and prohibitions. Every parent knows it's much easier to remove the poisons from under the sink than to constantly say, "No! Don't touch." Similar logic works in the child care center. The design of your environment can either help prevent disruptive and dangerous activities or encourage them. Your room arrangement can demand teacher intervention and teacher-initiated activities, or it can guide children to self-initiated discoveries.

Equipment and Materials

If you have the choice, will you purchase all your equipment or will you make some of it or all of it? The idea that people can make an impact on the environment will get transmitted to children with materials that are designed and made by people they know. Of course, there are some materials (like hardwood blocks) that are well designed and difficult to duplicate in their accuracy, durability, and safety, but many pieces of equipment (storage cabinets, tables) can be made as well as the commercial products, and many materials (puzzles, Lotto, books) can be made more attractive, and more relevant for your group, by your group.

In general, equipment for a child care center needs to be able to withstand a lot of use. You can buy a plastic truck for your child at home that may last as long as her or his interest, but it will be more economical to buy an expensive wooden truck for the center.

Materials for the center need to be varied and carefully chosen to meet the needs and interests of the children in your group. Children can be excited by the strange and unfamiliar, but the materials in the center should generally be chosen to reflect the culture and daily life of the surrounding community. (See resource section for equipment and materials to make and/or buy.)

Creating a Climate for Learning

Many centers open after simply deciding the ages of the children, the size of the group, the staffing pattern, and the design of the center. But in a short time there is a need for planning some basic routines and ground rules. The way you design your center, and the

J. J. Linsalata

equipment and materials you choose, create the environment for learning, but the "climate" for learning is created by the routines, the schedule, and the daily plan.

Routines are what happens every day: coming in, play, lunch, rest, going home, etc. They are somewhat similar for all the children in the group, and the schedule tells you when they happen. On the other hand, the daily plan is always different and can be designed for a group or for an individual child. For instance: Yesterday, late in the afternoon, Ronald asked to make play dough and we didn't have enough flour. Today (if he is still interested) we will go to the store, buy what we need, and make it. Other children can join if they want to. Or: Peter's mother is having a baby, and he seems concerned about both the physical changes in his mother's body and how the new baby will affect his life. Plan: Bring in books on reproduction and birth to read and discuss with Peter. A plan can also be for a group of children: Carl, Sandra, and Angelique will be going to public school in a couple of months; plan a trip to the neighborhood school, observe the different routines of standing on line, eating lunch in the cafeteria, etc., and discuss their impressions of what they see and their feelings about leaving the child care center. But no matter what the plan, if children's interests lead in a different direction, adults need to be willing to follow the children's lead with ideas of their own and suggestions and materials that enrich the play. The plan of each day reflects the over-all objectives and goals of the program. It is a flexible guide, not a rigid directive.

A typical day for a group of three- to five-year-olds might look like this:

As children come in they choose their own activities from the materials available for the day. A few want to finish a book they are making from magazine pictures of people at work; one boy wants to tell a story about the fire in his building last night and an adult volunteers to write it down. Others go to the water table that has been set up with basins, water, containers, egg beaters, and soap flakes. One adult reads a story to one child. Some children are using the blocks. At some point (around 10:00) a staff member initiates a special project of making pretzels for the afternoon snack and a group of five children join him.

At around 10:30 a snack of juice and crackers is put out on the table where children can help themselves. Those that are eating sit with an adult at the table. They are talking about their plans for the rest of the morning. Gradually all the children come to the tables for a snack.

Around 11:00 four children and one adult go out for a walk to find where different people in the group live. Most of the other children go outdoors. (There is a play area directly adjacent to the room which has slides, climbing bars, large wheel toys, etc.) A few children and one adult decide to stay in the room on the understanding that if the children want to they can join the others later.

After a while outdoors, a few children and one adult come inside and set up for lunch. Around 11:45 everyone comes in, washes up, and sits down in the library corner for a meeting, where they sing songs and talk about the day and where a teacher reads some of the children-made books to group. After this, they go to the table for lunch, where children are encouraged to help themselves. There is a lot of conversation. When children are finished they help clear the table and put out the cots.

Children are encouraged to nap or to play quietly, and by 1:00 almost all the children are asleep.

As children wake, they choose quiet games until everyone is up. By 2:30 all children are awake and they have the pretzels and juice for snack. The afternoon looks like the morning with a balance between child-initiated and adult-initiated activities, indoor and outdoor play.

In this program activities flow one into the other. Children are not continually asked to wait for the entire group or to work with everyone all the time. There are individual, small group and entire group activities, quiet/active, indoor/outdoor times, and transitions—from outdoors to lunch, from lunch to rest—that happen very smoothly and at the children's own pace.

In this program, cleanup is not a special time. Children are asked to put things away when they are finished with an activity. Before snack they are told, individually, that there will soon be a transition from one activity to the next: children with the most to clean up are notified first, some make arrangements to go back to activity after snack, or they gradually finish what they are doing, clean up, and join the rest of the group.

A day for adults: Each team needs to work out its own schedule so that each adult feels free to interact spontaneously with children while being responsible for certain activities and tasks.

In the example mentioned above, the adults' morning schedule might look like this:

ADULT X	ADULT Y	ADULT Z
Greets the children.		
Helps them with books and stories.	Works with children at water table.	Prepares whatever is necessary for snack.
	Reads stories to a small group of children.	Makes pretzels with children.
Notifies children of cleanup and snack. Helps with cleanup then joins group at snack.	Helps children with cleanup. Puts out snack and joins first group of children at snack.	Joins group at snack.
Goes outdoors with children.	Goes for walk with children.	
	Goes out in yard when they return.	Stays with children in block area.
Comes in with group to set up for lunch.	As the rest of children come in, helps them with washing hands.	
Begins meeting.	Joins meeting.	Joins meeting.
Lunch	Lunch	Lunch
When children finish lunch, helps them set up cots.		

J. J. Linsalata

Curriculum

The curriculum of the center is what you do with the children every day. It includes activities that are planned and provided in your center. It can be packaged into physical, social, emotional, and intellectual experiences, but to the child each activity can provide all these possibilities at once. Take water play: pouring water from one container to another can develop motor coordination, watching air bubbles form as a bottle is immersed is a scientific observation, sharing the water and the materials provide opportunities for social interaction and possibilities for cooperation and communication, and at the same time, feeling the water flow over one's hands is soothing and fun.

The curriculum can also be divided into content areas of language (written and spoken), math, science, creative expression, and social studies (or information about the world). But again, children experience many of these in different, less formal activities, every day. Reading, for instance, can be something the child does in the library corner when she or he sits down with a book, but it can also be finding her or his name in a job chart or asking an adult to write a sign saying DON'T TOUCH on her or his block building. Music can be learning a song with a group of children or making different sounds by banging different blocks together or humming a doll to sleep in one's arms. Understanding all the learning possibilities in a single activity, and the similar possibilities in different areas, can help us, as adults, provide a richer, more varied program.

Planning Activities for the First Few Weeks of School

The first few weeks (for some children it takes months) of school are largely devoted to the children's learning their way around: getting to know the people, the materials, the environment, and what is expected of them. The child is learning things like (depending on her or his age):

- What do I do if my diaper needs changing?
- How do I make the paint stop dripping?
- What do I do if Sarah hits me one more time?
- Can I tell Jim I don't want any mashed potatoes?

The activities in this beginning period should require a minimum of adult explanation or involvement, so that adults can be free to help children adjust to this new experience. Play dough, for instance, which is a mixture of flour, salt, and water, is a material that two- to four-year-olds enjoy manipulating. It requires very little, if any, supervision. On the other hand, making the dough from scratch requires fairly accurate measuring and is better left for later on. By the end of the year, some children will even be able to read the recipe.

You get ideas for new activities from your own interests and understanding of child development, but you also make plans based on the "cues" you get from children. Allow yourself time to look and listen. As children play with different materials, as they talk to you and others, or even from their nonverbal actions, you can get insights into their confusions, conflicts, and questions. You will learn to see the difference between what children are doing and what they are trying to do, and to plan accordingly.

Children Learn from the People Around Them

Children learn from each other, and the way you group them together in your center can either set the limits or expand the possibilities for their interactions. In many day care centers, groups are made up of children who all have their birthdays in the same year. But this seems alien to the way children live every day and the way they learn. On any city street, one sees preschool children mingling with kindergarten-age children at the same time they may be looking out for a toddler brother or sister. In fact, it would look rather strange to see a group of three-year-olds on one side of the street and a group of four-year-olds on the other. Clearly, they would mix and match themselves according to likes and dislikes, previous experience with each other, and personal preference.

With this in mind, some programs group children with an age spread of more than one year—for example, birth to eighteen months, eighteen months to three years, and three to five years old—with some overlapping, depending on the individual children. This kind of mixed-age or family grouping encourages children to learn from one another and to grow at their own pace.

Children also learn from adults. To a large extent the kind of person the child will become is determined by her or his interactions with adults in the early years. We can't treat children as less than human and then expect them to become confident, trusting, sensitive adults. We can't continually order children about, telling them we know what is right, and then expect them to have a strong self-image and sense of competence in solving problems and confronting challenges.

The school is a mighty force in influencing not only the excellence of intellect, but in shaping the feelings, attitudes, the values, the sense of self and the dreaming of what to be, the image of good and evil in the world about and the visions of what life of man with man might be.[4]

Your group can decide on an approach to learning, you can plan activities, you can *want* children to learn certain things, but what they *will* learn will largely be affected by the values and attitudes of the adults around them.

It is essential for the adults working with young children to know how children develop, what they go through, what they need, and how they learn. It can be an asset for the adults to have developed their skills and abilities working with children, but it is the way they *use* this

4. Barbara Biber, *Challenges Ahead for Early Childhood Education* (Washington, D.C.: National Association for the Education of Young Children, 1969), p. 8.

information and experience that is equally if not more important to the overall success of your program.

In a person-centered child care center, where everyone has the right to participate in the growth and direction of the community, there is little room for authoritarian teachers. The adults need to be resourceful, sensitive, and responsive individuals who are excited by the learning process and interested in the mutual exchange of skills, interests, ideas, discoveries, and dreams. The adults need to be able to adapt all they have learned to particular children at a special moment in time. They need to be able to design and prepare the environment, help establish routines, and plan activities that foster independence and success—success that is not measured by tests or competition but by individual strengths in cooperation with others. Take the example of a child doing a puzzle. If a child has chosen a puzzle that is clearly too difficult for him, rather than tell the child to put it away or let him sit there in frustration, an adult can help the child to focus on certain clues or suggest that she or he limit the amount of pieces that are taken out at one time. Or if a child spills juice, does the adult tell the child, "You did it again," with an expression of disappointment and does the adult run to get the sponge, or is there a sponge nearby so the child can do it instead? Does the adult in the center need to exert authority and reinforce a child's feeling of powerlessness, or does the adult do everything to support the development of the child's positive self-image?

The values of the adults are also transmitted through the kinds of rules they help establish, how the rules are set up, and how they are enforced. To many, the idea of free choice in a child care center means a total lack of rules or limits. It's the old confusion between freedom and license. Freedom is not without limits. Children experience the limits of their own capabilities at every stage of development. They experience the limits of space (natural and people-planned), and they experience the limits of living in a group with a certain culture and a certain set of values. Children need to

BOYS' WAGONS.

No. 29R58 Iron axles; body, 14x28 inches; wheels, 12 and 16 inches. Hardwood paneled body, landscape painting, scrolled and varnished, hub caps, high seat and dashboard. Iron braced, heavy iron axles in iron thimble skein, oval tires welded and shrunk on. Same as cut. Price, each..........**$1.95**
Shipping weight, 28 pounds.

Boys' Farm Wagon.

No. 29R62 Boys' Farm Wagon, with pole and shafts. Body, 18x36 inches, with hardwood frame. The sides and ends can be taken off, leaving bed with stakes. The gearing is made like a farm wagon, having bent hawns and adjustable reach; all parts are strongly ironed and braced; wheels are 14 and 20 inches; heavy welded tires; sand boxes and hub caps; has seat, handle and a pair of hardwood shafts for dog or goat. **It is handsomely ornamented with landscapes and scroll work. This wagon is the best in the market.** Price, each........**$5.00**
For Goat or Dog Harness, see Index.
Shipping weight, 54 pounds.

Dressed Dolls.

Exceptionally pretty; stylishly dressed; better values for less money than you ever bought them for before.

No. 29R715 Dressed Doll, Bisque head and flowing hair, steady eyes, jointed body, pretty costume. Length, 12 inches. **Shipping weight, 28 ounces.** Price..................**25c**

No. 29R719 Dressed Doll, jointed body, steady eyes, bisque head, flowing hair. Length, 14 inches. Pretty costume and hat. Excellent value. **Shipping weight, 36 ounces.** Price...................**50c**

No. 29R721 Stylishly Dressed Doll, similar to above, but larger body, steady eye and prettier costume, regular $1.00 value. 16 inches long. **Shipping weight, 42 oz.** Price.........................**75c**

No. 29R723 Handsomely Dressed Doll, bisque head, flowing curls, jointed body and moving eyes, new and pretty costumes. Length, 18 inches. Best value ever offered at the price. **Shipping weight, 42 ounces.** Price...........................**95c**

No. 29R725 Handsomely Dressed Doll, bisque head, flowing curls, jointed body and moving eyes. A very tastefully gotten up costume, and the highest grade doll that we sell. **Length, 20 inches. Shipping weight, 54 ounces.** Price........................**$1.50**

feel the adults are concerned about their safety and well-being. But they do not need arbitrary and adult-centered limits imposed on them.

Adults are powerful models of behavior and their attitudes will be the single most important influence on the children in your program. Women taking equal responsibility for every aspect of the program, and men working with children, changing diapers, holding them, smiling, and laughing with them will do more to affect the children than any story or discussion about sex roles. A staff of black, Latin, and white adults trying to get it together and dealing with their real differences and real problems will say more than any words or lectures against racism. You can't have an "open" classroom, no matter what the room looks like, if the adults hide their feelings and can't be honest with the children and one another.

Adults working in the center need to help one another to be self-critical and aware of how they are affecting the children. Did you tell a child you liked her painting because you saw a look of delight on her face or because you didn't see how she was struggling for something else? Did you stop two kids from fighting because someone was getting hurt or because your own feelings about violence and anger are too conflicted? Adults working in a child care center need to help one another examine their feelings about violence, sex, racism, death—all the issues that affect them and the children in the group. And this help needs to be given with love and respect.

If a center is run cooperatively, if it is controlled by the people directly affected—with each individual recognized as a contributing member of the group—children will be encouraged to work together. If the center is controlled by people they know, children will get the feeling that they too can control their own lives, that they too can have an impact on the world. If adults in the center respect their own feelings and try to become more human in their interactions with each other, if they try to mobilize their collective strength to build a community—then children will act that way too.

Lynn Phillips, from "Exactly Like Me," Lollipop Power

Liberating Young Children from Sex Roles

Phyllis Taube Greenleaf

When we were growing up the physically agile and aggressive girl was labeled "tomboy" and considered to be going through a temporary stage of development. The boy who cried or was too sensitive was labeled sissy and girlish. Tomboy girls soon learned to inhibit their spirit of adventure; sissy boys stopped crying. Female and male children learned their proper sex roles and so were considered well-adjusted and "normal."

The women's liberation movement has forced us to question whether our ideas about normal development are consistent with our goals for healthy development—for both sexes. The movement has made many women and men realize that our beliefs about normalcy are a basic part of the ideology of sexism, a system of ideas, values, and expectations that prescribes and therefore cripples the full development of both sexes. When a young girl learns it is not "feminine" to be strong and when a young boy learns it is not "masculine" to be emotional and when both the girl and boy begin to adjust their behavior to the normal expectations for their sex, the crippling process has begun. As they grow up, they will also learn that a normal relationship between a man and a woman is one in which the man is dominant and superior, while the woman is dependent and inferior. They will learn that a woman's role is to care for her children and husband, while the role of men is to support their families and achieve. From early childhood onward, we learn to accept this ideology of sexism. As adults we play our roles quite unconsciously and naturally.

Recently, a group of pre-school teachers discussed a children's book entitled *I'm Glad I'm a Boy, I'm Glad I'm a Girl,* written by Whitney Darrow, Jr., and published in 1970. The book, in simple, sunny terms, ascribes qualities of strength, leadership, creativity to boys; girls are characterized as followers, consumers, supporters—never *do*ers. The teachers felt that the book's clarity and simplicity regarding sex-role differences would be helpful to children's development. Most of the teachers believed that boys and girls should be socialized in different ways. Boys *should* be prepared to assume roles of leadership and action, while girls *should* be prepared to be more "feminine," which meant dependent and passive. Their attitudes toward the book probably would have been different had it blithely ascribed certain abilities and characteristics to black people, others to white, or certain talents to the rich, certain others to the poor.

At least intellectually, most teachers and parents do not believe in doctrines of class, race, and national superiority. Therefore few adults would intentionally select books for children that openly taught them that "black people

Boys playing, nineteenth century.

are stupid, while white people are smart." Nor do most adults consciously want to teach children national racism—that being North American makes one better than being Asian or African.

One could argue that in some respects all those statements contrasting whites and blacks, boys and girls, rich and poor, do indeed describe reality: the existing dominant-dependent relationships between those people with power and privilege and those without. But while children are learning about such realities, we also want them to learn that reality can be questioned and changed and that not everyone fits the pattern. We want children to have enough confidence in themselves to know that they can make new choices in their own lives.

Teaching Sex-Role Stereotypes

All adults have values that influence the way they work with and care for young children. Often certain values are unintentionally communicated. At other times teachers are fully conscious of their goals and very intentionally try to communicate them to children. In 1965 I intentionally dealt with the issue of race with the children and adults in the preschool where I taught. Having learned through study and experience that before the age of five, children already begin to accept our society's racist attitudes, I realized the importance of openly discussing this issue with the children. My goal was to help develop in children positive self-concepts that included an acceptance and respect for their own racial identity.

Yet while consciously trying to counter the learning of racial stereotypes and the ideology of racism, I unconsciously was teaching sex-role stereotypes and the ideology of sexism.

When I used to say, "I need some big strong boys to help me carry this table," I was communicating to all the children that I did not expect the girls to be physically strong, and that I assumed that all the boys were stronger than the girls. I expected the girls to set and clear the table for snack times. The lesson was well learned: "Boys are strong, girls are graceful." No girl ever offered her assistance in moving tables or other heavy objects. My expectations were fulfilled.

I encouraged the boys much more often than the girls to "channel their aggression" into hammering, sawing, or block building. If a group of boys excluded the girls in their dramatic play —chanting, "No girls here, no girls here"—I would smile, confident that this excluding behavior was normal to four-year-olds and therefore not harmful. Likewise, if some girls ex-

cluded the boys from cooking in the housekeeping corner, I felt no need to intervene in their "free" play. The children and I silently accepted the traditional pattern of male-female division of labor.

On the other hand, I would have intervened if a group of white kids excluded blacks by saying, "No blacks can play here," or a group of rich kids excluded poor kids from their play. But since I believed that boy-girl exclusive play was a normal part of developing a "healthy sex-role identity," it never occurred to me that children's exclusion of each other on the basis of sex could be harmful. Nor did I think that a girl's self-exclusion from "masculine" activities or a boy's self-exclusion from "female" activities was anything to be concerned about.

Yet believing in "free" choice, I never discouraged a child from "testing out" any role. In fact, a traditional goal of early childhood education has been to let kids test out different roles—occupation and sex—in preparation for later "normal" adjustment. We say they should have the opportunity to explore all areas of interest in order to develop physical and intellectual self-confidence. Yet while believing that it is normal to try out different roles in early childhood, we have failed to recognize that boys and girls might continue to enjoy and be challenged by those activities traditionally assigned to the opposite sex if it were not for the attitudes and expectations that adults express to them.[1]

Confronting Children's Acts of Exclusion

Early in the fall, three-year-olds Linda and Joanna were playing house in the outdoor kitchen. Larry, a somewhat shy boy, hesitantly walked into the playhouse to join them. He was instantly stopped by Joanna, who asserted confidently, "No, Larry, you can't play here. Boys don't cook." Linda nodded in agreement. Larry, looking somewhat rejected, began to retreat.

At this point the teacher said, in a matter of fact way, "Joanna, I know lots of men who like to cook, and I know many women who don't enjoy cooking."

1. Most of the experiences described in this article demonstrate that adults' actions with children regarding the issue of sex roles can bring about positive and visible change. However, it must be recognized that, given the social pressures of the media, family, etc., efforts to help children grow up in a new way can meet with frustration, and change is often slow and not as visible as in the experiences discussed here. In fact, working with children between the ages of two and four years gives one a rare opportunity to promote new attitudes and self-concepts, which is not the case when working with older kids.

Girls playing, nineteenth century.

The kids looked up at the teacher with puzzled and interested expressions.

"Yes, my daddy cooks," Linda proudly asserted to the other kids.

"You know, I'm a woman and I don't like to cook—at least not all the time. So my husband and I both cook," the teacher added.

Joanna especially looked baffled. Nevertheless, Larry joined the girls in cooking. For the moment Joanna accepted this.

Two boys in a four-year-old group were very competent at carpentry and worked with wood every day. The adults noticed how these boys continually made fun of two girls who occasionally joined them at the carpentry table. These two girls, who were less skilled, would leave the carpentry table when the boys made fun of them. They were obviously embarrassed by their incompetence; the boys could use the tools better than they.

Instead of confronting the boys for the way they made fun of the girls, the teacher decided to institute female and male periods at the carpentry table. Her purpose in doing this was to give the girls an opportunity to become more self-confident in woodworking without the pressure of the boys' ridicule and competition. (It should be mentioned that these two boys did not make fun of other boys who were as unskilled as the girls.)

After a few months of these male-female times at carpentry, the two girls who had initially showed so much interest in carpentry became as skilled as the boys who had made fun of them. And girls who had never participated before began to join in. Throughout this period the teachers, whether working with the boys or girls, gave lots of encouragement until each child had mastered the tools. Finally, the teachers never compared the work of different children but encouraged the children to assist each other. At the end of the year, all of the kids worked with the teachers building one structure—a collective achievement.

The next situation took place in an experimental elementary school; the children involved were in a "family group" that ranged in age from five to ten.

Seven-year-olds Eddy and John were engrossed in playing with hot wheels on an elaborate homemade ramp structure. After watching them race awhile, Linda, a sturdy five-year-old, walked up, picked up a car, and silently joined the boys in their racing.

"You can't play here, Linda," asserted one boy.

Without responding she continued playing

with her car. Both boys repeated their demand for her to leave, getting progressively louder and more annoyed. Over and over they repeated, "Girls don't play with cars!" While she didn't appear to be intimidated, she finally stood up, stared at them, holding on to one car. For a few moments she simply stood there and looked at them, unsure of what to do next.

At this point the teacher intervened, saying, "Girls can play with cars as well as boys can." The boys looked bothered by the teacher's statement.

"We'll talk more about this later, but right now I think you will have to let her play." Play resumed; although the boys played separately from Linda, excluding her from the racing and measuring.

At their regular group discussion time that day the teacher brought up the incident and asked the kids why it was that boys and girls did not play together.

"Sometimes we want to play alone," one boy said.

"Why do girls ever need to play with cars? They don't drive cars," another boy commented.

A nine-year-old girl responded, "Look, that's silly to say because ladies drive cars. Like Marian [the teacher], so we can play with cars too."

Another girl pointed out that one of the bus drivers was a woman. The teacher asked them about their own parents. It came out that mothers drove as often as fathers. The result of that discussion was to show that the boys' line of argument was simply not true: both men and women drive.

The teacher continued the discussion by asking, "Why do you think that boys usually play with cars and trucks and girls with dolls? I want you to go home and think about this for the next few days. Look at your toys and at your sisters' and brothers' and try to think why boys and girls play in different ways."

At the suggestion of a child the teacher reintroduced the issue a few days later. She began the discussion by asking if the children had noticed if their fathers ever helped out with the babies or with housework. Most of their fathers helped only on Mother's Day or when their mothers were sick. This happened whether both parents worked or not.

"How do fathers get that way? How come that happens?" the teacher asked.

"That's why young boys should take care of babies, 'cause they are going to be fathers and fathers should help too," one older girl replied.

"Yeah, that's why boys should play house with girls; they need to learn how to do that kind of thing," added another girl.

It was quite clear that the kids understood

DOLLY'S WASHING-DAY.

SLEEVES rolled up, and dimpled hands,
By her tiny tub she stands,
Busy as the golden bees,
Singing pretty melodies.
Lots of "pieces" she must do,
All, my dolly dear, for you;
Not one minute left for play:
This is dolly's washing-day.

Quite upset the play-house there;
And her dolly, prim and fair,
In the cradle lies alone,
Very quiet, be it known.
Little dresses hang to dry;
Dolly wears them by and by;
Earnest eyes — how bright are they,
All on dolly's washing-day.

that role playing in childhood taught people their adult roles.

"Look, remember our problem was the business of boys and girls playing with cars together?"

"But that's how it should be," insisted one boy.

"How did you learn that?"

"Tonka."

"Where do you see Tonka?"

"On TV. Only the boys play with the trucks."

Then proceeded a very involved forty-five-minute discussion about other things that kids see on TV regarding roles: mothers cooking with their girls, using Pillsbury; fathers fishing or hiking with their sons, smoking Kent, etc.

"Do you girls like to play with trucks?"

"I do." "Sure." "Yeah." "Not me." "Sometimes."

"And do you boys like to play with dolls?"

"Yeah." "Sure." "Sometimes." "Me too."

"Where do you do it?"

"I play with my sister's dolls," a few boys commented. The same was true of girls using their brothers' trucks. When the teacher suggested that the boys ask their parents for dolls, and the girls ask for trucks for their next birthdays, the response was a united "No" from all the kids. The teacher's final comment was to point out how early in their lives they had learned from their parents and TV what they could and could not do.

Throughout the year this topic cropped up in various ways. The kids, even though they didn't dramatically change their own behavior, certainly became aware of how they got that way.

In each of the above situations the adults' goals were to make every activity open to all the children and to help kids participate in all activities. These adults did not believe that children should be "free" to exclude, even if such behavior is normal in adult society.

The adults confronted the kids and, without preaching, opened up the incident for discussion, in effect, forcing integration in a reasonable but direct way. For some, like Joanna, it was disconcerting to be faced with an idea that did not fit into their pattern of thinking. The main value of the teachers' interventions into the cooking and racing was that it gave the children, who were directly involved or on the sidelines watching, some food for thought.

In the carpentry situation, the teacher felt that only with an initial period of separatism could there be a healthy integration. This teacher is now considering doing the same time division with the cooking-playhouse area, which is usually controlled by girls.

What all of the above situations shared were adults who chose to intervene into children's play when they excluded each other on the basis of sex. These adults confronted the children's acceptance of sex-role stereotypes and opened up the issue as a topic for group discussions. The last incident, especially, showed how it is possible for an adult to have an honest discussion about sexism without preaching or condemning. Although that incident happened with children over five, shorter versions of the same direct approach were used among younger children.

Helping Individual Children Break Out

The focus of this section will be on individual children whose behavior expresses an unspoken acceptance of sex-role stereotypes. In these cases the adults deal with problems of self-exclusion and even self-rejection that appear to be related to a child's attitude toward her or his sexual identity.

In the fall three-year-old Robin came to school dressed in delicate, carefully ironed dresses. She informed the teachers that she must not get dirty. Being neat and clean seemed to be tied up with being the pretty little girl that Robin knew she was. Most of her time was spent housekeeping, cooking, and playing with dolls. The rest of the time she engaged in sedentary activities: puzzles, Lotto, collage, browsing through books. She stayed clear of all physically vigorous activities. The teachers never saw her climb, hammer, ride a trike, or run fast. She would, however, control other children verbally —directing them to bring her this, do that—like a rich lady with servants to wait on her. But she never exerted power or strength with her body.

Although she seemed to be quite content participating only in those activities in which she felt confident, the teachers decided that it was important for Robin to branch out into activities that developed her physical strength and large motor coordination. They felt that her acceptance of the "female" role—to be clean, neat, and frail—coupled with her actual fears, inhibited her from entering into physically active play. In early winter, one teacher came up to Robin and suggested, "Robin, let's climb together to the top of the jungle gym."

"No, I don't like to climb," Robin answered firmly.

"I'll do it with you and help you, so you won't fall."

"I said *no,* I don't want to!"

About a week later, after this teacher had shown a lot of interest in Robin's housekeeping play, she again suggested that they climb together, this time adding, "You know, Robin, I know that you have strong arms and legs, and I'm sure you could be a good climber, once you started doing it a lot."

This time Robin nodded okay.

It seemed to take forever that first time she cautiously and awkwardly climbed the jungle gym. As she climbed, she kept repeating, "I'm going to fall." The teacher knew that Robin was afraid, but she also knew that Robin could make it. "You can do it, Robin; hold on firmly, and soon you will reach the top."

When Robin finally arrived at the top, she was extremely pleased with herself. Smiling with a victorious gleam in her eyes, she began calling out to the other kids to witness her accomplishment: "Look at me, look at me!"

By spring Robin was climbing the jungle gym and another higher structure with confidence and speed. She had also become competent in running and triking. At the same time she continued to participate in cooking and artwork. Her scope of play had expanded.

Boys playing, twentieth century.

After several casual discussions between the teachers and Robin's mother, Robin no longer wore dainty dresses to school. Instead she came in overalls and jerseys. It was also noticed that by the end of the year Robin didn't boss other kids as much.

The teachers used no fancy teaching methods to help Robin and her mother change. But they did express their attitude that it was important to be as agile with one's body as with words. The teachers encouraged and enjoyed her accomplishments with her. It should be added that a few of the boys needed the same kind of encouragement.

At the age of three a little girl named Jessica appeared insulted when her teacher commented to her when she was wearing a firehat, "Here comes Jessica, the firewoman."

"I'm not a firewoman, I'm a fire*man,*" she said sternly.

At first the teacher did not know how to respond. Then she said, "Jessica, it is true that right now not many people who put out fires are women. Most of them are men. But this is changing. You are a young girl now, but when you are older and become a woman, you could probably be a firewoman, if you wanted to."

"But I'm not a girl! I don't want to be a girl," Jessica answered with anger in her voice.

At this point the teacher felt at a loss. Fortunately for the frustrated teacher, Jessica ran off to continue playing fire*man* with her boy companions.

The teacher told Jessica's mother what had happened. The incident did not surprise the mother, as Jessica had already made the declaration to her parents that she was a boy and did not want to be a girl or to play with them. Both at school and at home Jessica avoided activities that most girls participated in—doll play, art, cooking, etc. She clearly preferred vigorous activities and the company of active boys.

The mother and teacher were not bothered by her preference for energetic play, but they were concerned about Jessica's rejection of her sexual identity. She seemed to believe that one had to be a boy to take part in "boy" activities. Girls did not belong in those activities, so therefore she decided—or wished herself—not to be a girl.

A later realization that Jessica had never gone to the bathroom at the center raised the question that her shyness about possibly being seen on the toilet could be related to her not wanting other children to know that she was a girl.

The teachers helped Jessica's parents to become more aware of the importance of assuring their daughter that she could be a person of action and still be a girl. Yet they knew what awaited Jessica in the public schools—sexually segregated sports, with the emphasis and prestige on boys' sports. Yet their daughter was a natural athlete, not a cheerleader or spectator type. They realized that unless they worked with other parents and teachers, who felt the same way, to change the schools, Jessica would have a lonely battle ahead.

While girls are usually not encouraged to develop themselves physically, boys are not encouraged to develop themselves emotionally. In fact, the capacity to be compassionate and the ability to take care of others—and babies in particular—have been considered instinctive qualities of women. Yet it is quite clear from watching young children from infancy on that boys can be as gentle and sensitive as girls.

Being deprived of the experience of playing with dolls, little boys have much less opportunity than girls to express and develop nurturant feelings. Furthermore, rarely in our society are older brothers or teen-age boys expected to be responsible for the care of younger children—at home or as neighborhood babysitters. By not encouraging boys to play with dolls or take care of babies and young children, adults are, in effect, promoting the development of emotional hardness and inhibition—qualities all too common in adult men, who, as fathers, cannot relate easily to their babies. The next incident illustrates the importance of dolls in the life of a three-year-old boy named Mark.

Mark was a bright, intense, physically aggressive boy. Usually he played alone, and when he made contact with another child, it was usually to take away a toy that he or she was using.

One day Mark seemed at loose ends. While normally able to get involved in one activity, on this day he went from activity to activity—rest-

Girls playing, twentieth century.

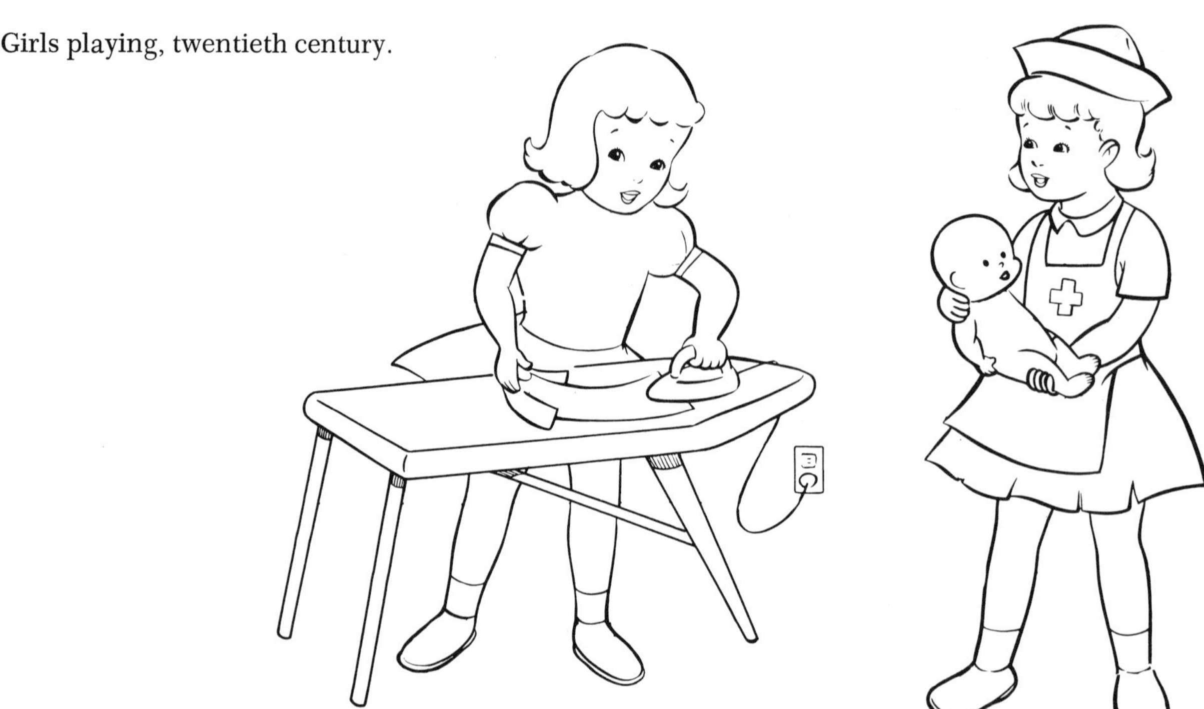

less, silent, and somber. All at once he ran to the cradle in the housekeeping area, picked up a baby doll, found a baby bottle, and sat down in a rocking chair. For the next fifteen minutes he rocked, talked, and sang to the baby doll, smiling frequently.

The adults who saw this happen made sure that Mark was not disturbed by the other kids, and they also left him alone. They had never in the six months at the center seen Mark as peaceful and affectionate as he was with that doll. For the remaining part of the day Mark played with the other kids in an unusually relaxed and flexible way.

In the following week one of the teachers described the incident to Mark's mother, and asked her if Mark ever played with dolls at home.

"Oh, yes, he often plays with his sister's dolls."

"Does Mark have any dolls of his own?"

"No, I've never thought of giving him one. And I know my husband would not permit it, or at least he would not approve."

In spite of her husband's attitude, she agreed with the teacher that it was important that her son be encouraged to play with dolls and that meant giving him his own dolls. Both the mother and the teacher felt that playing with dolls would help to free Mark emotionally. They were both aware that through doll play children could express feelings, both affectionate and hostile, that otherwise might not get expressed.

For the rest of the school year Mark continued to play with dolls, not as often as most of the girls, but more often than the other boys. The teachers noticed that Mark would choose to play with dolls at times when he was in a bad mood and feeling tense. His mother informed the teachers that Mark never played with dolls in front of his father; she felt that Mark did this to avoid his father's ridicule.

By the end of the year Mark, the solitary, intense achiever, was becoming a warmer, more relaxed social being, able to work independently as well as enjoy the company of his peers.

While Mark needed to develop the capacity to be sensitive to other people, Judy, in the following situation, needed to become more able to stand up for herself.

Judy and Jerry, two four-year-olds, were the oldest kids in a parent cooperative play group. Judy liked to please others. Her consideration for other children, her cooperative attitude with adults, and her capacity to get absorbed in art activities and doll play all made her an easy child to work with.

Jerry was the rough, tough leader of the group. His physical aggression and speed helped to give him that role. In the fall he continually picked on Judy—knocking her down, grabbing things from her, or shoving her out of the way. Her response to his aggression was a pitiful, defenseless wailing, calling to the adults for comfort. The adults' usual reaction was to get mad at Jerry, try to find out why he hit her, tell him it wasn't nice to hit people—he should use words instead—and then to comfort poor, frail Judy. In other words, Jerry could create a big event when he hit Judy.

Two of the mothers decided that instead of trying to stop Jerry from bullying Judy, it might be better for both kids if Judy would hit him back. They felt that Judy should be encouraged to defend herself. A few days later, one of these mothers saw Jerry shove Judy out of the way. Instead of bawling out Jerry, she quickly came up to Judy, who was on the verge of tears and said, "Say, Judy, you can hit him back when he does that to you."

"But it's not nice to hit."

"Maybe if Jerry knew you could hit back, he wouldn't bother you so much."

Judy looked at this mother with disbelief and confusion, and then commented with a somewhat put-on coyness, "Well, I don't really want to hit him anyway," and walked away.

A week after that conversation, as he was running through a museum, Jerry rammed into Judy full force, knocking her to the floor. At first she appeared stunned. Then all of a sudden, she got up, ran up to him and with a determined look on her face, she socked him hard on the back.

He turned around and stared at her. For the next few seconds they both stood still, staring at each other in silence. It seemed as though neither child could believe what had just happened. Then Jerry ran off.

The mother who had just watched the whole event, the same person who had encouraged Judy to fight back, came up to Judy, saying approvingly, "Judy, you can hit back when you need to! Now Jerry knows that you can defend yourself." Judy nodded and smiled, obviously pleased with herself.

After that event (as well as a few repeat performances), the parents noticed that Jerry and Judy played together more often, and that she participated more frequently in active play. Jerry's play became more constructive, especially when he was with Judy. He rarely hit her, and when he did, her typical response was to yell at him angrily. Angry words and the occasional use of force replaced her defenseless crying.

Their relationship became more give-and-take. He seemed to realize that a girl could be his equal. Judy only occasionally played the frail female role: she no longer seemed intimidated by his physical power. This probably grew out of a new recognition of her own strength. The other children in the group also benefitted from Judy's example. Though younger than Jerry, they began to get mad at him, at least occasionally, instead of being intimidated when he hit them.

What these mothers did in openly encouraging Judy to hit back goes against the "we-don't-hit-at-this-school" policy, the traditional

Vicki Breitbart

line toward physical aggression among professionals in early education. Teachers in nursery schools and day care centers have been trained to get the aggressor to "verbalize" feelings or to "channel" the aggressive energy into other activities. Attention is usually focused on stopping the child who uses physical force, rather than encouraging the kids who are intimidated to fight back.

Yet it is quite common for adults to quietly encourage "weakling" boys to fight back when attacked by other boys. Most parents will encourage their sons to stand up for themselves. But it is uncommon—especially among middle-income families—for parents to encourage girls to physically defend themselves against boys. Boys learn early in life that it is not proper to fight girls, frail creatures that they are. When a boy does hit a girl, the adult intervenes to stop him and protect her. His sin is not simply hitting, but hitting a girl.

By protecting girls instead of encouraging them to fight back, we are training them to accept the role of the retreating and impotent female. And while girls are trained to be defenseless, boys are pressured into being the brave defenders; they are not permitted to feel frightened or cry when in pain. "Big boys don't cry," we tell our boys, training them to control the expression of their emotions. As adults these big boys have little capacity to feel deeply and express those feelings freely—physically or verbally. Beginning in early childhood, boys learn to hold back feelings of hurt behind clenched teeth and determined eyes: instead of allowing their emotions to be expressed in words—asking for help, in tears—feeling the pain, or with their bodies—in warm embraces.

But regardless of our sex we need to develop strength—physical and emotional. But having strength does not mean that people will not experience moments and periods of weakness. What is most healthy is when a person can express and share her or his strengths and weaknesses with others, able to be independent yet also dependent. In fact, unless women can be as independent and strong as men, men and other women will not be able to depend on them.

The adults in the preceding section shared a fundamental goal: they all wanted to help children become self-expressive and confident, regardless of their sex. For this reason they attempted to help children break out of sex-role stereotypes. The teachers and parents wanted children to recognize that their sex types need not narrow their choices or inhibit the expression of their feelings. The adults attempted to free children from a stereotyped pattern or quality that was crippling to their development: Robin, from her physical inhibitions and concern about outward appearance; Mark, from his emotional sterility; Judy and Jerry, from their traditional dominant-submissive male-female pattern; and Jessica from her negative attitudes toward girlhood.

The teachers' actions with the children had a social as well as an individual impact: While becoming more physically competent, Robin also became less directive and manipulative with other kids; Mark's decreased tenseness and growing capacity to be affectionate contributed to the cooperative spirit of his group; Judy's actions in self-defense against Jerry were no doubt inspiring to the others. Not only did they learn that not all girls are sissies, but more important, they saw that standing up for oneself against a bully could result in a relationship of mutual respect and warmth. Finally, their budding egalitarian relationship changed the nature of leadership in the group.

Helping Jessica cope with and resolve her feelings of ambivalence toward being a girl presented a problem of a different order. Jessica did not need help in breaking out of a sex role or in asserting herself. But like many adult women, Jessica was struggling with a social problem that hurt her personally. She was aware that a woman's "role" is limiting and fairly predetermined, while men have a broader range of choice. She needed help in developing positive feelings about being a girl and becoming a woman. She needed to understand and resolve her conflicts about her future as a woman. Such ambivalent feelings can only be alleviated for Jessica and girls like her if they have adults in their lives who are living examples of people who have broken free of the prison of sex roles yet still feel positive about their own sexual identity.[2] The significance of having alternative adult models is discussed in the following section.

What Kind of Models Are We?

If children learn only at second hand that both men and women can be competent at woodwork or child care but never actually see a a woman using a hammer, or a man playing with a baby, they have learned only an abstract idea, a concept that does not mean much to their own experience. It has been well documented in child development research that the behavior of adult models—the real people who have some personal contact with the child—strongly influence children's ways of feeling, thinking, and behaving.

But unfortunately, what most children see at home and in school and centers supports the old values. The following four situations are typical examples of what children experience in the hidden curriculum of their early education.

One male teacher working in a parent cooperative told mothers he would not waste his time changing diapers or playing with the children under two. Each day the children saw him direct and criticize their mothers, who accepted his authority with silent resentment. If a mother made a suggestion or questioned some aspect of his program, he was visibly annoyed.

2. It is important to differentiate between sex role and sexual identity. A role is social behavior that is prescribed and defined by tradition. The individual "plays" her or his part in the play that has already been written. Identity relates to individuality, "unity and persistence of personality" to quote Webster's dictionary. Having a positive sexual identity would mean feeling good about yourself, enjoying your body, respecting yourself as a person who is female or male, and having the confidence and self-trust to express yourself in sexual relationships. In fact "role playing" will often come into conflict with a person's identity. For while identity relates to a person's self-concept, role relates to the behavior society expects from you on the basis of some category—be it sex type, race, age, income. Roles track us, and therefore cripple the development of personal identity.

After months of tension, the mothers decided to ask him to leave. His parting words, "Next time don't get a man for this job," confirmed their growing realization that being a male with professional credentials does not automatically give one the qualities of a good teacher of young children.

In a free school for older kids a highly inventive male teacher invited only boys to join him on his construction projects and related to girls and female teachers by flirting with them or telling them how pretty they looked. Though he worked cooperatively with the women teachers, his behavior was also seductive. Being the only male on the staff, he used his maleness to have special power over the other teachers.

The women teachers of a middle-class parent cooperative informed the fathers that when they worked in the school, they would not be expected to help with cleanup. This was done in order to keep the fathers involved. The mothers were expected to share all tasks with the staff. Unlike the fathers they had not complained about doing this. The female teachers were so delighted by the mere paternal presence that they were willing to do extra work on those days.

The message was clear: cleaning up was a demeaning task and men were too valuable to be concerned with such lowly chores. By implication, women were therefore less important than men.

The most common adult model for children in centers for young children is the woman teacher. A teacher of three-year-olds began some sewing projects with the kids. All the children were free to choose to sew, but she invited only the girls to join her. She simply assumed that the boys would not be interested. This same teacher would enthusiastically compliment the girls on their clothes and hairdos, rarely noticing a boy when he got a new shirt or a haircut.

Some alternatives do exist. The teachers of two parent cooperatives are examples:

In an all-day play group, the man and woman teacher share all the responsibilities for the children. Neither is the head teacher. (They

Vicki Breitbart

are paid equal salaries.) The kids see them planning and solving problems together, making decisions about field trips, cooking, giving and taking suggestions from each other. She often plays the doctor role in dramatic play; he cooks and cleans with the kids. Most important, these two people really like and respect each other. The woman teacher commented, "We really have an interesting relationship. Jack is more easygoing and affectionate than me. I tend to be more authoritarian. But we enjoy working together."

Another male teacher of a play group with kids from one to five is very conscious of his being a new kind of man. In his gentle way, he relates with warmth, patience, and flexibility to both the children and their parents. He cooks, builds, plays ball, tells stories, finger-paints, and changes diapers as a matter of course. Whether he is changing a diaper or leading the kids in singing, he takes his work seriously. He also really loves the kids.

Such firsthand experiences no doubt teach more powerfully than do words. Observing an egalitarian relationship between a man and a woman, watching your mother or female teacher change a tire and your father or male teacher change a diaper, seeing a woman carpenter build something in your school, meeting a male librarian, or having female and male doctors examine you, are experiences that embody an antisexist curriculum. Besides providing such living examples, teachers and parents can counter the learning of sex roles by being very selective about children's books, and by making sure that children recognize that TV and magazines (especially advertisements) portray an image of women and men that is both false and destructive.

Even those of us who are aware of the problem find it difficult to create a situation in our homes or schools that will give children experiences that can liberate them from sex roles. Yet perhaps the first step that we can take is to examine our own attitudes and behavior. Before we attempt to change children's behavior or our behavior with them, we have to examine how we feel about ourselves as women or men. Can we teach girls to respect themselves and take themselves seriously if we, as women, do not have the same attitudes toward ourselves? Nor can men help boys to become flexible, sensitive people if they cannot share decision making or express their emotions.

Once we have begun to change ourselves, we will be ready to help children to be more open people. In fact, our responses to children's acts of group exclusion or self-exclusion will come more naturally having dealt with our own attitudes and behavior. Most important, by beginning with ourselves we will be able to feel with the kids the difficulty and joy of breaking new ground.

When parents and teachers encourage children to develop self-trust, compassion, and egalitarian relationships, they are challenging the basic tenets of our capitalist society in which people learn to accept powerlessness, inequality, and competition as normal parts of life.

A girl is taught to accept the role of wife, mother, and homemaker. Her role is to be of service to her husband and children, to assist and help them in their development and work. Developing an identity apart from her husband and children is not part of that role—in fact, it contradicts it. Wife-mothers, taken as a whole—a caste, in fact—also serve the important role of pacification for the capitalist system. The security and warmth they provide their husbands make their families "refuges from the competitive, dehumanizing, impersonal world of modern capitalist technology."[3]

A boy is taught to accept the role of breadwinner for his own family. Most men (and women) workers work at jobs in order to survive—to buy food and clothing for their families and pay the rent or mortgage. Though they learned they could "make it" in the system by competing, they later found out that making it really

3. Linda Gordon, *Families,* pp. 1–2. New England Free Press. This pamphlet provides an excellent clear discussion of the function of the nuclear family, sex roles, and other forms of division of labor in a modern capitalist society.

means receiving a paycheck and getting through the day. Most workers, the majority of whom are men, do not even expect their work to be personally or socially meaningful. They view their work only as a means to an end (the paycheck), not as an activity that in and of itself is of worth. (An activity that has intrinsic worth to the individual or to society cannot be measured in dollars and cents. How can one measure whether teaching young children is "worth" more than designing a functional, beautiful hospital?)

The teachers described in this paper were trying to break down this system of roles, which depends on boys and girls learning to accept segregation from one another. Therefore, to begin with, their goal was to integrate children into activities previously dominated by the opposite sex, thus allowing them as individuals to develop and play more freely. Integration was considered only a short-term goal by the adults. The more fundamental goal was to help children work and play together as a group or collective. The example of carpentry demonstrated that when children had opportunities to achieve and become competent as separate individuals, they were later able to work together as equals—each using the skills and ideas he or she had developed when working alone. Again, letting children know that we value group achievement and collective work over private accomplishment is a clear challenge to capitalist ideology, in which individuals "make it" alone.

Mark was not encouraged to be self-seeking and competitive—basic values of an economic system based on private profit. Robin was not encouraged to depend upon being the pretty, passive female, qualities needed and promoted by our consumer culture. By encouraging Judy to physically defend herself against Jerry's bullyish behavior, the mothers were also confronting the power structure of the play group and expressing their nonacceptance of a status quo in which one person acts as though he has the "right" to dominate others. Jerry's unquestioned power to be boss of the play group was threatened when the "weaklings" began to rise up with angry words and actions.

Learning how to stand up for oneself, to become a self-determined person, is the opposite of learning to be passive and to follow without question the orders of the person in charge—whether he is the school bully, teacher, manager, or president.

Kids who can express and respect themselves, who are free from a dependency on sex roles, will have the strength to take control of their own lives and the capacity to make a revolution in our society.

Meg Leake, age 10

Politics in the Preschool

Anna Salter

There is a myth that preschool classrooms can be and often are neutral in their value orientation. The myth can be discerned most readily by the willingness of preschool educators to discard the whole question of values and to focus instead on such specific issues as daily curriculum. In this way they ignore the larger issue of what values a given curriculum and its method of presentation entail. It is the contention of this paper that preschool classrooms are in fact value-laden and that those values do not benefit children by being unconscious. Most teachers come from the middle class and are not always aware of the difference between middle-class and lower-class values. It is one thing to perpetrate certain values after examining them and deciding they have merit. It is another to ride roughshod over cultural differences and to perpetuate a class bias without even recognizing that fact.

Most of us as children were dealt with in authoritarian ways, at least by our schools. Our first response to a problematic situation is to deal with it in some manner akin to the way in which we were dealt with, usually with some modification. In similar manner we perpetrate both racist and sexist values, not by conscious choice but by the lack of a conscious commitment to overthrow the racism and sexism in ourselves and in our traditions.

Thus sexism in the classroom, for instance, goes largely unnoticed. Only recently have parents and teachers begun to look closely at the values represented, for example, in children's books, where all too often girls are portrayed as doll keepers in pink. Just the number of male central figures versus female is a statement in itself of who is the more interesting to read about. How often do you find female preschool literary figures engaged in the kind of active, rough-and-tumble, exploratory activities that young males are depicted as enjoying? The passivity of the female is depicted at a very early age. Women in the society at large are inevitably housekeepers, supermarket shoppers, and child raisers. Since these roles are presented so predominantly as female roles and others are not, women-in-the-kitchen begin to take on a natural cast as *the* appropriate role for a female. There are, in fact, serious questions about whether one half of the species is more suited to the menial labor that housekeeping involves than the other. Nonetheless, these questions are almost never raised in the preschool curriculum, which is a major force in forming the attitudes and conceptions of the preschool child. Mommies continue to sweep floors and wash milk bottles, while fathers function as visitors, much as friendly uncles who take their nephews to the zoo on Saturdays.

Lynn Phillips, from "Exactly Like Me," Lollipop Power

The argument against presenting women as active, fully participating members of the society at large, and fathers as having equal responsibility for the care of their children, is that it simply isn't that way. Women really are, whatever the merits, locked into stereotyped roles (as are men), and to give any other picture of this society would be to falsify. That sort of argument can best be evaluated by looking at its racial equivalent. Do you confront black children with images of blacks as poor, as locked into ghetto situations, as not having access to the educational superstructure which controls socioeconomic class in this country without any reference to why? Do you confront them with these kinds of realities without any reference to discrimination, and without any alternative models for the ways in which blacks can and often do function in this society, despite the incredible pressures against them? Do you expect children to draw from the images presented to them the fact that some things are the result of negative influences in our society and are subject to change, while others are not? Hardly! What happens is that children accept and internalize the roles given to them as natural and thus desirable. And the models you present of what women can be and what men can be are dynamite in terms of shaping attitudes that no amount of rational thought in later years will entirely dislodge.

Last year a five-year-old female student said to me when angry, "I'll get all the boys to burn the school down." She had, at that tender age when she was physically the equal of any male in the room, accepted an image of herself as passive and had attributed the power to act to males as a group. She was willing to use them to effect her own wishes. That seems to me to be not far at all from the values that support a situation where the wife achieves all income, status, and life style from her husband's relationship with the world. Her dependence on him is complete. The psychology of the "groupie," who lives explicitly through another human being, is only one step farther out on that continuum. It is not a model I would want my daughter to adopt. Thus it is crucial to me whether books portray women as capable of interacting with the world on their own, as capable of deriving status from their own efforts and of exercising autonomy and independence, or portray them as service units to males, who wield the power.

Is *Peter Pan* sexist? Indeed it is. Our male here is capable of flying. He has access to a whole fantastical world where he exhibits constantly his boldness and daring. Wendy, our female model, wants nothing more than to set up house for him and take care of the boys. In that situation, where the options are so enticing, where there is flying to be done, pirates to rout, and jungles to explore, Wendy prefers to stay in the underground den and read stories, presumably about such things. Of course there is Tinkerbell. But there you come to an ironic twist to the business of granting women competencies. Sadly enough those who possess them are often portrayed as being an entirely different species. Perhaps Peter Pan can fly. But he's a boy who can fly. Tinkerbell is a fairy and is part of the genre of fairies and witches and supernatural figures (Jeannie on TV) who are not really human at all and whose powers have nothing to do with their own efforts. And Tinkerbell, too, is a jealous fairy whose immature reaction to her attraction to Peter Pan (the real center of light and power in the story) nearly brings perdition. *Peter Pan* is hardly an exception. Snow White and Sleeping Beauty are brought back from death by a male (Prince Charming, no less). Cinderella is taken from rags to riches by our hero, and Little Red Riding Hood is saved by the hunter. Cinderella goes one step further. The distinguishing mark of Cinderella's worth as a person is her beauty, as compared to her stepsisters' ugliness. Only the *Wizard of Oz* differs, but even there our heroine is not portrayed as a leader of men, but of a robot, a lion, and a man of straw. There seems to be no literary end to active, assertive males with female accessories. You may make the decision that regardless, you prefer not to discard the traditional fairy tales for other reasons, namely the beauty and power of many of them, but it's an ostrich-like approach to pretend they do not carry messages or transmit values. They do, and if you do not present other values through other stimuli, you have tacitly

agreed to these values and must take responsibility for the attitudes they shape in children.

I will not speak so extensively on literary racism, for I have a conviction that whites attempt to talk too much about and for blacks and that unconscious bias makes much of what we say irrelevant or simply inaccurate. Nonetheless even as a middle-class white it seems obvious to me that any classroom that does not contain a considerable number of books with black heroes and *heroines* is fostering the image of a white world exclusive of blacks. Sadly enough the books that I have seen portraying blacks all too often take middle-class white kids and color them brown. Just as the first dolls purporting to be black carried white features, too many books portray a black middle-class existence, ignoring the fact that a high percentage of blacks in this country, because of racial discrimination, are trapped in poverty situations. Too few books portray one-parent families. Too few depict parents on welfare (if any). Are there books that show dirty kids? For many families, black and white, running water is not available and bathing not easily accomplished. There are all kinds of kids in this society looking for some sort of literary reflection of their existences, some sort of affirmation that they do exist and that their existence is a valid thing. It is one thing, as I propose, to show options to the role model assigned women as a group. It is another to deny by implication the existences of large numbers of children because they do not fit the current cultural stereotype of the middle-class, clean, nonaggressive kid.

Books are only one evidence of the value orientation of a classroom. Another area particularly worth considering (for there isn't space to deal with all areas equally) is the housekeeping area and the associated materials. By the time most children have reached preschool age they have already watched a good deal of television. Thus they have already internalized sex typing to a great extent. In particular, even if their own mommy is not part of the trend, they have seen countless mothers in the kitchen advertising inane products and countless male racing car drivers tooling off down the road with plastic smiling blondes beside them. To the extent that classrooms reproduce activities that have al-

Lynn Phillips, from "Exactly Like Me," Lollipop Power

ready been sex-typed, can they expect children to respond in any but stereotyped ways? Thus, girls will spend more time in the kitchen than boys, and the hot wheels that the teacher introduces will be mobbed by males. At the minimum I am saying that such divisions are not determined by biological differentiation, and thus are subject to scrutiny as to whether they are desirable or not. A more assertive position is that unless the teacher has some reason to desire such differentiation, it is her responsibility to mix the clues as to expectations. She could, for instance, put the housekeeping area (if she wants one at all) on the second floor of a climbing structure to encourage both climbing by females and housekeeping by males. Reproducing sex-typed activities in pure form—that is, having high heels and feminine clothes in the housekeeping area—makes a distinct statement to children. Adults should not be surprised if they respond to such statements.

The issue of dolls needs to be examined. Dolls of one color and dolls without genitals deny by implication the existence of both race and sexuality in human beings. Do black babies not exist? Are they not important? Do babies not have genitals? Is there some reason for pretending they don't?

More generally, whether or not the classroom is equipped with reconverted junk or with shiny new toys indicates what the school values. Given a generally favorable adjustment to school, that which is assigned value by the school has some power for the child. It is particularly crucial in programs involving poor children that children be exposed to the creative possibilities in materials which they might find in their neighborhoods or in their homes. To imply to children that the only toys worth having are those that come in boxes is not to help them at all to learn to deal with the potentialities in their own environments. It is to not even interest them in trying, and not to mention at all the fact that there are very few cases where a particular toy is worth more than a handmade or scrounged equivalent. For children who already perceive the discrepancy between their homes and the materialistic values of the culture at large (particularly through TV), it is one more statement that they and their families do not have what it takes. For middle-class children the inclusion of manufactured America in the classroom is less devastating, but it merely serves to perpetuate a culture already suffocating in its own materialism.

Before the introduction of the teachers into the situation, before the curriculum for the day or week has been decided, before questions of discipline and schedule arise, the materials that comprise the stable environment of the preschool classroom make an endless number of statements to children. The statements are no less registered because children are not conscious of their form. Indeed, if children were conscious of the alternatives to these statements, they would hold far less power than they do.

It should be clear by now that daily curriculum is no less loaded than more indirect teaching devices. When a unit is presented on the family, are black and white units presented? Are mixed units? Are one-parent families and families with strong grandmother figures dealt with? Are communes and co-ops presented as options? Are all mothers married? Are all fathers present? It is possible to do some sorting within these available options. The point is to be conscious of the fact that options do exist, and thus what you present represents a decision and expresses a value judgment.

Is a curriculum unit on Africa important? Is it important enough to go to the trouble to get material for wraps, and to introduce African foods, musical instruments, and other facets of different African cultures? When does it become important to show the heritage of a people brainwashed into thinking they have had none? when you have one black child? two? or none? And if you use that same time and energy to devote to a unit on good manners, is it possible to deny the values underlying your actions?

Cultural and class differences are ignored in other ways. The middle-class reliance on verbal communication has been well documented, as is the fact that this is less true of lower socioeconomic groups. I do not dispute the appropriateness of language development to the preschool classroom, but I do think the form in which it is presented is significant. Teachers who ask questions indiscriminately of children with limited language skills can be perceived as threatening. If the point is to encourage children with poor language skills to talk, it is worth considering that the whole business of asking questions implies a high degree of reliance on verbal expression. Not to know the answer to a question or how to express it is to be put very much on the spot. Ritualistic questions such as "how are you," which have ritualistic answers, can be particularly threatening if you don't know the form. A child can be made quite inadvertently to feel stupid, and the result is to inhibit communication on the part of the child. I have worked in a program which dealt with this issue by having teachers initially only make statements to children. "I'm glad you came to school today. You're wearing a red jacket. It's the same color as the shelf." Often singing was used to describe what children were doing as they were doing it. "Johnny is sliding down the slide."

In a program that solely contains low-income kids, teachers become aware of their middle-class orientation more quickly, but all too often programs that contain both low-income and middle-class kids are focused, without conscious commitment, in favor of middle-class children. (Most teachers, after all, come from the middle class.) Middle-class children in them prosper, and well they might, for the classroom expresses values to which they are accustomed and which reflect favorably on their families and on themselves.

The issue of politeness is a case in point. The whole concept of sharing rests on believing there really is enough, that one really will get a turn. For children who have grown up in a situation of scarcity there is no reason to automatically accept that. Sharing and being polite about it is less important and should be less important for such children than assertiveness. The real danger for children growing up in a society manifestly hostile to their existence and their needs is passivity. The odds against them will increase as they grow, and they will need all the belief they can muster in their own capacity to

Vicki Breitbart

meet their needs. True, you can teach children different ways of meeting their needs, and sharing is a valid way. Children need friends, and help in learning how to hold them. But there is a real difference in teaching children to share because you demonstrate that sharing is a problem-solving device and, on the other hand, bewildering children and increasing their negative self-image by emphasizing that "nice children share." It is the difference in respecting the needs the child perceives her- or himself as having and her or his assertiveness in trying to meet them, and at the other extreme, imputing a negative morality to actions which, within the context of the child's life, make ultimate good sense.

Authoritarianism is transmitted to kids in its more subtle forms by teachers who find it more efficient, and who do not see the reasons for working out a problem with a child. The conformity and passivity which strictly controlled sit-in-your-seat type classroom situations inculcate should be well understood by now. It is interesting to consider, however, that the end result is probably not just people who take orders, but people who are more than willing to give them. Inevitably, what children learn from a scolding is not the object of the scolding but that one way to interact with people is to scold them. But even in a presumably "free" classroom, where children have free access to materials and where there is a free flow of movement, all too often problems are solved by teachers' saying, "Give him the truck, Tommy. He had it first." There are options. Teachers can say, "You've got a problem. He had the truck and you wanted it. Now you could tell him you want it when he's finished. Or I could help you look for another truck. But I don't think he's going to let you keep it because he looks pretty mad to me." There is teacher intervention to be sure. But the difference is in giving the child options to choose from and in focusing the situation so that the child has to come to grips with the external results of her or his actions—namely the response of the other kid. Problem solving with children can range from providing a very narrow set of options for a child with few skills to helping a kid with many skills generate her or his own solutions.

Jane Melnick

The difference between the two types of approaches can be illustrated by reference to a situation where a child, previous to her or his school entrance, has lived in a minimally stimulating environment. Very often children with few skills in choosing will be unable to focus, differentiate, and sort activities when confronted with a highly stimulating environment. One solution in dealing with a child thus immobilized is to say, "Go paint today," thus making the choice for her or him. Another is to say, "When I come in in the morning, I stop and look to see what there is to do. Today I see blocks, and woodworking, and painting [pointing]. Sometimes when I can't decide what I want to do, I take a walk around the room. Wanta come?" If you start walking you will sooner or later lose the child at some activity. The object is not to make decisions for children but to give them decision-making models that will serve them when authority figures are not present.

The point of all this is that whenever there are options to choose from, the model you present represents a value judgment. In the cases above there are clearly options. In a society that is sexist, racist, authoritarian, and elitist, the options that we choose, if we choose them without consideration, are likely to be all too often sexist, racist, authoritarian, and elitist. The fact that we were raised on *Peter Pan* doesn't make it any less sexist; it just makes us less likely to recognize that fact. My argument is simply that we are politicizing kids all the time and refuse to take responsibility for our choices by denying we are making them. Inevitably in people's minds the term "politicizing" raises the specter of children carrying peace signs and protesting the invasion of Cambodia. I do not support such activities, but not on the grounds that they are political in nature. Children cannot, I believe, deal conceptually with groups as large as nations and cannot, perhaps, deal with groups much larger than those they come in contact with constantly. Thus, to ask children to accept on authority concepts they are incapable of evaluating is to be guilty of gross authoritarianism. We cannot teach children to memorize the concept of freedom; we must illustrate it whenever possible by allowing them the maximum number of options in a given situation. I would rather have someone give my child a choice between telling another child she wanted the truck when finished or finding another one, than have that person give my child a lecture on why we should get out of Vietnam. Needless to say, I feel precisely the same way about the American flag and the Pledge of Allegiance. In this case, the issue is not whose politics they represent, but the breadth of the political concern.

We must make some decisions about whether we want the same sort of society we have had, or whether we want to try to eliminate some of its more inhumane features. And we must translate these decisions into the environments that shape our children. The alternative is not a valueless environment, but an environment that systematically inculcates values which our history should have shown us thwarts and oppresses human potential instead of freeing it.

M.S.R.

Epilogue

Child care has become one of the biggest issues in this country. At the same time, men and women are setting up their own underground centers, executives from General Motors, Polaroid, and Pepsi-Cola are meeting to discuss their involvement in child care; and companies set up to provide child care services on a profit-making basis are going public on the stock market. A meeting of all the people interested in child care would bring together bankers, business executives, and government officials as well as women in the women's liberation movement, activists in black, Latin, Indian, and Asian communities, and a lot more people simply identifying themselves as angry women and men. Quite a group! Probably the only thing they could all agree on is the need for more child care.

In a recent debate in Congress, the terms "fascist" and "revolutionary" were both used in reference to a program of universal child care. And it can go either way. Child care programs can be a way to force-feed society's prejudices to its young or it can be a liberating experience for everyone involved. Child care alternatives can be used to regiment children and track women into oppressive work, or they can be part of a larger struggle for self-determination.

If we simply demand *more* day care, our children's lives can be bartered for part of our own. Group child care can be used to force women to work outside the home as well as in the home, with little reward in either place, to be manipulated in and out of the labor force only in the interest of profit. And just as after World War II, more group child care that is not run by the people who use it can be closed down or phased out whenever government or industry desires.[1] More group child care can be just another way for others to control our lives.

> *It's not enough to say that child care should be the responsibility of the whole society where people's needs are twisted to serve a privileged few. We live in the United States, which perpetuates itself by exploiting, oppressing and discriminating against millions of people every day the world over.*[2]

People can only be truly satisfied with

1. It is no coincidence that the announcement of new eligibility requirements that severely restrict the use of federal funds came at the same time the Vietnam War was ended and the troops returned, and the government began putting an emphasis on jobs for vets.

2. *Notes on Child Care* (New York: Women's Union Child Care Collective). Vol. I, p. i.

J. J. Linsalata

the kind of child care a society provides when they feel satisfied with that society and their role in it. How can you trust the care of your child to a society that makes you feel alienated, powerless, and angry a lot of the time? Yet at the same time, we cannot wait for a new society before we change our lives. If what we have learned from looking at child care here and in other countries is that child care mirrors the values and goals of a society, it is also true that the child care we create can help shape the future we want.

Child care alternatives that are set up for a privileged few, that duplicate the isolation of the nuclear family, or that reinforce the stereotypes and prejudices that exist now will not change anything. But creating child care alternatives that are part of a growing community, where differences are respected and not used to pit one group against another—these alternatives will have long-range implications. Ultimately, they can affect all relationships in this and future societies: family, sex, property, etc. Sharing the responsibility for children can challenge the ideological assumptions of individualism and competition. Everyone sharing child care can break down the feeling of possessiveness and the concept of ownership: *My* child is *my* problem and therefore *I* must conform to whatever demands the system makes of *me* so that *I* can care for *my* child. Everyone sharing child care will also demand new work routines in which all adults (male and female) have time to be part of child rearing. This in turn will challenge the organization of a society that not only gives women the exclusive responsibility for child care but also deprives men of its joys.

The gap between the ways we feel now, what we see around us, and what we want seems enormous. But the difficulty is not in knowing what we want but in getting together with other people to begin to create it. As we begin to break through the prejudices and false divisions imposed on us—divisions that have alienated us from our own feelings and needs and isolated us from other people with common concerns—as we rechannel our anger away from ourselves and against those who deserve it, we can free our energies to make the changes necessary to resolve our common problems. We can begin to create alternatives where children can feel secure; where they can develop confidence, independence, and compassion for others; where we can help shape the environment; where we can spend time if we want to or leave children with people we trust; where we can care for children without having to give up our right to our own development.

All child care alternatives will seem imperfect if measured against our need for child care available at all times, for all children, publicly supported, and controlled by the people directly affected. But nobody expects it to be given to us. And our attempts to break through the limits of our roles and join with other people in providing care for our children will help give us an understanding of what it will take to get what we want. New forms of child care that we create and control can help us begin to change our lives and change the ways we feel about ourselves and each other. They can help make us all more human.

Talking about our experience in setting up the Children's Storefront, a group of us wrote:

The Storefront was responsible for changing people's lives. It made activists of many of us who would have been turned off by endless pre-planning meetings. From our talks we had never realized the extent to which child care was not only a necessity for women with children, but for many women was an opportunity for productive work that the society and the movement generally do not provide.

It was a chance not only to express our beliefs but to begin to make them visible and real. It was a glimpse of what it means to work collectively; to be involved with one's mind, feelings, and body at the same time. It gave us a sense that if we do not accept the myth and the lies about our own powerlessness, and the definitions of the way things have to be, there is a real and better alternative. It gave us a sense of real power because it showed us that people working together can create and build what we want and need. If what we want does not exist, then we can, and must, make it exist.

Vicki Breitbart

M.S.R.

Resources

Contents

Day Care Licensing

	Group Day Care Facility (G) and Family Day Care Facility (F)						
	Welfare Agency		Health Department		Department of Education		Voluntary Licensing Only
	G	F	G	F	G	F	
ALABAMA	x	x					
ALASKA	x	x					
ARIZONA			x	x			
ARKANSAS	x	x					
CALIFORNIA	x	x					
COLORADO	x	x					
CONNECTICUT		x	x				
DELAWARE	x	x					
DISTRICT OF COLUMBIA			x	x			
FLORIDA	x	x					
GEORGIA	x	x					
HAWAII	x	x					
IDAHO	x	x					
ILLINOIS	x	x					
INDIANA	x	x					

	Welfare Agency		Health Department		Department of Education		Voluntary Licensing Only
	G	F	G	F	G	F	
IOWA	x	x					
KANSAS			x	x			
KENTUCKY	x	x					
LOUISIANA	x	x					x
MAINE	x	x					
MARYLAND		x	x				
MASSACHUSETTS		x	x	x			
MICHIGAN	x	x					
MINNESOTA	x	x					
MISSISSIPPI	x	x					x
MISSOURI	x	x					
MONTANA	x	x					
NEBRASKA	x	x					
NEVADA	x						
NEW HAMPSHIRE	x	x					
NEW JERSEY					x		
NEW MEXICO			x	x			
NEW YORK	x	x					
NORTH CAROLINA	x	x					x

	Welfare Agency		Health Department	Department of Education	Voluntary Licensing Only
NORTH DAKOTA	x	x			
OHIO	x	x			
OKLAHOMA	x	x			
OREGON	x				
PENNSYLVANIA	x	x			
PUERTO RICO	x	x			
RHODE ISLAND	x	x			
SOUTH CAROLINA	x	x			
SOUTH DAKOTA	x	x			
TENNESSEE	x	x			
TEXAS	x	x			
UTAH	x	x			
VERMONT	x	x			
VIRGINIA	x	x			
WASHINGTON	x	x			
WEST VIRGINIA	x				
WISCONSIN	x				
WYOMING	x	x			
VIRGIN ISLANDS	x	x			

Directory of Licensing Agencies

ALABAMA
Supervisor of Child Caring Institutions and Agencies
State Department of Pensions and Security
64 North Union Street
Montgomery, Alabama 36104
(205) 269–6731

ALASKA
Division of Public Welfare
Department of Health and Welfare
Pouch H
Juneau, Alaska 99801
(907) 586–5401

ARIZONA
Child Day Care Health Consultant
Maternal and Child Health Division
Arizona State Department of Health
Arizona State Office Building
1624 West Adams Street
Phoenix, Arizona 85007
(602) 271–4521 (General Information)

ARKANSAS
Day Care Specialist
Department of Public Welfare
P.O. Box 1437
Little Rock, Arkansas 72202
(501) 371–2085

CALIFORNIA
Social Service Consultant
Adoptions and Foster Care Bureau
Department of Social Welfare
744 P Street
Sacramento, California 95814
(916) 445–4500

COLORADO
Supervisor
Licensing and Standards
Division of Welfare
1575 Sherman Street
Denver, Colorado 80203
(303) 892–2561 (General Information)

CONNECTICUT
Director of Community Health
Connecticut State Health Department
79 Elm Street
Hartford, Connecticut 06106
(203) 566–4282

DELAWARE
Chief
Bureau of Child Development
P.O. Box 309
Wilmington, Delaware 19899
(302) 764–8180 (Ext. 304)

DISTRICT OF COLUMBIA
Child Care Specialist
801 North Capitol Street, Room 501
Washington, D.C. 20001
(202) 629–2152

FLORIDA
Supervisor, Day Care Unit
Division of Family Services
5920 Expressway, P.O. Box 2050
Jacksonville, Florida 32203
(904) 725–3080

GEORGIA
Chief, Licensing Section
Division for Children and Youth
State Department of Family and Children Services
613 Trinity-Washington Building
Atlanta, Georgia 30334
(404) 656–4468

HAWAII
State Department of Social Services
Assistant Program Development Administrator, Day Care
P.O. Box 339
Honolulu, Hawaii 96809
(808) 548–2211

IDAHO
Director, Bureau of Family and Children's Services
State Department of Public Assistance
Box 1189
Boise, Idaho 83701
(208) 344–5811

ILLINOIS
Office of the Director
Department of Children and Family Services
Springfield, Illinois 62706
(217) 528–8406

INDIANA
Department of Public Welfare
100 N. Senate Avenue, Room #701
Indianapolis, Indiana 46204
(317) 633–6650

IOWA
Day Care Supervisor
Department of Social Services
Lucas State Office Building
Des Moines, Iowa 50319
(515) 281–5453 (General Information)

KANSAS
Director
Division of Child Welfare
State Department of Social Welfare
State Office Building
Topeka, Kansas 66612
(913) 296–3959 (General Information)

KENTUCKY
Department of Child Welfare
Chief, Office of Special Services
403 Wapping Street
Frankfort, Kentucky 40601
(502) 562–4650

LOUISIANA
Department of Public Welfare
Director of Child Welfare
P.O. Box 44065
Baton Rouge, Louisiana 70804
(504) 389–6036

MAINE
Licensing Supervisor
Department of Health and Welfare
State House
Augusta, Maine 04330
(207) 289–3456

MARYLAND
Child Day Care Center Coordinator
State Department of Health
301 W. Preston Street
Baltimore, Maryland 21201
(301) 383–2668

MASSACHUSETTS (Group Day Care Licensing)
Day Care Coordinator–Day Care Advisory Unit
Department of Public Health
88 Broad Street
Boston, Massachusetts 02110
(617) 727–5196

MASSACHUSETTS (Family Day Care Licensing)
Day Care Unit
Department of Public Welfare
600 Washington Street
Boston, Massachusetts 02111
(617) 727–6112

MICHIGAN
State Department of Social Services
Bureau of Family and Children's Services
Director
300 South Capitol
Lansing, Michigan 48926
(517) 373–2076

MINNESOTA
Day Care Supervisor
Day Care Section
Child Welfare Division
Department of Public Welfare
Centennial Building
St. Paul, Minnesota 55101
(612) 221–2528

MISSISSIPPI
Day Care Supervisor
Division of Family and Children's Services
State Department of Public Welfare
P.O. Box 4321
Fondren Station
Jackson, Mississippi 39216
(601) 362–9608

MISSOURI
Chief
Bureau of Family and Children's Services
State Department of Public Health and Welfare
Broadway State Office Building
Jefferson City, Missouri 65101
(314) 635–8111

MONTANA
Licensing Specialist
Department of Public Welfare
P.O. Box 1723
Helena, Montana 59601
(406) 449–3470

NEBRASKA
Child Welfare Consultant
Department of Public Welfare
1526 K Street, Fourth Floor
Lincoln, Nebraska 68508
(402) 471–2369

NEVADA
Adoptions and Licensing Specialist
Welfare Division
201 South Fall Street
Carson City, Nevada 89701
(702) 882–7412

NEW HAMPSHIRE
Chief, Children and Family Services
Division of Welfare
Concord, New Hampshire 03301
(603) 271–2522
(This state has no licensing rules.)

NEW JERSEY
Associate Consultant
State Department of Education
Early Childhood Department
225 W. State Street
Trenton, New Jersey 08625
(609) 292–4362

NEW MEXICO
Licensing Section
Health Facilities Services Division
Health and Social Services Department
P.O. Box 2348
Santa Fe, New Mexico 87501
(505) 827–2107

NEW YORK
Day Care Consultant
New York State Department of Social Services
1450 Western Avenue
Albany, New York 12203

NORTH CAROLINA
State of North Carolina
Department of Social Services
Raleigh, North Carolina 27602
(919) 829–3387

NORTH DAKOTA
Director of Social Services
Capitol Building
Bismarck, North Dakota 58501
(701) 224–2310

OHIO
Chief
Bureau of Day Care Services
Division of Welfare Services
Oak and Ninth
Columbus, Ohio 43215
(614) 469–2686

OKLAHOMA
Administrative Assistant, Children's Services
State Department of Public Welfare
P.O. Box 25352
Oklahoma City, Oklahoma 73125
(405) 521–3646

OREGON
Supervisor
Day Care Unit
Public Welfare Division
Public Service Building
Salem, Oregon 97310
(503) 364–2171

PENNSYLVANIA
Licensing Program Supervisor
Office of Family Services
Health and Welfare Building
Harrisburg, Pennsylvania 17120
(717) 787–4882

RHODE ISLAND
Office of the Director
Department of Social Welfare
1 Washington Avenue
Providence, Rhode Island 02905
(401) 467–7550

SOUTH CAROLINA
Chief
Children and Family Services Division
P.O. Box 1520
Columbia, South Carolina 29202
(803) 758–3151

SOUTH DAKOTA
Consultant
State Department of Public Welfare
Pierre, South Dakota 57501
(605) 224–3491

TENNESSEE
Supervisor of Licensing
Department of Public Welfare
State Office Building
Nashville, Tennessee 37219
(615) 741–2306

TEXAS
Consultant on Child Development and Day Care
State Department of Public Welfare
John H. Reagan Building
Austin, Texas 78701
(512) 475–4238

UTAH
Day Care, Licensing and Adoption Specialist
Bureau of Family and Children Services
Division of Family Services
231 E. Fourth South
Salt Lake City, Utah 84111
(801) 486–1811

VERMONT
Day Care Operations Unit
Chief Licenser
Vermont State Office of Economic Opportunity
43 State Street
Montpelier, Vermont 05602
(802) 223–2311 (Ext. 437)

VIRGINIA
Intake Supervisor
Department of Welfare
429 S. Belvedere Street
Richmond, Virginia 23220
(703) 770–5078

WASHINGTON
Supervisor
Services to Child Care Agencies
Family and Children's Services
Division of Public Assistance
P.O. Box 1162
Olympia, Washington 98501
(206) 753–7039 (General Information)

WEST VIRGINIA
Day Care Unit
State Department of Welfare
Division of Social Services
Room 824
1900 Washington Street East
Charleston, West Virginia 25305
(304) 348–2400

WISCONSIN
Director
Division of Family Services
State Office Building
Department of Health and Social Services
Madison, Wisconsin 53702
(608) 266–3416

WYOMING
Division of Public Assistance and Social Services
State Office Building
Cheyenne, Wyoming 82001
(307) 777–7561

Standards and Costs of Day Care (For a Full Day in a Center)*

PROGRAM ELEMENT	LEVELS OF QUALITY					
	MINIMUM		ACCEPTABLE		DESIRABLE	
	Description	Annual cost per child	Description	Annual cost per child	Description	Annual cost per child
1. Food (meals and snacks)	One meal and snacks	$140	Two meals and snacks	$210	Two meals and snacks	$210
2. Transportation	Provided at parent expense		Provided by center	60	Provided by center	60
3. Medical and dental services	Examinations and referral services	20	Examinations and referral services	20	Examinations, treatment when not otherwise available, and health education	60
4. Work with parents	Little or none except on problem cases	10	General parent activities plus limited counseling services	30	Parent education, family-type activities, full counseling services	70
5. Facilities and utilities (rental)	Space meeting state and local licensing requirements	90	Same as minimum	90	Space providing more generous room for activities plus room for work with parents	110
6. Clothing and other emergency needs	As necessary	30	As necessary	20	As necessary	20
7. Supplies and materials	Custodial program	20	General developmental program	50	Individualized developmental program	75
8. Equipment (annual replacement costs)	Custodial program	20	General developmental program	12	Individualized developmental program	15

* From Office of Economic Opportunity.

	MINIMUM		ACCEPTABLE		DESIRABLE	
9. *Staff* a. Classroom professional ($6,600)	One per 20 children	$275	One per 15 children	$405	One per 15 children	$405
b. Classroom nonprofessional ($4,400)	Two per 20 children	320	Two per 15 children	420	Three per 15 children	640
c. Social service professional ($6,600)	One per 150 children	65	One per 100 children	65	One per 100 children	65
d. Community, social service, parent, or health aides ($4,400)	None	—	One per 100 children	20	Two per 100 children	45
e. Business and maintenance ($4,000)	Two per 100 children	80	Three per 100 children	120	Three per 100 children	120
f. Special resource (psychology, music, art, consultants, etc.) ($6,600)	Urgent need only	20	One per 100 children	60	Two per 100 children	120
g. Supervision	One per 100 children	80	Two per 100 children	160	Two per 100 children	160
10. Training	Approximately 10% of salary cost	75	Approximately 10% of salary cost	120	Approximately 10% of salary cost	145
TOTAL PER CHILD		$1,245		$1,862		$2,320
Estimated federal cost (in millions)		$747–872		$1,117–1,303		$1,392–1,624

NOTE: *This analysis is based on centers providing service ten to twelve hours a day, five days a week.*

Budget for Operating a Cooperative Day Care Center

Average monthly expenses based on the budget of an on-going program for 16 children, ages 2 to 5 years old.

Staff	One full-time (6 hours a day). Other teachers are parent and nonparent volunteers.	$400
Rent	800 sq. ft. (50 sq. ft. per child) plus kitchen, bathrooms, and outdoor play area. Includes heat, electricity, telephone (in-coming service and out-going emergency calls).	180
Food	Approximately 50¢ a day per person for one meal and two snacks for 16 children and 3 adults (food purchased through food co-op)	190
Supplies		
Maintenance	Paper towels, toilet paper, cleaning supplies, etc.	30
Educational	Paper, pastes, paint, etc. (most of these supplies are made or donated).	50
Pampers	Approximately 40¢ a child per day for 8 children.	64
Petty Cash	Transportation, emergencies, etc.	20
TOTAL		$934

Funding Sources and Aids

Annual Register of Grant Support. Academic Media, Inc. Los Angeles, California 90053. Grant support programs of government agencies, foundations, businesses, etc.

Federal Funds for Day Care Projects. U.S. Department of Labor, Women's Bureau, 1969. Describes different federal programs that can fund some aspect of day care.

Foundation Directory. Russell Sage Foundation, 230 Park Avenue, New York, New York 10017. This is a reference book of 8,000 foundations, their addresses, and what kinds of activities they usually fund.

How to Raise Money for Community Action, How to Apply for Grants. Scholarship, Education and Defense Fund for Racial Equality, 164 Madison Avenue, New York, New York 10016.

Organizations: For Assistance and/or Written Materials

Association for Childhood Education International
3615 Wisconsin Avenue N.W.
Washington, D.C. 20016

Bank Street College of Education
Publications Department
Day Care Consultation Service and Center for Day Care Training
610 West 112th Street
New York, New York 10025

Black Child Development Institute
1028 Connecticut Ave. N.W., Suite 514
Washington, D.C. 20036

Bureau of Child Development and Parent Education
New York State Department of Education
Albany, New York 12201

Canadian Welfare Council Research Branch
55 Pardale Avenue
Ottawa 3, Ontario

Child Study Association of America
9 East Eighty-ninth Street, New York, New York 10028

Child Welfare League of America
44 East Twenty-third Street
New York, New York 10010

Children's Foundation
1026 Seventeenth Street N.W.
Washington, D.C. 20036
(*Information on Special Food Service Program of National School Lunch Act*)

Day Care and Child Development Council of America
1401 K Street N.W.
Washington, D.C. 20005

Educational Development Center
55 Chapel Street
Cambridge, Massachusetts 02138

Educational Facilities Laboratories
477 Madison Avenue
New York, New York 10022

Educational Resources Information Center (ERIC)
U.S. Department of Health, Education and Welfare
Office of Education
Washington, D.C. 20202

Interstate Research Association
3210 Grace Street N.W.
Washington, D.C.
(*Bilingual bicultural child care*)

National Association for the Education of Young Children
1834 Connecticut Avenue N.W.
Washington, D.C. 20009

National Parents Federation for Day Care and Child Development
429 Lewis Street
Somerset, New Jersey 08873

National Welfare Rights Organization
1424 Sixteenth Street N.W.
Washington, D.C. 20036

New England Free Press
791 Tremont Street
Boston, Massachusetts 02118

N.O.W. (National Organization for Women)
Task Force on Child Care

45 Newbury Street
Boston, Massachusetts 02116

R.E.P. (Radical Education Project)
Box 561-A
Detroit, Michigan 48232

Women's Action Alliance
370 Lexington Avenue, Room 313
New York, New York 10017

Government Agencies

Child Nutrition Division
U.S. Department of Agriculture
Washington, D.C. 20250

Office of Child Development
U.S. Department of Health, Education and Welfare
400 Sixth Street S.W.
Washington, D.C. 20201

Office of Economic Opportunity
1200 Nineteenth Street N.W.
Washington, D.C. 20036

Social and Rehabilitation Service
Community Services Administration
330 C Street S.W.
Washington, D.C. 20201
(*Title IVA funding*)

Women's Bureau
U.S. Department of Labor
Washington, D.C. 20210

Suppliers of Equipment and Materials

Looking at other child care centers is the best way to learn what children do and what materials they use. But catalogues are helpful. They can also give you ideas of things to make or buy. Sometimes the same equipment is available at the local 5-and-10 or stationery store at lower prices.

These major suppliers will send you free catalogues. Tell them you are a child care center and the ages of the children in your program.

Childcraft Education Corp.
964 Third Avenue
New York, New York 10002

Child Life
Highland Street
Holliston, Massachusetts 01746

Community Playthings
Department 2
Rifton, New York 12471

Creative Playthings
Princeton, New Jersey

Crowell, Collier and Macmillan, Inc.
at these local addresses:

School Materials, Inc.
2124 W. Eighty-second Place
Chicago, Illinois 60620

School Materials, Inc.
200 W. First Street
Austin, Texas 78701

American School, Inc.
2301 Black Street
Denver, Colorado 80205

American School of New Mexico, Inc.
3204 Candelaria Road, NE
Albuquerque, New Mexico 87107

Arts and Crafts, Inc.
9520 Baltimore Avenue
College Park, Maryland 29741

Camobsco, Inc.
342 Western Avenue
Boston, Massachusetts 02135

Standard School, Inc.
1945 Hoover Court
Birmingham, Alabama 35226

Standard School, Inc.
5817 Florida Avenue
Tampa, Florida 33604

Houghton Mifflin Company
53 West Forty-third Street
New York, New York 10035

or at:
3108 Piedmont Road NE
Atlanta, Georgia 30305

6626 Oakbrook Boulevard
Dallas, Texas 75235

777 California Avenue
Palo Alto, California

110 Tremont Street
Boston, Massachusetts 02107

J. L. Hammett Co.
Hammett Place
Braintree, Massachusetts 02184

or at:
290 Main Street
Cambridge, Massachusetts 02142

165 Water Street
Lyons, New York 14489

2393 Vauxhall Road
Union, New Jersey 07083

or at their retail store at:
48 Canal Street
Boston, Massachusetts 02114

Judy Materials
General Learning Corp.
Early Learning Division
310 N. Second Street
Minneapolis, Minnesota 55401

Macmillan Co.
Early Childhood Discovery Materials
School Division
866 Third Avenue
New York, New York 10022

McGraw-Hill Co.
8171 Redwood Highway
Navato, California 94947

or at:
Manchester Road
Manchester, Missouri 63011

Princeton Road
Hightstown, New Jersey 08520

NOVO Educational Toys Corp.
585 Avenue of the Americas
New York, New York 10001

Selective Education Equipment
3 Bridge Street
Newton, Massachusetts 02158

Teaching Aids
A Division of A. Daigg and Co.
159 W. Kinzie Street
Chicago, Illinois 60610

Xerox Corp.
P.O. Box 381
Beacon, New York 12508

or at:
3330 Wilshire Avenue
St. Charles, Missouri 63301

7225 S.W. 109th Terrace
Miami, Florida 33156

26970 Harvester Road
Malibu, California 90269

Equipment and Materials to Make

The advantage of this type of smock is that it can be tied in front by the child.

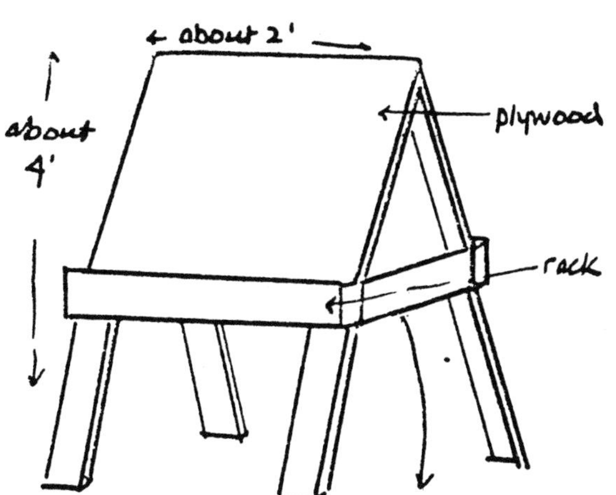

This is a double standing easel. To make easel collapsible, use heavy cord instead of wood here and add hinges on top.

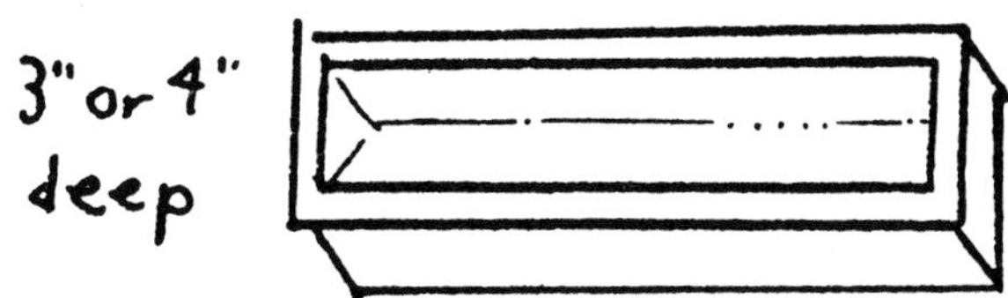

This paint rack is attached to the easel. Put cans of paint in it for the children to use.

A Way to Hang Easels

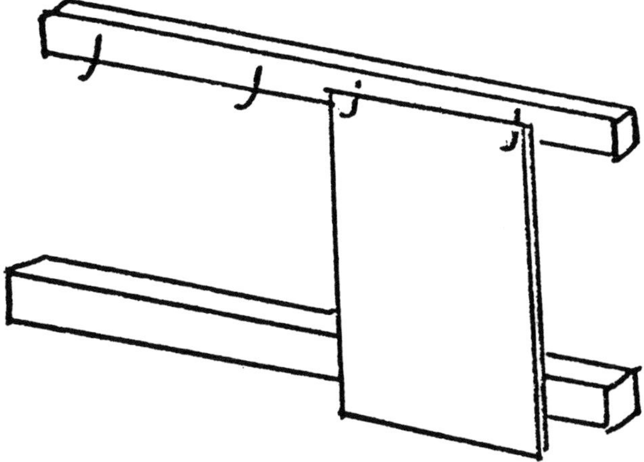

You can nail two strips of wood on the wall to hang easels on. The top strip should be 1" x 1" and about 4 feet from the floor. The bottom strip should be 2" x 4" and about 2½ feet from the floor. On the top strip hang large pieces of wood or cardboard to use for easels.

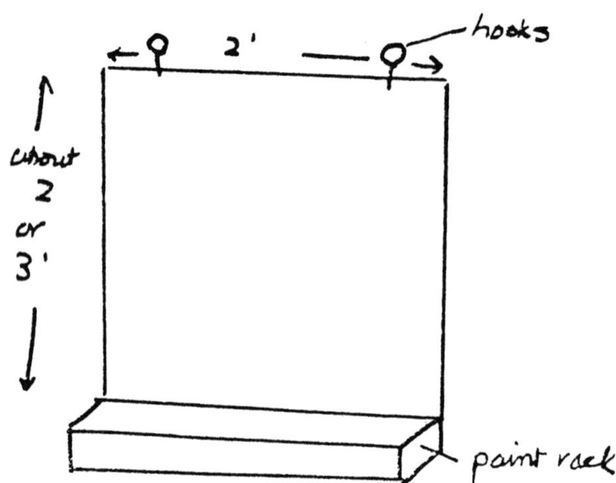

You can cover easel with oilcloth for easy cleaning, and use clothespins to hold painting paper.

Storage Cabinets

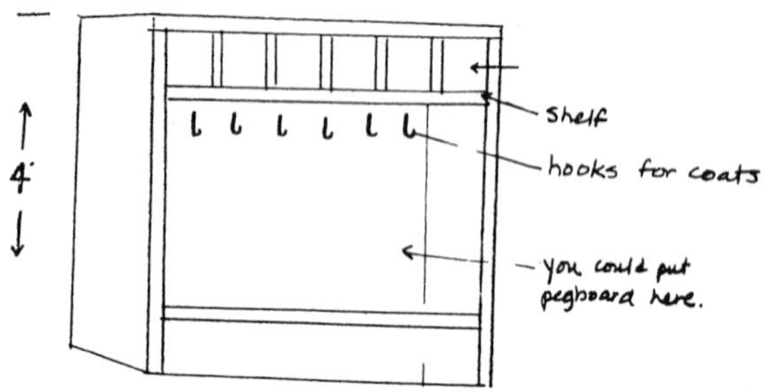

partitions so that each child has a special place to keep things

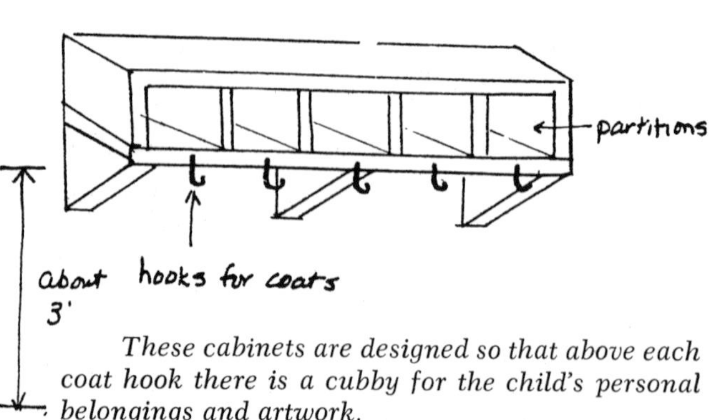

These cabinets are designed so that above each coat hook there is a cubby for the child's personal belongings and artwork.

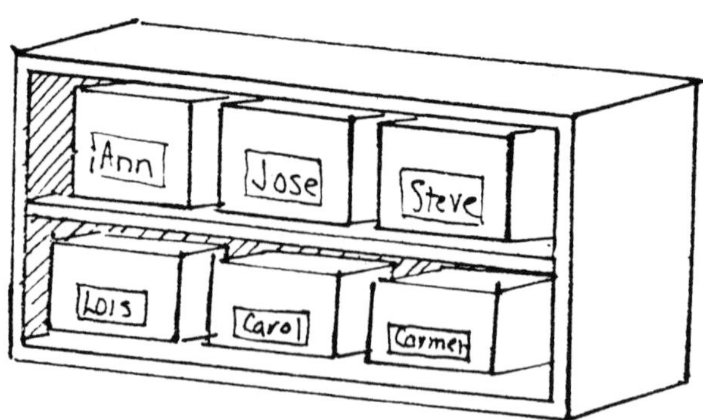

For younger children, you can use cartons on shelves instead of cubbies.

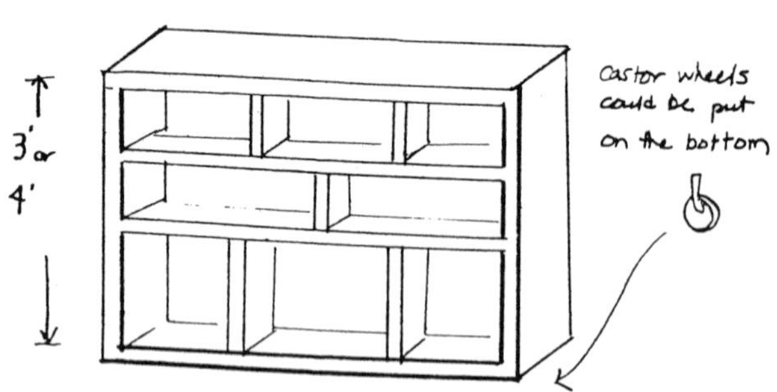

These cabinets are for materials in different interest areas.

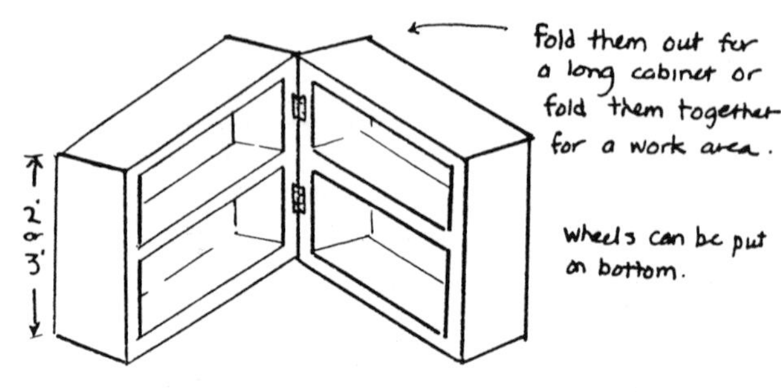

These cabinets are useful if you have to put everything away every night or on weekends. They are joined together with hinges and have wheels on the bottom. During the day you can put them at right angles or open them out for one long cabinet.

You can decide how big to make these storage cabinets, how many shelves you need, and where to put dividers.

Tables

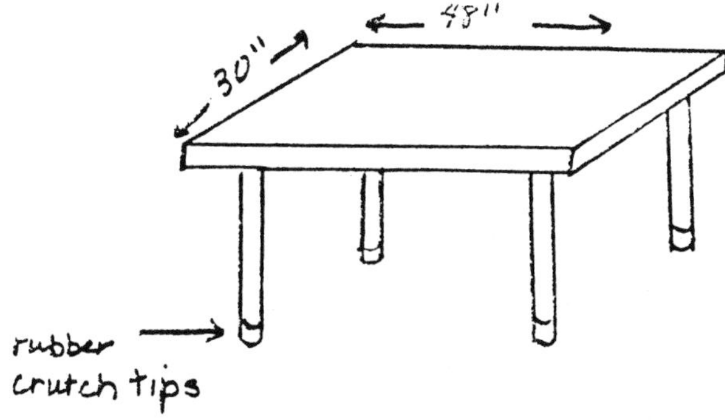

The pipe flanges are screwed into the bottom of the plywood.

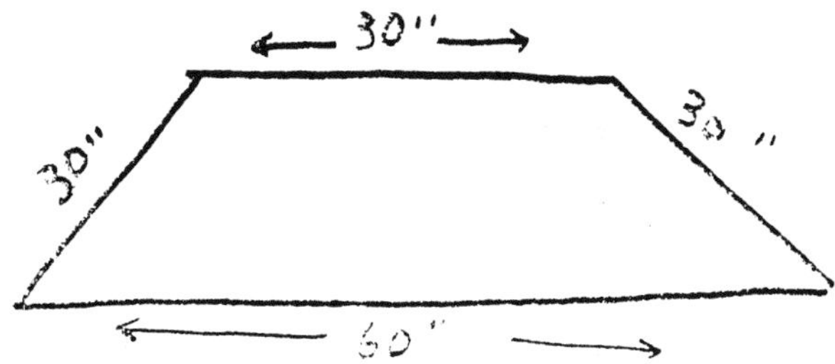

Table tops can also be cut in the shape of a trapezoid.

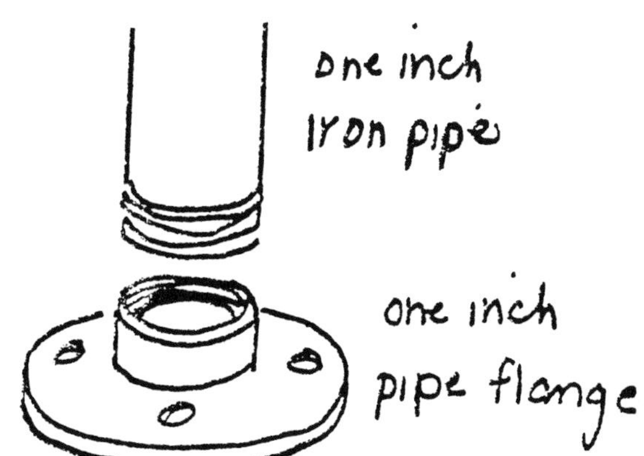

The iron pipes screw into flanges. Rubber crutch tips fit on the bottom of the iron pipe legs.

Depending upon the heights you want for the table legs, lengths of pipe can be cut 18″ to 30″.

Room Dividers

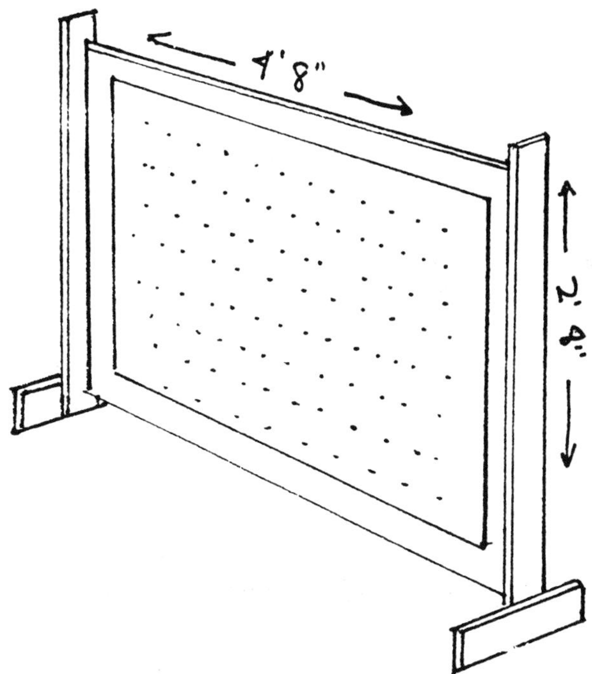

If dividers are made of pegboard, they can be used to display children's work, or to hang up dress-up clothes for dramatic play.

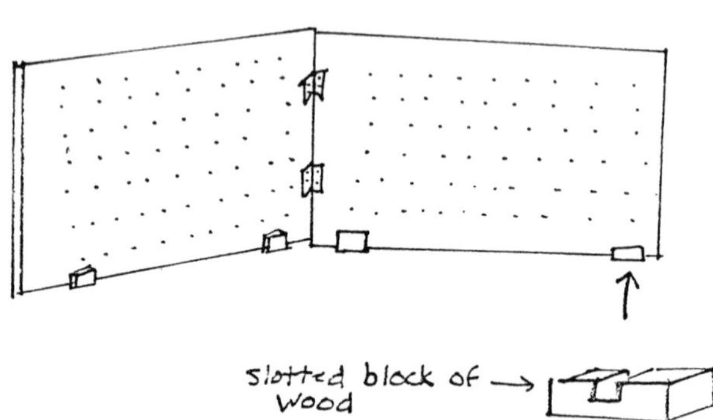

Two pieces of pegboard attached with hinges make a corner or enclosed space.

Rocking and Climbing Toy

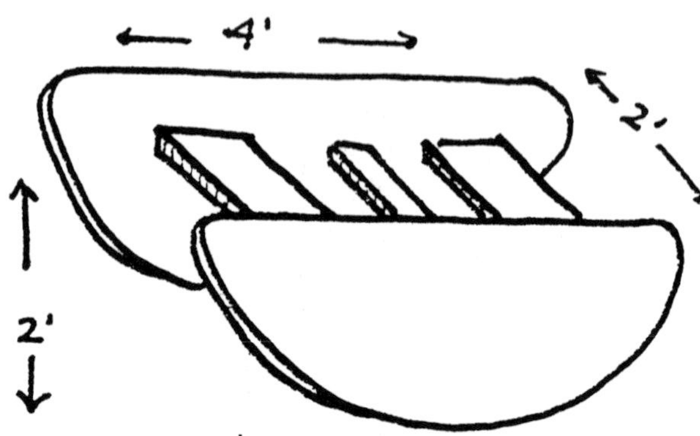

Turn this rocking toy over for climbing toy.

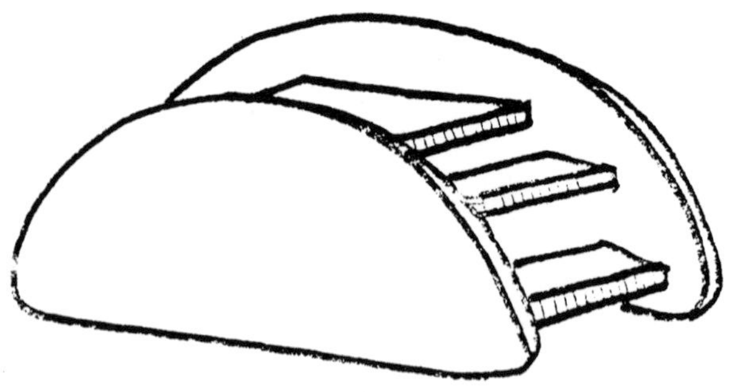

Play Materials

PLAY DOUGH

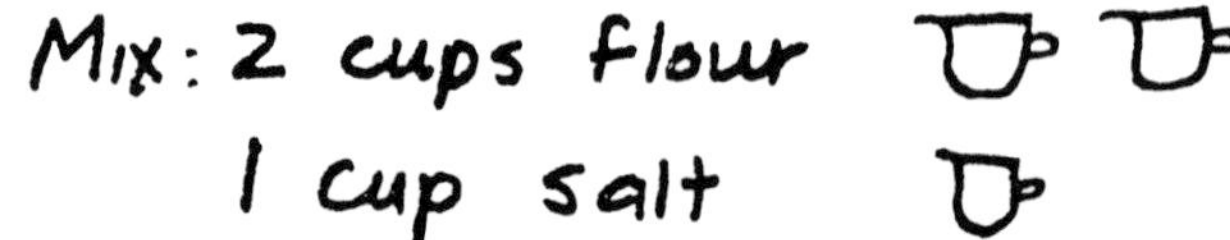

Add water very slowly to make dough that can be used without sticking to hands. You can add food coloring.

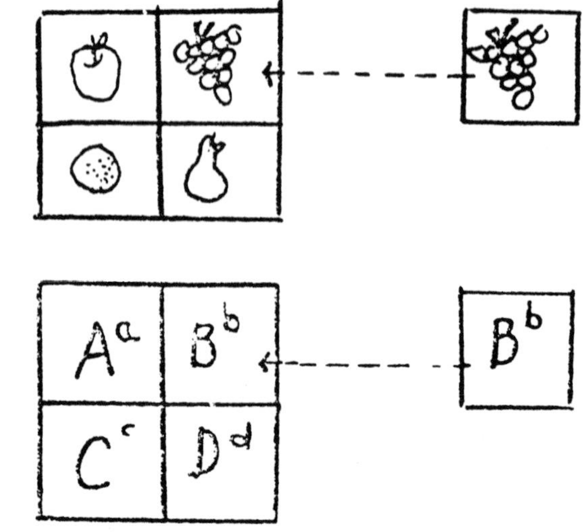

LOTTO

Children match pictures on small cards to identical pictures on large cards. You can use names, letters, numbers, etc.

FINGER PAINT

Mix liquid starch and soap flakes with an egg beater until you have the desired texture. Or: *Mix flour and salt with water until it is the consistency of thick gravy. You can add food coloring to these mixtures, too.*

In finger painting the process is more important than the product. You can put the paint directly on a table or large piece of oilcloth or plastic. If you want a print, lay a piece of paper on your design, rub the back and lift.

PUZZLES

You need 2 *pieces of thick cardboard the same size. Mount a picture (drawing, photograph) on one piece, leaving a good size border all around. Cut out the picture, leaving a frame. (You can use an x-acto knife or single-edged razor blade.) Glue the frame on to second piece of cardboard.*

*Varnish or cover picture with clear contact paper and cut into pieces (*2 *or* 3 *for two- and three-year-olds,* 5 *to* 7 *for four- and five-year-olds).*

If pieces are hard to take out of frame, cut a small hole in the back of the frame.

WORDS

Draw or cut out picture from magazine (children can choose their own words and pictures). Print word on card and leave enough spaces under word so children can match the letters to make the word.

*This is another way of matching picture to word. Instead of pictures, you can have an amount of apples (three) on top and numeral below (*3*).*

You can also use children's names. If you wish, names can be under photographs of the children.

FLANNEL BOARD

Bend or attach large pieces of sturdy cardboard or oaktag to make the shape above. Cover the front and back with flannel.

Cut shapes of different-colored felt, or pictures from magazines backed with felt or sandpaper so children can stick them on board to make designs, tell stories, or work on math concepts.

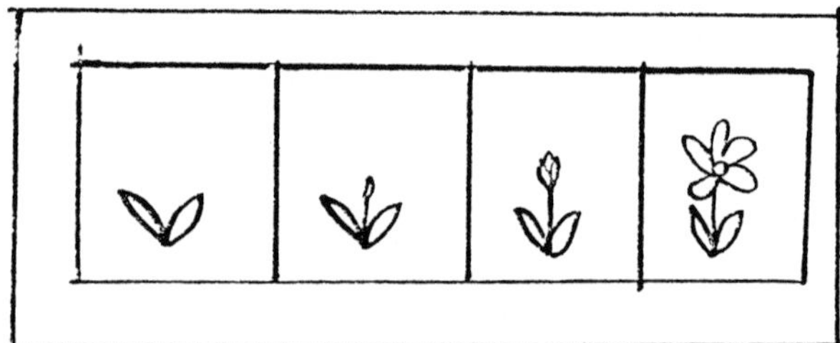

SEQUENCE CARDS

You can use any three or four pictures that can be ordered. Draw the first picture directly on a piece of cardboard. Mark places for the three other cards. Some children can tell you why they placed the small cards in a certain order.

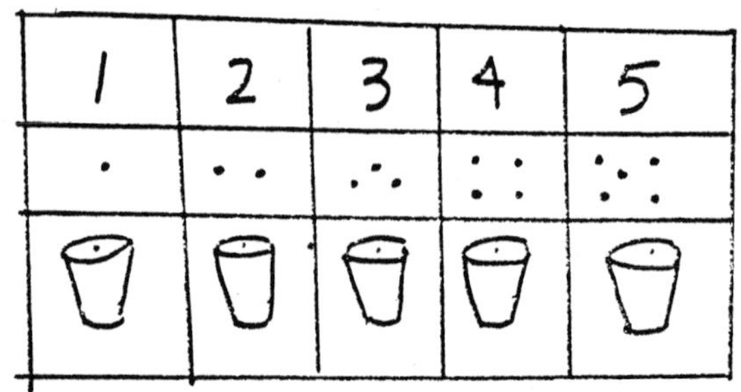

MATH GAME

On a piece of sturdy oaktag or cardboard, make a row of numerals, another row showing different amounts, and attach cups to third row with paper fasteners. Children can put the correct number of pebbles, buttons, etc. on objects in different cups. They can check themselves by matching objects in cup to number of dots directly above.

BLACKBOARD WALLS

Chalkboard-finish paint will transform any flat surface into a chalkboard. Comes in black and green at approximately $5 a quart, and two coats will cover about 50 square feet.

Michele — Michele
Robert
Mike
Felipe
John — John
Nancy
Sandra

NAME CARDS

Write all the names in the group on a large sheet of oaktag—include adults and children. As people come in in the morning they find their name from the envelope below, and put it in the pocket next to their name on the chart.

Adding person's photograph next to her or his name makes it easier to find matching card.

TEXTURE CARDS

Cut pairs of cards. Cover them with rough, smooth, or fuzzy pieces of cloth or paper. Children match textures that are the same. Some materials you can use: velvet, suede, leather, sandpaper, burlap.

BOOKS

You and children can make books about anything and everything. With cardboard covers covered with clear plastic, reinforcements around the holes and metal loose-leaf rings to hold pages together, books will last a fairly long time.

PUPPETS

Small paper bags become puppets if children draw eyes, nose, mouth on front and cut two holes on side. You can add string or wool for hair, buttons for eyes, etc. Large bags with holes cut for eyes can be decorated and fitted over child's head. Some children will dislike anything over their heads, but others will enjoy this.

J. J. Linsalata

Bibliographies

Selected Books and Pamphlets

Bettelheim, Bruno. *Children of the Dream.* New York: Macmillan, 1969.

This book is a vivid description of child-rearing practices on the kibbutz. Although I disagree with Bettelheim's opinion that the kibbutz experience is relevant primarily to the "culturally deprived child," the observations and information in this book are valuable.

Biber, Barbara. *Challenges Ahead for Early Childhood Education.* Washington, D.C.: National Association for the Education of Young Children, 1969. $1.75.

Written for professionals, this pamphlet advocates a balance between tradition and radical new demands on the education of young children—between "the maintenance of standards with the needs of a crisis situation."

Cade, Toni, ed. *The Black Woman: An Anthology.* New York: Signet Books, 1970. 95¢.

Different voices, all talking about the life of the black woman in America and the struggles for liberation. Particularly strong on the issue of child care are articles on motherhood and racism in education.

Child Care Bulletin Series. Nos. 1–8. Washington, D.C.: Day Care and Child Development Council of America, 1971.[1]

Each of these bulletins summarizes a recent research study or report in the field of child care.

Children Are Waiting. The Report of the Early Childhood Development Task Force. New York City, 1970.

This report surveys the day care situation in New York City and makes specific recommendations for the expansion of quality programs.

Gordon, Linda. *Families.* Boston: New England Free Press, 1970.

This pamphlet is a radical analysis of the functions of the family in a capitalist society.

[1] Whenever material is available from the Day Care and Child Development Council of America it is indicated by the initials DCCDCA.

Gotberg, Edith H., ed. *Day Care: Resources for Decision.* Office of Economic Opportunity, Office of Planning, Research and Evaluation. Available DCCDCA. $4.

Includes descriptions of child care in Denmark, Czechoslovakia, Israel, and other countries. There are also sections on Adult Involvement and Program Supports, including health, nutrition, and social work in programs in the United States.

Hawkins, D. F., Curran, J. R., and Jordan, J. W. *Industry-Related Day Care: The KLH Child Development Center,* Part I. Needham, Mass.: Social Administration Research Institute, 1969.

The development and progress of one of the country's leading experiments in industry-related day care. Discusses the motivation for this demonstration project.

Howe, Louise Kapp, ed. *The Future of the Family.* New York: Simon and Schuster, 1972.

Excellent collection of articles about the members of today's family (Part I) and transforming the family (Part II).

Industry and Day Care. Chicago, Illinois: Urban Research Corporation, 1970.

A report on the first conference on industry and day care, which brought together representatives from government, business, industry, and community child care centers.

Keyserling, Mary Dubler. *Windows on Day Care.* New York: National Council of Jewish Women, 1972.

A thorough survey of the availability and quality of a variety of day care services in this country.

Mitchell, Juliet. *Woman's Estate.* New York: Pantheon, 1972.

A thorough description of the organization and politics of the women's liberation movement here and in western Europe, as well as the author's own theory of women's oppression.

New University Conference. *Classes and Schools: A Radical Definition for Teachers.* Chicago Teachers Center, 852 West Belmont Ave., Chicago, Illinois 60657.

Although this is directed at elementary school teachers, the radical perspective in this pamphlet is relevant to anyone working with children. It is a theoretical framework for understanding the political nature of education in this country.

Notes on Child Care, Vol. I and II. New York: Women's Liberation Child Care Collective. Available from the New York Women's Liberation Center, 243 West 20th Street, New York, New York 10011.

Volume I (1970) contains articles on government plans, university-based child care, cooperative nurseries, and a Saturday day care service in New York. Volume II (1971) has additional articles as well as some practical ideas about setting up and designing a center.

Nye, Ivan, F., and Hoffman, Louis W., eds. *The Employed Mother in America.* Chicago: Rand McNally, 1963.

Several studies of women who work and the children of working women.

Ruderman, Florence. *Child Care and Working Mothers.* New York: Child Welfare League of America, 1968.

Describes the causes and the effects of the negative image of child care. She is a strong advocate of child care for human development.

Sidel, Ruth. *Women and Child Care in China.* New York: Hill and Wang, 1972.

Traces the development of the Chinese woman's role from the "bitter past" to the present. This book was written after the author's visit to China; it has a lot of information, but the last few chapters are the most inspiring.

Wortis, Sheli. *Child-Rearing and Women's Liberation.* Boston: Boston Area Child Care Action Group, 12 Glenwood, Cambridge, Mass. 02139. 1970.

This pamphlet is an argument against women's primary identification as mother, and for people-controlled alternative child care.

Articles

Babcox, Deborah. "Liberation of Children." *Up from Under,* May/June 1970.

Breitbart, Vicki, and Leman, Beverly. "Women Who Take Care of Children: Why Child Care." *Up from Under,* January/February 1971.

Edmiston, Susan. "The Psychology of Day Care." *New York Magazine,* April 5, 1971.

Ellis, Katherine, and Petchesky, Rosalind. "Politics of Day Care." *Social Policy,* Vol. 3, Nos. 4 and 5 (November/December 1972 and January/February 1973).

Featherstone, Joseph. "The Day Care Problem: Kentucky Fried Children." *The New Republic,* September 12, 1970.

Jensen, Gordon D. "Day Care Centers in Europe: A Focus on Consequences for Mental Health." *Mental Hygiene,* October 1971.

Leiner, Marvin, and Ubell, Robert. "Day Care in Cuba: Children Are the Revolution." *Saturday Review,* April 1, 1972.

Mead, Margaret. "Some Theoretical Considerations on the Problem of Mother-Child Separation." *American Journal of Orthopsychiatry,* Vol. 24, No. 3 (1954).

Miller, Lindsay. "Day Care Battle." New York *Post,* March 13–18, 1972.

Wortis, Sheli. "The Acceptance of the Concept of Maternal Role by Behavioral Scientists: Its Effects on Women." *American Journal of Orthopsychiatry,* Vol. 41, No. 5 (1971).

Additional Readings on Alternative Education

Dennison, George. *The Lives of Children: The Story of the First Street School.* New York: Random House, 1969.

Graubard, Allen. *Free the Children: Radical Return and the Free School Movement.* New York: Pantheon, 1972.

Illich, Ivan. *Deschooling Society.* New York: Harper & Row, 1971.

Kozol, Jonathan. *Free Schools.* Boston: Houghton Mifflin, 1972.

Rasberry, Salli, and Greenway, Robert. *Rasberry Exercises: How to Start Your Own School . . . and Make a Book.* Freestone, California: Freestone Publishing Co., 1970.

Guides for Establishing a Child Care Program

Auerbach, Aline, and Roche, Sandra. *Creating a Preschool Center: Parent Development in an Integrated Neighborhood Project.* New York: John Wiley and Sons, Inc., 1971.

Description of the development of a child care program with a lot of parent involvement.

Campus Day Care: Issues and Resources. Child Welfare League.

Short, concise how-to pamphlet for universities and colleges.

Child Development Manuals. Office of Child Development, 1972. Available DCCDCA. 50¢ for handling.

Different pamphlets on aspects of day care including: (1) Statement of Principle, (4) Serving School Age Children, (5) Staff Training, (6) Health Services, (7) Administration.

Evans, E. Belle; Shub, Beth; and Weinstein, Marlence. *Day Care: How to Plan, Develop, and Operate a Day Care Center.* Boston: Beacon Press, 1971.

Excellent as a practical guide for setting up a cooperative and/or publicly funded day care center. Includes budgets, curriculum, and teacher-training programs.

How to Start a Child Care Center. Women's Action Alliance.

Concise step-by-step guide for starting a program.

Manual on Organizing, Financing, and Administration of Day Care Centers in New York City for Community Groups, Their Lawyers, and Other Advisors. New York: Day Care Consultation Service, Bank Street College of Education, 1972. $5.50.

This is what it says it is. Although it was written specifically for New York City, there is useful information on writing bylaws, pros and cons of drop-in care, and curriculum for a child care center.

Musco, T. G. *. . . and Instructions for Those Interested in Day Care.* Copies available from author at Self Help Center, Box 34, Calverton, New York 11933. Money goes to the Day Care Center. $2.

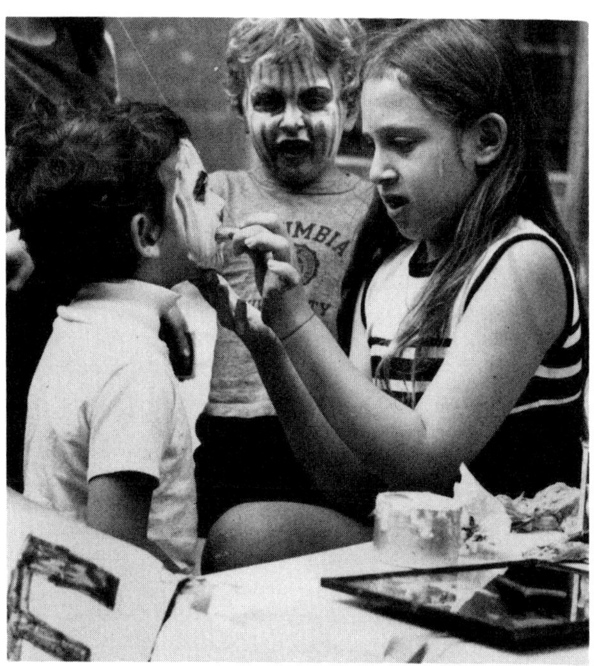

Not as complete as the Manual, *also written for one locale, but applicable elsewhere. At first the charts in this guide seem more confusing than helpful, but it turns out to be a clear, simple guide.*

Project Head Start Rainbow Series. Office of Economic Opportunity, Washington, D.C.

These pamphlets cover every aspect of Head Start. The most useful ones are probably the Daily Program I, II, and III and Nutrition.

Taylor, Katherine Whiteside. *Parents and Children Learn Together.* New York: Teachers College Press, Columbia University, 1967. $4.95.

Geared to a middle-class audience but contains ideas about child development and parent education and suggestions for organizing and running a cooperative child care program that are relevant to all groups.

Winn, Marie, and Porcer, Mary Ann. *The Playgroup Book.* Baltimore, Maryland: Penguin Books, 1967. $1.95.

Makes the false assumption that everyone has a "playroom" for their children and it talks specifically about an in-home cooperative arrangement, but has good specific suggestions for materials and activities for children three to six years old in all settings.

Specifically for Infants and Toddlers

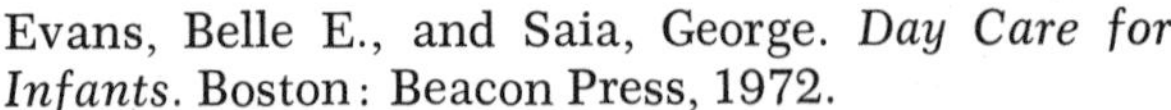

Evans, Belle E., and Saia, George. *Day Care for Infants.* Boston: Beacon Press, 1972.

This is an argument and guide for setting up a quality program for children under three.

Handbook: Campus Community Day Care Center. A pull-out section of *This Magazine Is About Schools.* Vol. 5, No. 2 (Spring 1972).

Written by the people involved in the program, it includes why they set it up as well as practical tips on how to change a diaper, how to plan a day, and activities for children.

Parent and Child Center: A Guide for the Development of Parent and Child Centers. Office of Child Development, ULS. Department of Health, Education and Welfare, Washington, D.C. 20201.

Parent and child centers include day care and "home intervention" for infants and their families.

Serving Infants. Child Development #2. Washington, D.C.: Office of Child Development, 1972.

Has an excellent section on equipment and activities for infants.

Description of Early Childhood Programs

Curran, Joseph R., and Jordan, John W. *The KLH Experience: An Evaluative Report of Day Care in Action.* KLH Development Center, Inc. 38 Landsdown St., Cambridge, Massachusetts 02139.

Evaluation of an industry-related day care program.

Keister, Mary Elizabeth. *The Good Life for Infants and Toddlers: Group Care of Infants.* National Association of Education of Young Children. 1970. Available DCCDCA. $1.50.

A report on a demonstration project of quality care for infants and toddlers at the University of North Carolina.

Pines, Maya. *Revolution in Learning.* New York: Harper & Row, 1967. 95¢.

A report on the current emphasis on cognitive development of the young child. Includes descriptions of Bereiter-Engelmann program and infant program in Syracuse.

Preschool Breakthrough: What Works in Early Childhood. National School Publications Relations Association. Available DCCDCA. $4.

Includes short descriptions of 11 preschool programs in the United States.

Swenson, Janet P. *Alternatives in Quality Child Care.* DCCDCA, 1972. $3.50.

(Available in Spanish and English.) Good descriptions of a variety of approaches to care and learning of the young child, plus sketches of different programs.

Different Approaches to Early Childhood Education

Biber, Barbara; Shapiro, Edna; and Wickens, David. *Promoting Cognitive Growth: A Developmental Interaction Point of View.* Washington, D.C.: National Association for the Education of Young Children. $2.50.

"A humanist approach." The authors analyze events in the preschool as they relate to the over-all educational goals of the program for children three to five years old.

Brown, Mary, and Precious, Norman. *The Integrated Day in the Primary School.* New York: Agathon Press, Inc. $2.45.

Sections on the environment and the teacher-child interaction are clear descriptions of the British Infant School "open classroom."

Lavetelli, Celia S. *Piaget's Theory Applied to an Early Childhood Curriculum.* Boston: A Center for Media Development, Inc., Books.

Short description of Piaget's theory and specific activities in the classroom.

Orem, R. C. *A Montessori Handbook.* New York: Capricorn Books, 1966.

A very practical guide to activities and equipment in a Montessori program.

Planning Space for Children

[1] Thanks to Phyllis Taube Greenleaf, Margie Bakken, and Susan Kanor for their contributions to the following sections of this Bibliography.

A Small World of Play and Learning. LINC Press. Learning Institute of North Carolina, 1106 Lamond Avenue, Durham, North Carolina 27701.

Practical guide for setting up play areas for children. Clear, concise, and very good.

Kritchevsky, Sybil, and Prescott, Elizabeth. *Planning Environments of Young Children.* Washington, D.C.: National Association for Education of Young Children. $1.50.

Excellent pamphlet on space arrangements and play equipment for children's programs. Emphasis on outdoor space, but could be helpful in arranging activity areas. Grew out of a study that indicated adults have less need to be restrictive with children when space contains equipment and materials that are complex enough to challenge and involve kids.

Materials and Equipment for the Children's Center

Early Childhood Education Study. Advisory on Open Education. 90 Sherman Street, Cambridge, Massachusetts.
Booklets on building equipment:
Cardboard Carpentry Introduction. A 38-page picture book giving ideas of kinds of equipment that can be built from triple-strength corrugated cardboard. 60¢
Building with Cardboard. A booklet showing how to work with cardboard. Includes instructions and designs for tables, bookcases, stools, easels, playhouses, and puppet stages. 60¢
Building with Tubes. A booklet showing how to work with heavy cardboard tubes, which are normally discarded by business and industry, to make stools, tables, cubbies, shelves, etc. 60¢

Elementary Science Study, 55 Chapel Street, Newton, Massachusetts 02158
Musical Instruments Recipe Book. $1
Whistles and Strings. $1

From the Ground Up: A Book of Ideas for Pre-School Equipment. CDGM. Vincent Building, 203 W. Capital Street, Jackson, Mississippi.

Everything in this book was designed and made by people in the local community for their community-run center.

Matterson, E. C. *Play and Playthings for the Preschool Child.* Baltimore, Maryland: Penguin Books, 1967. $1.95

Straight, informative text on activities and materials for children—sand, water, clay, wood, musical instruments, lists of children's books. Also has diagrams showing how to build equipment.

Pre-School Equipment: For a Multi-Use Center. Prepared by Stone Mountain Education Projects, Inc., Roaring Brook Farm, Conway, Massachusetts 01341. Send $2 to Stone Mountain, 60 Broad Street, Westfield, Massachusetts 01085.

Ideas for equipment that is "portable, inexpensive to make, provides its own storage." Useful for programs that share space with other groups and have to store or move their equipment after every schoolday or -week.

Planning Curriculums

This list includes only pamphlets that are both useful and relatively inexpensive.

Beginnings. Nuffield Mathematics Project. New York: John Wiley and Sons, Inc., 1967.

Blance, Ellen; Cook, Ann; and Mack, Herb. *Cooking in the Open Classroom,* and *Reading in the Open Classroom.* Community Resources Institute, 270 West Ninety-sixth Street, New York, New York 10025.

Cobb, Vicki. *Science Experiments You Can Eat.* New York: J. B. Lippincott Co., 1972. $1.95.

Cole, Ann; Haas, Carolyn; Bushnell, Faith, and Weinberger, Betty. *I Saw a Purple Cow and 100 Other Recipes for Learning.* Boston: Little, Brown and Co., 1972. $2.95.

Hirsch, Elizabeth. *Transition Periods: Stumbling Blocks of Education.* Early Childhood Education Council of New York City, 196 Bleecker Street, New York, New York 10012. 75¢

Hochman, Vivienne, and Greenwald, Mildred. *Science Experiences in Early Childhood Education.* New York: Bank Street Publications, 1969.

McKee, Paul. *Primer for Parents: How Your Child Learns to Read.* Boston: Houghton Mifflin, 1966. 15¢

Neuman, Donald. "Sciencing for Young Children." *Young Children* (April 1972), pp. 215–26.

Vicki Breitbart

Sheviakov, George. *Anger in Children: Causes, Characteristics and Considerations.* National Education Association, 1201 16th Street N.W., Washington, D.C. 20036. 75¢

Starks, Esther. *Block Building.* Washington, D.C.: National Education Association, 1960. $1.

Periodicals

There are numerous magazines, journals, and periodicals on child development, education, and child care. Some you may be interested in are:

Big Rock Candy Mountain. Published six times a year by: Potoloa Institute, Inc. 1115 Merril Street, Menlo Park, California 94025. *Has ideas for making equipment and places to order materials.*

Childhood Education. Published by the Association for Childhood Education International. Membership in the organization includes the magazine. $12 annual. $4 undergraduate students.

Children Today. Issued six times a year by the Children's Bureau, U.S. Department of Health, Education and Welfare. Subscription is $2.

Voice for Children. Newsletter of the Day Care and Child Development Council of America. Included in the membership in the organization. From $5 for parents or students on up.

Young Children. Issued six times a year by the National Association for Education of Young Children. Members of the Association receive the magazine as part of the membership, or you can subscribe for $10 a year.

There are several Women's Liberation publications, but those I know that usually carry articles on child care are:

Ms. For subscription send $9 to 123 Garden Street, Marion, Ohio 43302.

Second Wave. Box 303 Kenmore Station, Boston, Massachusetts 02215. $3 for a year.

Up from Under. 339 Lafayette Street, New York, New York 10012. $3 for five issues.

Women: A Journal of Liberation. 3028 Greenmount Avenue, Baltimore, Maryland 21218. $4 for four issues.

For more information on periodicals, resources, and contacts in the women's liberation movement:

Mushroom Effect: A Directory of Women's Liberation. P.O. Box 6024, Albany, Georgia 94704. 50¢

The Whole Woman Catalog. P.O. Box 11711, Portsmouth, New Hampshire 03801.

Bibliographies of Children's Books

These are sources for books that show children of different ethnic and racial groups and/or men and women taking nonstereotypical roles.

Black Experience in Children's Books. New York Public Library, Office of Children's Services. 8 East Fortieth Street, New York, New York 10016. 50¢

China Books and Periodicals. 2929 Twenty-fourth Street, San Francisco, California, or 125 Fifth Avenue, New York, New York.

Circle Associates. Afro-American Studies Resources Center. 126 Warren Avenue, Roxbury, Massachusetts. They have lists available of children's books which emphasize ethnic and racial diversity.

Feminist Press. Box 334, Old Westbury, New York 11568.

Little Ms. Muffet Fights Back. Feminists on Children's Media. P.O. Box 4315, Grand Central Station, New York, New York 10010. 50¢ plus a 4″ x 9″ self-addressed stamped (16¢) envelope.

Lollipop Power. P.O. Box 1171, Chapel Hill, North Carolina 27514.

Ms. 370 Lexington Ave., New York, New York. The Spring 1972 issue contained a bibliography on pp. 30–2, or you can send directly to their office for a more complete list.

Additional Bibliographies

Annotated Bibliography on Early Childhood. Educational Facilities Laboratories, New York, New York, 1970.

Bibliography on Early Childhood. U.S. Department of Health, Education and Welfare, Project Head Start, 1969.

Selected Bibliography on Day Care Services. U.S. Department of Health, Education and Welfare, 1965.

Women: A Bibliography. c/o Lucinda Cisler, 102 West Eightieth Street, New York, New York 10024. 50¢ for a single copy.

Resources for Non-Sexist Education

Children's Books

This list was compiled by Phyllis Taube Greenleaf. It is "a list of books for young children that express to children, either through their stories or illustrations, a nontraditional concept of what it can mean to be a girl or boy, man or woman."

Abramovitz, Anita. *Winifred.* Austin, Tex.: Steck-Vaughn, 1971.

Blos, Joan, and Miles, Betty. *Just Think!* New York: Alfred A. Knopf, 1971.

Chorao, Kay. *The Repair of Uncle Toe.* New York: Farrar, Straus & Giroux, 1972.

Conford, Ellen. *Impossible Possum.* Boston: Little, Brown, 1971.

Danish, Barbara. *The Dragon and the Doctor.* Old Westbury, New York: Feminist Press, 1971.

Eichler, Margrit. *Martin's Father.* Chapel Hill, N.C.: Lollipop Power, 1971.

Goldreich, Esther, and Goldreich, Gloria. *What Can She Be? A Veterinarian.* New York: Lothrop, Lee & Shepard, 1972.

Mao-chiu, Chang. *The Little Doctor.* San Francisco: China Books and Periodicals, 1965.

Merriam, Eve. *Mommies at Work.* New York: Alfred A. Knopf, 1961.

Preston, Edna M. *The Temper Tantrum Book.* New York: Viking, 1969.

Reich, Hanns, ed. *Children and Their Fathers* and *Children and Their Mothers.* New York: Hill & Wang, 1962 and 1964.

Shulevitz, Uri. *Rain, Rain Rivers.* New York: Farrar, Straus & Giroux, 1969.

Shulman, Alix. *Finders Keepers.* Scarsdale, N.Y.: Bradbury, 1971.

Udry, Janice May. *Moon Jumpers.* Illustrated by Maurice Sendak. New York: Harper & Row, 1959.

Zolotow, Charlotte. *William's Doll.* Illustrated by William Pene duBois. New York: Harper & Row, 1972.

Record

Free to Be . . . You and Me. Bell Records. Available from *Ms.* Magazine, Dept. R, 370 Lexington Avenue, N.Y., N.Y. 10017. $6.50

Songs like "Parents Are People," "Sisters and Brothers," sung by Marlo Thomas, Diana Sands, Harry Belafonte, and Rosie Grier, among others.

Pictures

Women in Nontraditional Jobs. Feminist Resources for Equal Education. P.O. Box 185, Saxonville Station, Framingham, Massachusetts 01701. $2.50 for set of 8.

Films

This is only a partial list of the major distributors of films on early childhood.

ACI Films, Inc.
35 West Forty-fifth Street
New York, New York 10036

Bank Street Films
267 West Twenty-fifth Street
New York. New York 10001

CATEC Consultants
2754 San Gabriel
San Bernardino, California 92404

EDC Film Library
Educational Development Center
55 Chapel Street
Newton, Massachusetts 02160

Educational Facilities Laboratories
477 Madison Avenue
New York, New York 10022

McGraw-Hill
1221 Avenue of the Americas
New York, New York 10020

Modern Talking Pictures
1212 Avenue of the Americas
New York, New York 10036

New York University Film Library
26 Washington Place
New York, New York 10003

Odeon Films, Inc.
22 West Forty-eighth Street
New York, New York 10036

Polymorph Films, Inc.
331 Newbury Street
Boston, Massachusetts 02115

Pyramid Films
Box 1048
Santa Monica, California 90406

Time-Life Films
43 West Sixteenth Street
New York, New York 10011

Vassar Film Program
Department of Psychology
Vassar College
Poughkeepsie, New York 12601

University of California
Extension Media Center
Berkeley, California 94720

It is also worthwhile getting in touch with:

Bureau of Audio-Visual Education at your state university. Your state's Department of Mental Health Film Library.

Westinghouse TV has produced a film on community-controlled day care called "Chance for a Lifetime." It is available through Westinghouse TV (Group W) or your local NET station.

Sources of Materials for Infant and Toddler Programs

The following are ongoing programs that publish program descriptions, manuals, and/or curriculum materials.

The Children's Center
Project Director
100 Walnut Place
Syracuse University
Syracuse, New York 13210

The Demonstration Project in Group Care of the Infant
University of North Carolina
Greensboro, North Carolina 27412

Educational Intervention at Home by Mothers of Infants
Institute for Research on Exceptional Children
Department of Special Education
402 East Healey Street
Champaign, Illinois 61820

Mother-Child Home Program
Director
Mother-Child Home Program
30 Albany Avenue
Freeport, New York 11520

Parent Education Program
Project Director
Institute for Development of Human Resources
College of Education
University of Florida
Gainesville, Florida 32601

Also available: By Ira Gordon, project director of Parent Education Program: *Baby Learning Through Baby Play: A Parent's Guide for the First Two Years.* New York: St. Martin's Press, 1970. $3.95.

Ypsilanti-Carnegie Infant Education Project
High/Scope Educational Research Foundation
125 N. Huron
Ypsilanti, Michigan 48197

A NOTE ON THE TYPE

The text of this book by Vicki Breitbart was set on the Linotype in a face called Primer. The complete range of sizes of Primer was first made available in 1954, although the pilot size of 12 point was ready as early as 1951. The design of the face makes general reference to Linotype Century—long a serviceable type, totally lacking in manner or frills of any kind—but brilliantly corrects its characterless quality.

The various articles extracted by Ms. Breitbart for us in this book have been set in Helvetica, perhaps the most widely accepted and generally acclaimed sans-serif face of all time. Designed by M. Miedinger in the 1950's in Switzerland and named for its country of origin, Helvetica was first introduced in America in 1963.

The book was composed by H. Wolff Book Manufacturing Co., Inc. Printed and bound by Halliday Lithographic Corporation, West Hanover, Massachusetts.